American Labor Since the New Deal

American Labor Since the New Deal

Edited with an Introduction by
Melvyn Dubofsky

A NEW YORK TIMES BOOK

Quadrangle Books
CHICAGO

The publishers are grateful to the contributors herein
for permission to reprint their articles.

Abel

Contents

3. Workers in an Affluent Society: 1946–1960

4. Workers and Unions Since 1960

5. Labor Today

viii • *Contents*

American Labor Since the New Deal

Introduction

TWO SCENES separated by some thirty-six years encapsulate the experience of the American working class since the election in 1932 of Franklin D. Roosevelt to the presidency. In the summer of 1934 on the streets of Minneapolis, Minnesota, police shot workers running out of ambush; across the state line in the smaller industrial city of Kohler, Wisconsin, National Guardsmen and private guards savagely beat and maimed striking workers; and two thousand miles away, in the shadows of the Golden Gate and Bay bridges, San Francisco's "men in blue" clubbed and tear-gassed protesting longshoremen.

The other scene occurred in the spring of 1970 in New York City, where unionized construction workers rushed to the defense of the established order by clubbing and beating young anti-war protesters. What had happened over the course of four decades to transform American workers from victims of the "system" to its defenders?

I

In March 1933, despite the brave words of Franklin Roosevelt's inaugural address, American workers had much to fear. For almost four years they had suffered bitterly, victims of the worst economic depression in the nation's history. Between 1929 and 1932 unemployment had risen from 1.5 to 12.8 million, and by Inauguration

Day, 1933, some estimates placed the figure as high as 15 million. Millions more worked short time for reduced wages. Mortgage hammers and Ford tractors pushed Okies off the land, whereupon they fled west—as John Steinbeck has poignantly told us—only to be exploited by California ranchers and pursued by sheriffs' deputies. The urban unemployed scavenged in garbage cans and anxiously sought a warm place to sleep, perhaps in a subway car or a jail cell. Thousands of young men, and women too, took to the road in desperate search for a nonexistent pot of gold. The President of the United States, Herbert Hoover, used the Army to rout a harmless "army" of unemployed World War I veterans from a camp on the banks of the Potomac, where they had come to seek bonus payments from Congress. An impotent, anachronistic labor movement could barely defend the worker's place in American society. It was indeed a time of defeat and frustration.

Only a true patrician like Franklin Roosevelt could have said on a public platform that there was nothing to fear but fear itself. In truth, most Americans had abundant reason to be anxious about the present and more so about the future. And precious little was offered to comfort those with cause to worry, least of all by the organized labor movement. The American Federation of Labor (AFL), which since the 1890's had been the almost unchallenged voice of the national labor movement, had no cure for the misery of most workers. It did gather statistics revealing the nature and extent of unemployment, and it called upon employers to reduce the work week to thirty hours in order to spread available employment among a larger share of the work force. But reducing the hours of work without maintaining existing daily wage levels only served to pool misery, more men laboring to earn the same total wage package and hence less income for each individual worker. In 1932 the AFL refused to support Franklin Roosevelt; indeed, many old-guard trade unionists had favored the re-election of Herbert Hoover. Only after a heated debate and by the narrowest margin did the AFL's executive council in 1932 sanction a federal unemployment compensation program. And the executive council still drew the line against legislation providing maximum hours for men, minimum wages, and social security.

To most labor leaders the Great Depression was neither a great opportunity for change nor a threat to the existence of the labor movement. The AFL had had the good fortune to survive previous depressions, and bad times, its leaders reasoned, were scarcely the occasions to go out and organize the masses—whom they considered to be unorganizable even in good times. In 1929, after a decade of prosperity, the AFL and most of its trade-union affiliates were weaker and smaller than they had been in 1919 at the end of World War I. And by March 1933, after four years of depression, they seemed impotent. As Roosevelt took the oath of office on that wet, chilly March day, only the most ludicrous visionary could have prophesied what the next five years would bring the labor movement and the American worker.

By a remarkable combination of rhetoric, action, and promises, the New Deal released that most explosive of human aspirations: hope! Where despair had brought apathy, hope stirred militancy. Roosevelt and his New Dealers immediately offered relief to the needy and promised (through a myriad of federal agencies and projects, each with its own unique alphabetical title) jobs for the able-bodied. During the famous "hundred days," Roosevelt rushed through a special session of Congress a wide variety of substantial reform legislation, including one measure, the National Industrial Recovery Act (NIRA) that carried major implications for the labor movement and for American workers. Under Section 7a of the NIRA, the federal government for the first time in peacetime American history sanctioned the right of workers to organize into trade unions of their own choice and to bargain collectively with employers.

II

The more aggressive and astute among the nation's labor leaders promptly used Section 7a to enroll restive and militant workers into the ranks of trade unionism. John L. Lewis, president of the United Mine Workers of America, once the nation's largest union but under the leadership of Lewis the worst victim of the trade-union decline of the 1920's and the depression, rushed his organizers into the coal camps and towns of Pennsylvania, West Virginia, Kentucky, Ohio, Indiana, and Illinois. There they told the miners that President Roosevelt *wanted* them to join the union. The miners complied, joining the union by the tens of thousands and building the foundation for the United Mine Workers and John L. Lewis' later penetration of the mass-production industries. What Lewis accomplished among the coal miners, Sidney Hillman did among the men's clothing workers whom he organized into the Amalgamated Clothing Workers of America (ACWA) and David Dubinsky did among the ladies' garment workers in the International Ladies' Garment Workers' Union (ILGWU). Hillman's and Dubinsky's unions were also lifted out of the doldrums of depression, and joined with the UMWA to demand the organization of mass-production workers.

While the coal miners and the garment workers were the most notable and successful beneficiaries of Section 7a, they were scarcely alone among American workers in their response to early New Deal reforms. Auto workers in Detroit, steel workers in Pittsburgh, Gary, and Youngstown, rubber workers in Akron, teamsters in the Twin Cities, longshoremen in San Francisco, and millions of other workers scattered across the nation suddenly looked to unions for their salvation.

Employers did not respond peaceably to this upsurge among the rank and file, triggered by the promise of the New Deal. Management wasted no time in fighting back. Using every weapon at their disposal, including company unions, psychological persuasion, forcible repression, and the wide loopholes available even in Section 7a, employers at first repulsed the trade-union offensive.

Management's response revealed with striking clarity Roosevelt's less than enthusiastic desire to stimulate independent trade unionism, as well as the AFL's impotence. Wracked by jurisdictional disputes, lethargic leadership (Lewis, Hillman, and Dubinsky belonged to a select minority of labor leaders), and a pessimistic outlook, the AFL failed to offer mass-production workers the guidance they needed, the policies they wanted, and the type of unions they demanded. Roosevelt, more in need of cooperation from industrialists than workers (and their unions) in his plans for restoring the nation to economic health, generally deferred to the desires of corporate leaders on matters of interpretation or conflict in labor-management relations. Thus it was not surprising that workers soon began to refer to the National Recovery Administration (NRA, the agency that administered the NIRA) as the "National Run Around," and that few mourned when in 1935 the Supreme Court declared the NIRA unconstitutional.

While employers might temporarily defeat the trade-union thrust, they could not extinguish the flame of hope ignited by the original promise of the New Deal. The workers refused to languish in apathy as they had from 1929 to 1932; they rose up and fought back militantly, and sometimes violently. In St. Paul and Minneapolis the teamsters, under the leadership of the Dunne brothers (William, Vincent, Miles, and Grant) and Farrell Dobbs, old radicals and by 1934 members of the Trotskyite Socialist Labor party, took to the streets in a series of carefully planned and calculated moves to fight police and state militia sent into the Twin Cities by a liberal Farmer-Labor party Governor. In this case, militancy and solidarity brought the striking teamsters' union recognition and victory. Ironically, the strategy developed by the radical Dobbs and the Dunne brothers would later be used by Jimmy Hoffa to build a more powerful national union of teamsters—but one with a shrunken social conscience and slight concern for a basic reformation of society. Meanwhile, in San Francisco, Harry Bridges, one of the most controversial and misunderstood labor leaders of the time, had welded together the West Coast's waterfront and maritime workers into a militant labor front—solid enough to shut the waterfront tight and even tie up the whole city through a peaceful but effective general strike. In the face of management-hired gunmen and strike-breakers, relentless police repression, and a red scare fostered by newspapers and public officials, Bridges and his followers remained sufficiently united to win union-controlled hiring halls which ended the "shape-up"; a wage increase; and a basic six-hour day with greatly increased overtime rates. Not just in the Twin Cities and San Francisco but everywhere across the nation by the end of 1934 and on into 1935, labor revolts flared in the streets and shops, dissatisfaction with New Deal labor policy increased, and businessmen more and more turned against "that man" in the White

House. The time was ripe for the reformers in Washington, those to the left of the President, to shift labor policy in a more radical direction.

III

Ever since the passage of the NIRA, a small coterie of influential reformers, administrators, and Congressmen in Washington had been aware of the weaknesses in Section 7a and eager to strengthen the hand of labor in its struggles with management. None was more influential and more certain of what he desired than New York Senator Robert Wagner, who since his service on the New York State Factory Investigating Commission of 1911–1915 had been a warm and ardent advocate of labor's right to organize. Well before the Supreme Court declared the NIRA unconstitutional, Wagner had introduced during the 1934 session of Congress new labor legislation that would pass into law during the 1935 session * as the National Labor Relations Act (Wagner Act). Not an entirely new approach to labor relations, the Wagner Act nonetheless defined precisely and forbade a number of unfair labor practices used by employers. Among other features, it outlawed company unions, sanctioned majority union representation through federally supervised worker elections (thus employers could no longer Balkanize their workers through schemes of proportional representation which divided laborers in a single plant among several competing and hence impotent trade unions), officially certified union bargaining agents, and required management to bargain with them in good faith. Most important, it provided machinery to enforce its decisions. A three-man National Labor Relations Board (NLRB) was granted the power to seek injunctions against uncooperative employers. In short, the Wagner Act fully legitimated labor's right to organize and provided a New Deal for trade unionism.

But the New Deal could only establish the governmental and

---

* This same session of Congress (probably the most significant of all New Deal sessions) passed three other notable reforms: the Social Security Act, the Wealth Tax (making personal and corporate income taxes higher and more progressive), and the Public Utilities Holding Company Act.

legal environment within which the organization of workers might proceed. It remained entirely up to the leaders of labor and to the rank and file whether workers in fact would be organized. Only in retrospect can the achievement of mass unionization be made to appear easy or inevitable.

Although almost everyone in the labor movement by 1935 maintained that the mass-production workers should be organized, they could not agree on how to organize them and in what types of unions. This was so because labor leaders were primarily men of power who wished to extend their own spheres of influence and hence tended to perceive many organizing schemes as threats to existing power relationships in the labor movement. Wracked by self-doubt and fearful of what change might mean, the old leaders were in no position to overcome recalcitrant employers in the mass-production industries. Indeed, the leaders of the AFL and its affiliated unions had already failed again and again during 1933 and 1934 to preserve and expand union inroads among auto, steel, and rubber workers. To workers who preferred industrial unions,* AFL spokesmen could promise nothing better than temporary federal labor unions (in effect, wards of the AFL) and the ultimate prospect of being divided up among separate craft unions. To militant workers eager to test their strength in strike action against employers, and to organizers convinced that only such militant action would win mass recruits, AFL officials counseled moderation and accommodation with employers. To workers long divided among themselves by ethnic and racial factors, the AFL sent organizers who could tell the following story: "My wife can always tell from the smell of my clothes what breed of foreigners I've been hanging out with." No wonder the AFL organizing campaign had stalled in 1934, and that thousands of workers had taken to the streets under non-AFL and sometimes quite radical leadership.

As younger and more aggressive labor leaders continued to urge the organization of mass-production workers, they discovered an unsurpassed field commander inside the old guard of the labor movement: John L. Lewis. At the 1934 AFL convention these

---

* That is, unions which encompassed all workers within a single plant or industry, regardless of craft or task.

Young Turks had come close to passing a resolution approving industrial unionism, and they were determined to win their point at the 1935 convention. Even the president of the AFL, mild and meek William Green, appeared to be moving with the times when he noted of the auto workers: "They are mass minded. They ask me over and over again, Are you going to divide us up? I cannot change that state of mind. It is there. We cannot organize them on any other basis." Yet, in the end, Green deferred to the wishes of such old-fashioned craft-union leaders as A. P. Wharton of the International Association of Machinists, "Big Bill" Hutcheson of the Brotherhood of Carpenters and Joiners, and Dan Tobin of the Teamsters, and he refused to push industrial unionism. At the 1935 AFL convention the old-time leaders again had the might, if not the right, and they roundly defeated Lewis and his younger lieutenants on the industrial-union question. During one particularly heated moment, Lewis and Bill Hutcheson came to blows; the punches signaled the start of a civil war in labor's ranks.

After their defeat on the industrial-union question, Lewis and his supporters wasted no time in forming within the AFL a Committee on Industrial Organization (CIO). At first the only publicly stated purpose of this committee was to lobby for industrial unionism within the AFL and to help mass-production workers form trade unions. But this narrow role failed to recognize Lewis' vaulting ambition. Once on the road to independent action and in command of his own national organization, Lewis, a supreme egotist, could scarcely consider uncertain compromises, let alone surrender. Suspicious of all change and dedicated to the defense of their separate labor fiefdoms, the craft-union barons considered Lewis a traitor to the cause and proceeded to treat him as such. Accusing the CIO's supporters of the most heinous crimes in labor's book—acting as an enemy of the labor movement, dual unionism, and even communist sympathies—the AFL executive council in the summer of 1936 ordered all unions then affiliated with the Committee on Industrial Organization to withdraw or stand suspended from the AFL. Lewis and his allies remained obdurate, having in their own minds nothing to compromise or surrender. Consequently the 1936 AFL convention, meeting without such suspended unions as the United Mine Workers, the International Ladies' Garment Workers, and the Amalgamated Clothing Workers (the three great beneficiaries of New Deal reforms), overwhelmingly sanctioned the executive council's suspension of recalcitrant CIO supporters. The convention's action removed the last restraints on Lewis and the CIO, which then proceeded not only to organize the unorganized but also to challenge the AFL in its existing areas of jurisdiction and to establish competing national, state, and local labor bodies. After November 1936, labor waged a civil war with no holds barred.

IV

Success blessed the CIO quickly and in an unprecedented manner. Shortly after the Lewis faction left the AFL, auto workers in Flint, Michigan, the heart of the General Motors empire, directly challenged the largest and most profitable industrial corporation in the world. In what was perhaps the most significant single industrial conflict of the 1930's, if not in American history, workers organized by the United Auto Workers (UAW), a CIO affiliate, defeated an apparently impregnable adversary with surprising new tactics. On December 30, 1936, without warning, auto workers sat down on the job and occupied Fisher Body Plant No. 1 in Flint. There they remained, provisioned and supported by their allies on the outside, until General Motors conceded. Inside the plant they created a community that provided solidarity and a sense of purpose, and offered its members education, entertainment, and athletics. So united were the strikers inside and outside the factory gates that they were able to rout the police who attempted to dislodge them in the famous "battle of the running Bulls." Before long UAW members, using tactics of which any army commander would have been proud, sat in and seized a second plant, the vital Chevy No. 4. This second group of sit-downers also determined to remain inside until victory was theirs. General Motors was unable to resume production, to import strike-breakers, or to obtain a commitment from federal or state authorities to evict trespassers from private property regardless of the human cost. Management thus had no choice but to negotiate and ultimately to concede what its spokesmen had once insisted was unthinkable.

On February 11, 1937, John L. Lewis could proudly wave the agreement he had just signed with General Motors' executives, compelling that major corporation for the first time to recognize an international union and to bargain collectively with it. Three weeks before the victory was won, the *New York Times* had head-lined: FUTURE OF C.I.O. HANGS ON AUTO STRIKE RESULT. And afterward, the secretary of the Communist party of Michigan noted: "The auto workers have cleared the way in planting the flag of unionism over the great factories of this country."

The shock waves from Flint reverberated throughout American society. As the year 1937 wore on, hospital workers, pencil makers, janitors, dog catchers, sailors, Woolworth girls, and gar-bage collectors, among others, sat down. In January there were 25 sit-down strikes, in February 47, and in March what had be-come an epidemic struck 170 firms. Moreover, in March 1937, United States Steel, without even passing through the ritual of industrial warfare, signed a contract with the CIO's Steel Workers' Organization Committee (SWOC). As in autos and steel, CIO affiliates and wards between 1937 and 1940 successfully pene-trated rubber, electrical goods, and meat packing.

By October 1937, when it transformed itself from a temporary committee into a permanent organization (Congress of Industrial Organization), the CIO had thirty-two affiliates with a claimed membership of four million, a figure already larger on paper than that of the AFL. Winning the affection and devotion of idealistic young people, gaining the support of dedicated communist trade unionists, becoming the cynosure of radical intellectuals, stirring workers to militant action, and led by the commanding labor leader of the twentieth century, John L. Lewis, the CIO seemed to be riding a powerful wave, one that would carry it into a future of its own making. "Around mammoth modern mills and at bleak old factories," wrote one observer, "on ships and on piers, at offices and in public gathering-places, men and women roared, 'C.I.O.! C.I.O.!' . . . Labor was on the march as it had never been before in the history of the Republic."

But 1937 proved to be high tide for the CIO. Its very success proved in a sense its undoing. The sit-down strikes after Flint created a sharp reaction among large and concerned sectors of the public. Already by late 1937, and more so in 1938, strong political opposition had developed against the New Deal, and the CIO, obviously in the vanguard of the reform crusade, was among the first institutions to suffer. When in the spring of 1937 the Steel Workers challenged the companies that formed the coalition known as Little Steel in an effort to win a collective-bargaining agreement, they were forced to strike for recognition. Little Steel, using the time-honored tactics of anti-union employers—labor spies, private guards, company armories, strike-breakers, back-to-work committees, and community pressures—repelled the union drive at a cost of 18 killed and 168 injured. When Lewis appealed to Roosevelt for help, the President, resorting to Shakespeare, responded, "A plague on both your houses." The CIO wave had crested.

Meanwhile, the AFL leadership proved that old dogs could learn new tricks. Watching the successes of the CIO, they realized that the unorganized could indeed be organized; and why should they decline the opportunity to gain new members, an increased treasury, and greater institutional power? AFL affiliates, more numerous, usually more stable, and spread more evenly across the nation than their competitors in the CIO, vigorously sought members and no longer made fine distinctions between the more and the less skilled, between craft and industrial unions. In fact, the larger and more successful AFL affiliates became to all intents and purposes industrial unions with an inclusive rather than exclusive membership base. Not associated directly with the militancy stirred by the CIO, firm critics of the sit-down tactics, and traditional enemies of communist subversion, AFL unions sometimes appeared a good bargain to employers—better to deal with a known commodity than to negotiate with the volatile and possibly even communist CIO. Using every weapon its leaders could command, the AFL grew until by 1941 its total membership far surpassed that of the CIO.

By 1941 few essential economic and organizational issues separated AFL from CIO affiliates. The struggle between the two national labor giants continued, but it was obviously waged as much over power as about principles, values, or objectives.

The differences that remained, largely on issues secondary to trade unionism,* and reflecting the ethnic composition, age level, and radical influences in the CIO, might have been compromised. But neither Lewis nor Philip Murray, his successor as president of the CIO, would accept second place in a reunited labor federation; nor could William Green conceive of himself stepping down as head of the AFL. Reasons of power and ego, as well as divergent trade-union philosophies, kept labor divided.

V

On the eve of United States entry into World War II, the country for the first time in its history had a mass labor movement which had successfully organized the basic industries. As a result of New Deal reforms which had sanctioned the emergence of independent trade unions, and National Labor Relations Board decisions which had generally favored organized labor, particularly the CIO's mass-production unions, total union membership had risen from 2,805,000 in 1933 to 8,410,000 in 1941, some 23 per cent of all nonagricultural workers. This growth was most marked in the manufacturing, mining, transportation, and construction industries, where blue-collar workers comprised the overwhelming majority of the labor force. White-collar workers in the service trades and in public employment remained largely outside the unions, as did millions of migratory farm workers and domestics who had been excluded from coverage under the basic New Deal labor reforms.

What the triumph of unionism meant for individual workers was also evident. Wage rates in unionized industries rose much more rapidly than in unorganized sectors of the economy, and trade-union members received protection against arbitrary rulings by foremen and supervisors through institutionalized procedures for the amelioration of job grievances. A measure of what was called "industrial democracy" had been won. As one worker on

* Mainly in the areas of politics and civil rights and largely a function of the CIO's debt to the New Deal; communist and radical influences among affiliates; its mass membership among ethnic groups; and its consistent efforts to recruit black workers.

the line in Flint put it, "We are now treated as human beings and not as part of the machinery." For most organized workers, and for a substantial proportion of the unorganized, New Deal measures provided an added measure of assistance. The social security legislation of 1935 (the first benefits were paid out in 1940) offered some protection, minimal as it may have been, against old age, death in the family, crippling illness, and unemployment. And the Fair Labor Standards Act of 1938 set for certain industries a floor below which hourly wages could not fall and a ceiling above which hours could not rise; it also forbade or restricted the employment of children.

Grateful workers rewarded their political patrons. Organized labor had become a vital part of the Democratic party coalition, as the CIO's heavy financial and moral backing for Roosevelt during the election of 1936 had revealed. What the CIO initiated politically, the AFL soon imitated, it too becoming a cog in the Roosevelt political machinery. So completely had Roosevelt won the loyalty of American workers that when, in the autumn of 1940, John L. Lewis made a dramatic radio address in which he advised workers to vote for Wendell Willkie, the Republican presidential candidate, and threatened to resign as president of the CIO if Roosevelt were re-elected, scarcely a dent was made in working-class support for the Democrats. Even Lewis' own coal miners voted overwhelmingly for Roosevelt, and the imperious union leader was not allowed to forget his threat to resign as president of the CIO. Just as workers repudiated Lewis, a leader who had done so much for them in the thirties, old socialists drifted away from the political party of their first loyalty and also entered the New Deal coalition. The New Deal buried what remained of a once vital socialist movement, and American communists, despite folk myths regarding their omnipotence, never posed a threat to the established political order.

What the New Deal failed to accomplish for organized labor, and what workers failed to win for themselves, the coming of world war brought. In peacetime both Henry Ford and the executives of Little Steel had repulsed the trade-union advance. But as America geared up for wartime production in 1940, pressures from the workers below and from Washington officials above compelled first Ford and later Little Steel to recognize the principle of the union shop and the check-off of union dues by management. Trade unionism thus conquered the last major anti-union corporations. The tide which had begun to run against trade unionism in 1937–1938 now receded.

Government needed labor-management harmony to run the war effort efficiently, and of course went about obtaining it. Following precedents established during World War I, Roosevelt in 1941 created a Defense Mediation Board to cope with industrial conflict in industries vital to the war effort. And in January 1942 the President appointed a twelve-man National War Labor Board (NWLB) * with total jurisdiction over industrial relations. Just as Woodrow Wilson had appointed Samuel Gompers to vital defense agencies and relied on his advice in labor matters, Roosevelt brought Sidney Hillman of the CIO Amalgamated Clothing Workers to Washington to serve as spokesman for organized labor. What war had done to make the AFL respectable in 1917, a second war accomplished for the CIO in 1941.

The economic realities of modern war also favored organized labor. With millions of men being conscripted into the armed services and industrial plants operating at full capacity after a full decade of depression, surplus labor was soaked up. With a market available at a profitable price for all it produced, management had no desire or interest in combatting trade unionism. At first cost-plus government contracts allowed employers to pass rising labor costs on to consumers, and subsequently, after the Office of Price Administration (OPA) was established to set prices and wages, business no longer faced a threatened cost-push/price-pull. Management could, and did, live equably with trade unionism.

American unions and employers wrote a notable industrial-relations record during the war years. Despite regular difficulties with John L. Lewis and his coal miners, the United States lost less time due to strikes (most of which were unauthorized) than did wartime England. The chairman of the War Labor Board observed that "it is the best this nation or any other nation has ever done in wartime or peacetime." And President Roosevelt added: "That

---

* Four employer members, another four representing trade unions, and four representatives of the public.

record has never before been equalled in this country. It is as good or better than the record of any of our allies in wartime."

The unions had every reason to cooperate in the war effort as organizational gains flowed their way. Decisions by the War Labor Board during the spring and summer of 1942 practically assured the unions of all the membership gains won during the thirties. These decisions, which established for the duration of the war the "maintenance of membership" principle, in effect made it difficult for a worker once enrolled in a union to leave voluntarily * and almost impossible for employers to reduce substantially the organized portion of their work force. "Maintenance of membership" was especially important to CIO affiliates, most of which lacked union- or closed-shop security contracts—arrangements under which all employees had to be union members either at the time of employment or shortly thereafter. AFL unions were less affected by the decisions since they typically operated under union- or closed-shop contracts, which remained untouched by wartime federal labor policies. The proportion of eligible workers covered by collective-bargaining agreements thus rose from 30 per cent in 1941 to 48 per cent by 1945, with some 3,900,000 workers bound by "maintenance of membership" clauses. The exigencies of war and the activities of the War Labor Board also accustomed employers to living and dealing with trade unions on a regular basis. By the war's end organized labor could count between fourteen and fifteen million members, a percentage of the total labor force that was to be exceeded only for a short time during the Korean War. By 1945 the CIO and its mass-production unions were ten years old and still thriving.

Equally important was the impact of the war on the structure and shape of the labor force. As is often the case, some of the most significant changes were those least perceptible to contemporary observers. Obviously, the war created full employment for the first time in a decade, and made available additional income from overtime wages. Although actual hourly wage rates failed to

---

* Most union clauses included an escape period, generally the first fifteen days of the contract period, when the individual worker retained the right to leave the union. Some clauses allowed workers to leave the union but required them to pay union dues for the duration of the contract.

rise significantly, total income did as a result of full employment. This was even more true for the unorganized and the poorly paid who in peacetime lacked union protection and were thus most severely affected by cyclical and seasonal patterns of employment. Less obviously, the war substantially altered attitudes and expectations among two long-exploited groups in American society: blacks and women. With able-bodied men drained off to war, blacks began to fill jobs once reserved for whites, and women took up men's work. "Rosie the Riveter" was a common sight from 1941 to 1945, yet few Americans took the time to consider what the ultimate impact of such jobs might be on the female consciousness. If women could do the same work as men and, as the war propaganda agencies informed them, equally well, what did that fact portend for the future of male-female relations and expectations? At the same time, in war-production centers everywhere in the land, black men and women provided an increasing amount of the labor necessary for the war effort. The urban black beachheads and ghettos that had expanded so enormously during World War I filled to overflowing and sometimes burst at the seams from 1941 to 1945. The blacks' role in the war effort, which they too were told was absolutely vital, necessarily affected their consciousness and expectations; but this fact was usually ignored except when a city such as Detroit in 1943 erupted in racial conflict. Even then, scapegoating rather than analysis and understanding of the changes wrought by war was the common response. After the experience of war, black-white relations could never again be the same. World War II, in its impact on women and blacks, had planted a time bomb that a decade or two later would explode.

VI

Ironically, the end of the war brought as much anxiety as comfort to organized labor and to American workers. In 1946 Americans still suffered from what might be called a depression trauma. The peacetime experience most firmly fixed in their minds was that of the Great Depression of the 1930's. With the war over, industrial production curtailed, and millions of veterans returning home, would the nation once again witness rising unemployment and growing breadlines? Many thought so, and feared the conversion of the economy from war to peacetime production. Trade unionists also had reason to be pessimistic. They recalled employers' opposition to union organization before the war, and had to suspect—particularly the CIO unions that had not negotiated a peacetime contract since 1938–1939, as well as some newer AFL affiliates—that employers would now seek to deflate union power. Worried as union leaders were about defending their prewar and wartime membership gains, they also had to bear in mind the aspirations created among their members during the war. For most union members were now convinced that, as a result of War Labor Board rulings, they had lost ground during the crisis in their struggle to raise wages; and now that the war was over they wanted to be rewarded materially for their sacrifices and extraordinary production efforts.

The result of such fears and hopes was an explosion of labor discontent and a series of major strikes in the winter of 1945–1946. Practically every major industry—from autos and steel to coal and railroads—and most minor ones were hit by strikes. Yet the conflicts followed a similar pattern, though one not entirely expected. Employers had apparently learned how to live with unions, for in 1945–1946 they did not try to operate their plants during strikes or to break the unions; instead, they accepted the fact of trade unionism and negotiated with the unions in a series of hard but peaceful bargaining sessions.

Actually there were good reasons for this new relationship. Employers discovered that instead of being surrounded by surplus labor and a glutted market, their potential market was immense, the supply of labor stayed tight, and it was still quite easy to pass the cost of wage increases on to consumers. Moreover, the 18 per cent wage increase negotiated in the steel industry became the pattern that federal mediators and officials, including President Truman, fastened onto other industries, and it was an award well within the financial capacity of business to pay. When the Republican-dominated Congress elected in 1946 began to dismantle the wartime wage and price controls, prices promptly outran wages; no matter how hard unions pressed their monetary demands, wages could never thereafter quite catch up with prices.

Inflationary pressure notwithstanding, labor-management relations remained generally harmonious as compared with the pre-war era. This new period of labor peace was capped off by the 1948 agreement between the United Auto Workers and General Motors, which provided both for an annual cost-of-living adjust-ment in wages and automatic annual wage increases based on gains in productivity estimated at 3 per cent. Inflation was thus built into the labor contract itself. But few Americans complained while the United States dominated the global economy through the Marshall Plan, foreign aid, and overseas corporate investment, all of which kept the domestic economy booming, the labor market tight, and job security excellent. With the outbreak of the Korean War in June 1950 and the immense growth in military expendi-tures that followed, unemployment was further reduced and union membership climbed to a peak of eighteen million.

The Age of Affluence had arrived, the American Century could be celebrated. Sociologists soon began to focus their attention on working-class life in suburbia, where every worker allegedly had a weedless lawn, one—or perhaps even two—cars in his garage, television sets in every room, and beefsteak on his table. The great discovery was then announced to the American public: the work-ingman was now middle class in substance as well as in mentality. He could consume middle-class goods as well as harbor middle-class dreams. As long as the welfare-warfare state (that combina-tion of federal expenditures—in uneven proportions—on aid to the needy and the mighty) maintained a market for American in-dustries and kept employment high, poverty, it was proudly an-nounced, had been conquered. Or so it seemed from 1946 to 1960.

VII

The "abolition" of poverty and the creation of permanent pros-perity was not an unmixed blessing for the labor movement. After all, with wages rising (and wasn't that the real cause of inflation?), workers able to enjoy the same creature comforts as other Ameri-cans, and job security a fact, were not trade unions growing too powerful? If not too powerful in fact, too imperious in attitude? During the war, when John L. Lewis had several times called the coal miners out on strike, Congress was moved to pass anti-strike legislation that was vetoed by the President. The strike wave of 1945–1946, which scarcely left an American home unaffected, reinforced the popular image of organized labor's omnipotence, and a stream of newspaper and magazine articles contributed to that image.

It was high time, the critics of labor and most Republican politicians insisted, to redress the balance of power between unions and employers. The Wagner Act, it was asserted, had given labor preponderant power; new legislation was needed to protect both employers and individual workers against the abuse of the unions. This the Republican Congress of 1947 provided in the form of the Taft-Hartley Act, basically a revision of the National Labor Relations Act of 1935. Passed over President Truman's veto and immediately labeled the "Slave Labor Act" by its union critics, Taft-Hartley, for all its clauses and specific limitation on union power, had at most a marginal impact on the already established unions. It was after the passage of the act that the labor movement achieved its peak membership from 1951 to 1953, and the subsequent decline in trade unionism was a process of gradual erosion which had little to do with hostile legislation. What Taft-Hartley did do, however, was to render more difficult the recruitment of union members in such traditionally anti-union regions as the South and the prairie states, where the new law sanctioned "right-to-work" statutes (basically anti-union devices outlawing closed- and union-shop contracts) which thwarted union advance in those regions. Ironically, the established unions—especially the building trades and teamsters—which in theory were most hampered by Taft-Hartley's restrictions on secondary boycotts and jurisdictional strikes, proved to be among the few unions to grow and thrive after the passage of the law.

More troublesome to organized labor than congressional legislation or an unfavorable political environment (as reflected in the election of Dwight D. Eisenhower to the presidency in 1952) were domestic difficulties in its own house. Not that such troubles were unrelated to politics generally. The Cold War struggle with Soviet Russia and its internal repercussions in the age of Joe McCarthy had its impact on the labor movement. The AFL had been red-baiting the CIO since 1936, and such AFL leaders as

John Frey, Matthew Woll, and David Dubinsky had been hunting communists in the labor movement well before the Senator from Wisconsin knew that there were such political animals. On the communist issue the AFL unions could appear before Congress and an increasingly hysterical public with clean hands. Not so the CIO! It had willingly used communist organizers during the 1930's, and in several of its more important affiliates, such as the United Electrical Workers, communists had risen to positions of power. Despite what they had contributed to the growth of the CIO in the 1930's and how capable some of the alleged communist union leaders in fact were, Philip Murray, president of the CIO, and Walter Reuther, elected president of the UAW in 1946, reacted to the growing anti-communist hysteria by declaring war on "the reds" within the CIO. The result of their declaration of war was the expulsion in 1948–1949 of eleven reputedly communist unions with a membership of between 500,000 and one million from the CIO, and the replacement of several with competing unions. (The CIO never really recovered from this blow, which eliminated its final distinction from the AFL.)

Relatively unscathed by the communist issue, the AFL had its own internal problems. If the CIO had been infiltrated with communists, the AFL was rife with gangsters—or so it seemed to the public. Hearings in New York revealed that the International Longshoremen's Association, especially its Brooklyn and Hoboken branches, was run by criminals who exploited shippers as well as their own union members.* A leader of the Operating Engineers' Union in the New York metropolitan area was to end his days in state prison, and officials of the Carpenters', the Bakers', and the Teamsters' unions, among others, were soon in legal trouble. Before long, AFL conventions had to consider action against so-called corrupt, or criminal, unions as a regular item of business.

As more and more examples of trade-union crime and corruption filtered through the media and into the public consciousness, it was only a matter of time until Congress chose to investigate the problem. With investigations of communism losing their

---

* In 1953 the AFL suspended the ILA from Federation ranks.

effect by the mid-fifties, conservative politicians needed a new bogeyman to scare the voters. Senator John McClellan of Arkansas discovered it in a corrupt labor movement. In a series of hearings which began in 1957 and were skillfully conducted by the ambitious young counsel of the Select Senate Investigating Committee on Labor-Management Relations, Robert Kennedy, the full scope of corruption and crime in the labor movement was laid before the public. As it turned out, while McClellan and his Senatorial colleagues were generally sympathetic to AFL witnesses and hostile to those from the CIO, most of the illegal activities uncovered were committed by AFL affiliates. The most notable object and victim of the McClellan hearings was the Teamsters' Union and its leader James R. "Jimmy" Hoffa. Hoffa, made notorious by these congressional investigations, became in the late 1950's as much the symbol of the American labor movement as John L. Lewis had been in the thirties and Walter Reuther immediately after World War II. As a result of such investigations and Hoffa's unrepentant behavior, the merged AFL-CIO in 1957 expelled the Teamsters' Union from the organization. It is worth noting, however, for what it may reveal about American values, that the unions expelled by the CIO for communist influence died or declined in power; the Teamsters' Union, ridden with corruption, after its expulsion remained the single largest and most powerful trade union in the nation, and grew still larger.

The internal problems of the CIO and the AFL, and the unfavorable politics of the fifties as reflected in anti-union legislation, a Republican President, and congressional investigations of the labor movement, brought union officials to realize that in unity lay strength. By the early 1950's there were no longer any substantial structural or ideological differences between the AFL and the CIO. And when William Green and Philip Murray died within weeks of each other in 1952, there were no strong personal reasons for the existence of two separate national labor centers. The obvious followed. Serious negotiations resumed between AFL and CIO leaders, and by 1955 a mutually acceptable merger was accomplished. In the reunited labor movement, George Meany of the AFL became president of the AFL-CIO, as befit the leader of the larger and more successful organization, and Walter Reuther agreed to serve as first vice-president. Founded by leaders who pledged an aggressive and militant labor movement that would organize the unorganized, the AFL-CIO was in fact a defensive reaction to trade unionism's fading public image and an effort to preserve what already had been won.

The merged AFL-CIO represented a mature labor movement that behaved, in the words of economist Richard Lester, as a "sleepy monopoly." Prevailing union-shop contracts guaranteed a secure union membership and stability in union income regardless of membership satisfaction. This stability enabled labor leaders to increase their power and their own security of tenure in office, both of which were based on maintaining amicable relations with employers. Union officials and corporate managers together developed a vested interest in mutual survival and the avoidance of strikes. If strikes came, in those industries that had long accepted unionism, they ran their course as placidly as the conflicts of the 1930's had once been turbulent. Labor leaders and business executives preferred to sacrifice potentially troublesome economic gains for ease and convenience in administering their respective institutions. As unions grew and collective bargaining became increasingly complex, union officials, like their counterparts in business and government, became bureaucrats whose first obligation was to preserve and protect the institution they served—in their case the trade union. As a result, labor leaders became more concerned with maintaining their own powers and privileges than with organizing the unorganized, contributing to innovative trends in unionism, or promoting the general welfare. They had become, in truth, smooth-working members of John Kenneth Galbraith's "New Industrial State," a junior but vital part of the "technostructure."

VIII

Just when the labor movement seemed most secure and ordinary workers most affluent, a concatenation of basic changes in the American social and economic structure threatened to undermine hard-won security and dearly bought affluence. The last years of the Eisenhower era (1955–1960) brought the results of conservative fiscal and monetary policies vividly home to many workers and trade unionists. Rising unemployment became a permanent, accepted, and, some conservative economists even maintained, necessary part of the American system. Without a foreign war, such as the one in Korea, to soak up excess labor and capital, the reserve army of unemployed men and women served as a check on union wage demands. As unemployment rose steeply after 1953 and then seemed to stabilize at between 4 and 6 per cent of the work force, unions found it much more difficult to negotiate attractive new labor contracts.

Unemployment, however, did not strike all sectors of the population equally. The nonwhite, the less educated, the young, and the least skilled bore the brunt of economic recession. Nonwhites still tended to be last hired and first fired, and together with youths formed the largest proportion of the population with limited education and few job skills. Not surprisingly, at the start of John F. Kennedy's administration (1961–1963), unemployment among blacks and youths became a major issue in domestic policy.

And a new spectre came to haunt the workingman: automation. The substitution of machines for men in many basic sectors of the economy hit with unequal force the same social groups most affected by rising unemployment. Again, the nonwhite, the less educated, and the unskilled felt the effects of technological change. Mere brawn became a surplus commodity on the labor market. The apparent conjunction of rising costs, failing profits, and the availability of a new technology in the late fifties and early sixties moreover impelled employers, wherever possible, to replace relatively expensive and temperamental human laborers with less costly and more predictable machines. Structural unemployment thus complicated and aggravated the impact of cyclical unemployment.

For the first time since their rise to power during the New Deal, such great industrial unions as the UAW and the Steel Workers suffered membership losses. The story is told of how Harlow Curtice, president of General Motors, took Walter Reuther, president of the UAW, for a tour of an auto assembly plant. The corporation executive, ecstatic about the new automated machinery operating on the plant floor below, turned to the union leader and said, "Walter, in the future the UAW will not be able to call the machines out on strike." To which Reuther responded, "Will the machines be able to buy your automobiles?" This repartee, however, offered no solace to workers who were replaced on the line by machines and who were too old or too unskilled to find employment elsewhere.

Automation also accelerated a change in the structure of the labor force that had long been in process. Since at least the 1920's, and perhaps even earlier, the nonmanual portion of the work force had been growing at a more rapid rate than the blue-collar sector, the traditional stronghold of organized labor. By the 1950's not only was white-collar employment still rising, but manual labor as a proportion of the work force was absolutely declining. New jobs became most abundant in public service, the retail trades, and clerical office work, all occupations traditionally immune to mass unionization.

Yet as employment rose in those areas, the labor movement necessarily had to seek its new recruits there. And unions in fact had their greatest success in gaining members among governmental employees whose positions on the public payroll proved unresponsive to rising price levels. Throughout the fifties and sixties wages in public service rose much less rapidly than those in private employment. As a result, schoolteachers, government clerks, and other public servants joined trade unions and even engaged in militant strikes. It was no longer unusual to see schoolteachers walking picket lines, and, despite state laws forbidding strikes by public servants, for civil servants to tie up vital public services. Neither rain, nor snow, nor sleet, nor war might delay the United States mail, but in the spring of 1970 a strike by Post Office employees did so. Unable to gain a much-needed wage increase through the usual lobbying tactics used by federal employees, the letter-carriers resorted to action more customary among industrial workers—and by striking in defiance of the law, they won their wage increase.

Other long-neglected sectors of the labor force also became militant. For more than half a century migratory farm workers had remained the most exploited part of the working class. Invariably, labor and welfare legislation, whether federal or state, had ignored farm workers. Not for them were minimum-wage laws, restrictions on child labor, social security, or the Wagner Act. Not for them were trade unions—indeed, most labor leaders considered the farm workers unorganizable, as they had once considered the mass-production workers before the New Deal. After all, every effort to organize the migratories in the past had ended in failure.

But with the rediscovery of poverty in America during the Kennedy years and the publication of Michael Harrington's *The Other America* (1962), farm workers and other exploited Americans were pushed into the spotlight. Television documentaries and newspaper features highlighted the plight of the migrants. John Steinbeck's *Grapes of Wrath* was being replayed in the 1960's, only this time Chicano * workers replaced Okies as the objects of public concern. Finding a leader in César Chavez, himself a Mexican-American, the migrant farm workers of the West Coast organized themselves into a union (United Farm Workers' Organizing Committee) and carried on a relatively successful struggle against the California grape growers. Using such traditional union tactics as strikes and pickets, Chavez's followers harassed their employers. Equally important to their success, however, was a boycott of California-grown grapes by aroused, sympathetic, or guilt-ridden middle-class consumers in the cities of America. Pressed by their workers on one side and their consumers on the other, California grape growers in 1967 began to sign contracts with the Chavez organization. Buoyed by his success in the vineyards, Chavez in 1970 pushed on in an attempt to win labor contracts from California's numerous other commercial agricultural interests.

Much as its militant new recruits among white-collar workers and migrant farm hands may have pleased the labor movement, most of its officials could scarcely have considered the other developments of the late fifties and sixties an unmixed blessing; nor could they look forward to the seventies with pleasure. Old patterns in American working-class history had begun to reassert themselves in the 1950's. David Riesman has remarked: "No other large industrial society has substituted color and ethnicity for social class as the basis of stratification and hence of tension." Almost a century earlier, in attempting to explain the failure of trade

* Americans of Latin, mostly Mexican, derivation.

unionism and radical politics among American workers, Friedrich Engels had observed: "Your bourgeoisie knows even better than the Austrian government how to play off one nationality against another. . . . The bourgeoisie need only wait passively, and the dissimilar elements of the working class fall apart again." Which seemed to be the story of the fifties and sixties.

The rise of black consciousness and militancy in the mid-fifties had paradoxically proved to be a problem rather than a gain for the labor movement. Instead of black workers' directing all their militancy against employers, a good share of it was aimed at white workers and their union officials—and not without good reason. In trade after trade where blacks formed an increasing share of the labor force, union offices remained by and large lily-white. And in those sectors of the economy where the highest wages were paid—the construction trades in particular—unions tended also to be lily-white in membership. Indeed, in most of the largest and most successful building trades' unions, blacks could not even qualify for membership. So instead of black and white workers uniting to fight their employers, the reverse too often occurred. Herbert Hill, the NAACP's labor adviser, clashed publicly with George Meany and officials of the International Ladies' Garment Workers' Union; Hill regularly accused Meany and the labor movement he represented of institutional racism. A. Philip Randolph, founder of the Negro-American Labor Council, one-time socialist, and long-time leader of black trade unionism, also found himself frequently at odds with Meany and the leadership of the AFL-CIO. In New York City, white members of the local teachers' union in 1968 found themselves in effect at war with some of their black "brothers" and on strike against a part of the black community. In Detroit, militant black workers organized in such groups as DRUM (Dodge Revolutionary Union Movement) seemed to be devoting more time to fighting the leadership of the UAW than to taking on General Motors, Ford, or Chrysler.

At a time when the working class and the labor movement needed unity as never before to cope with problems of unemployment, automation, and inflation, the racial division loomed formidable. At a time when workers, students, and reformers might have been cooperating to oppose President Richard Nixon's social policies, construction workers took to the streets of New York to attack anti-war protesters. At a time (1965–1970) when wages and buying power simply refused to keep pace with prices, too many workers preferred to think only of themselves and their individual consumption desires. As one labor leader remarked of his followers: "They don't give a damn about anyone else. They see everybody getting away with murder and they don't want to be left out." At a time when old-fashioned collective bargaining seemed unable to solve the most pressing working-class problems, unions struck, as the auto workers did against General Motors in 1970, and won fat contracts because, as one union official noted: "The trouble is you ask for the moon and you wind up getting it." Alas, for most workers wages simply failed to keep pace with prices—between October 1969 and October 1970 take-home pay fell 2 per cent, and it lagged behind 1965 real wage levels even though national productivity had risen some 15 per cent over the same period.

Thus, some three decades after the end of the New Deal and organized labor's rise to national prominence, the American labor movement and the working classes found themselves in a strange predicament. On the one hand, George Meany in a 1969 Labor Day interview could take pride in the successes of the labor movement since 1933 and in what he characterized as the middle-class consciousness and status of the ordinary union member. On the other hand, more and more ordinary dues-paying union members found themselves unable to afford the style of life that Madison Avenue told them they must have in order to be good Americans. And while the Meanys took justified pride in the labor movement they had built and led, trade unionism appeared incapable of significant new growth or of doing much about the unemployment, low wages, and poverty that afflicted substantial numbers of the working class. It was a labor movement that could, on the one hand, struggle against such pillars of the established economic order as General Electric and General Motors, and yet, on the other hand, defend with equal enthusiasm the local police and the American presidency. It was a labor movement uncertain of where it should move, built on a working class that lacked a clear social identity. And it was a labor movement and a working class in which ethnic and racial tensions had assumed an explosive, if not a new, shape. In what direction the internally divided and apparently anomic American working classes and their unions would move in the last quarter of the twentieth century, only the most foolish or venturesome would dare guess.

Part 1

A NEW DEAL FOR LABOR: 1933–1938

THE FOLLOWING selections offer a glimpse at the turbulence that characterized American life in the 1930's, and how workers, their unions, and their leaders contributed to the unrest. Russell Porter's dispatches from San Francisco capture the militancy and solidarity of that city's working class, as well as employers' and public officials' deep anxiety about the methods and objectives of labor protest. News reports covering industrial conflicts in St. Paul-Minneapolis and Kohler, Wisconsin, further indicate the widespread geographical base of working-class protest, the stringent measures used by employers and authorities to contain it, and the considerable violence that often resulted.

The violent strikes of the year 1934 were largely a result of the refusal by American employers to countenance the organization of their workers into independent trade unions with which they would have to bargain collectively. Early New Deal labor legislation had failed to protect the individual worker's right to join a union. This failure was sensed in Washington, where reform politicians were eager to move workers off the streets and to return labor-management confrontations to negotiating rooms. Senator Robert F.

Wagner's essay offers an insight into the values and motives of the man who sponsored the 1935 National Labor Relations Act. It strikingly reveals how an advanced New Dealer perceived the basic social and economic realities of American life and how he intended to bring those realities in line with American ideals. Wagner's proposals and values also raise questions about the basic character and intent of the New Deal.

The Wagner Act and the opportunities it provided for the unionization of mass-production workers precipitated a split within the American Federation of Labor. The news story of November 24, 1935, describes the resignation of John L. Lewis as an AFL vice-president after the defeat of the industrial unionists at that year's convention. Louis Stark analyzes the subsequent split in the labor movement from an historical and contemporary perspective. His article leads one to inquire if the trade-union rupture was inevitable and whether the AFL, as constituted in 1935, was indeed incapable of organizing the mass-production workers.

Lewis' resignation caused the recently founded Committee on Industrial Organization to go its own way, a decision soon vindicated by the Flint sit-down strike of 1937. The news stories included in this section present some sense of the tactics and feelings of the sit-downers in Flint, and especially of the combination of planning and spontaneity that marked the conflict. In his article, Russell Porter discusses the larger implications of the struggle in Flint and inquires whether the sit-down strike was a tactic capable of extensive imitation as well as a means to alter American society fundamentally. Are Porter's generally sober estimates of the effect and value of sit-down strikes valid?

The victory of the United Auto Workers in Flint guaranteed the CIO's future as an independent national labor organization. Aside from its mere independence, did the CIO offer anything to the American worker different from the traditional aims of the AFL? Indeed, did the CIO represent a new direction in the history of the American labor movement? Russell Porter seeks to answer those questions in his portrait of the CIO as it appeared in 1937. Although Porter indicates certain specific differences between the CIO and the AFL, his overall conclusions suggest that on basic issues the CIO remained well within the bounds of traditional American labor policies and objectives. S. J. Woolf's sympathetic portrait of and interview with John L. Lewis captures the CIO chieftain's basic concepts about the labor movement's place in American society. It also helps us to distinguish between the CIO's objectives as an institution and Lewis' as an individual. Comparing Porter on the CIO to Woolf on Lewis, one naturally wonders precisely to what extent Lewis' ideas and values shaped the labor movement.

Just as the New Deal years began with turbulent industrial conflict, they ended for labor on a violent note. The defeat of trade unionism by the Little Steel companies in 1937 revealed strikingly the restraints under which workers and unions still functioned after five years of New Deal reforms. News reports from Chicago, which describe the notorious Memorial Day massacre of 1937, indicate the persistence of violence in American industrial relations and the continued use of anti-communist rhetoric to justify the most brutal forms of repression.

Strike Paralyzes
San Francisco Life

by Russell B. Porter

SAN FRANCISCO, JULY 16.

THE FIRST day of San Francisco's general strike, which went into effect at 8 o'clock this morning, saw a modification by strike leaders of the transit tie-up, and, to some extent, of the food blockade. There were no mass disorders or looting, and although numerous cases of violence were reported they were sporadic and of a minor nature.

Late in the day, after having completely tied up all transportation, except for those private automobiles which could obtain gas; having paralyzed many retail trades and businesses and having seriously inconvenienced the 1,300,000 residents of the metropolitan area in getting to work and in obtaining food and gasoline and such services as the laundry, tailor and barber shops supply, the general strike committee eased up materially in its interference with the normal life and business of the city.

The strike picket lines which had been thrown across the highways leading into the city from adjacent farm areas let food trucks convoyed by policemen pass unmolested. This removed one of the chief fears of violence, as it had been generally understood that serious trouble would follow any attempt to stop food trucks guarded by the public authorities.

The food trucks allowed to pass the picket lines received "permits" from the strike committee, which announced that more permits would be issued tomorrow so that "no one in San Francisco shall go hungry."

At the same time the strike leaders announced that they had no intention of trying to starve out the city. They also indicated that they intended to let all or most of the city's restaurants re-open, inasmuch as the limitation of restaurant services today to nineteen places designated by the union clearly proved inadequate. Long lines waiting on sidewalks outside the favored eating places so attested.

The strike committee also released its grip on the city's transportation by telling the employes of the Municipal Railway to return to work and cautioning against any violence against the city-owned street-car lines. This removed a danger which had been regarded fully as threatening as the possibility of stopping the convoyed food trucks.

Just before the strike committee acted on the Municipal Railway problem the public utilities committee had informed the carmen that they must return to work immediately or forfeit their jobs and civil service standing. It was widely believed that if the men did not return to their posts strike-breakers, many of whom are said to be in the city, would be put on the cars, guarded by policemen and special deputies, and that bloodshed certainly would follow.

Service was resumed on the Municipal Railway this evening, with regular employes operating the cars, protected by policemen. The cars were not molested. It was expected that about 50 per cent of the usual service would be restored before the night was over and that normal operations on this line would be effective tomorrow.

While the strike leaders thus pursued a course obviously designed to keep public opinion from rising against them, State and city officials were taking determined steps to keep the city supplied with food and other necessaries of life, as well as with transportation facilities, before the growing food shortage should become acute, and before the city's industry and commerce should become hopelessly crippled.

The authorities also made public comprehensive plans to protect the city against any attempt by irresponsible elements to take advantage of possible chaos and confusion growing out of the general strike for the purpose either of subversive attacks against the government or of rioting and looting.

Governor Frank F. Merriam, who ordered full police protection for the food trucks, also sent 2,600 additional National Guardsmen into the city early today, with tanks and artillery units, in addition to the infantrymen and machine gunners already on hand. There were 4,500 National Guard troops on duty here tonight. During the day, they extended their zone of control from the dock district to the produce area, where they set up sand-bag barricades and machine-gun nests.

"If I err in performing my duty at this time," said Governor Merriam, "I propose to err on the side of public interest."

The Governor warned that "rioting or any sporadic or concerted movements having the aspects of insurrection will be vigorously, summarily and uncompromisingly suppressed; and that any person or persons attempting to interfere with the transportation of the necessities of life or with the maintenance of law and order will do so at their own risk and peril."

Governor Merriam's action in sending more troops followed a proclamation by Mayor Angelo J. Rossi in which the Mayor declared such action necessary in view of fear by the chief of police that disorder could not be prevented otherwise. The Mayor charged that the existing situation was largely due to Communist activities.

Besides continuing to swear in additional policemen, Mayor Rossi and the police officials began the organization of a citizens' committee of 500 to cooperate with the authorities in keeping open the transportation and distribution of foodstuffs. F. M. McAuliffe, president of the San Francisco Bar Association, was named chairman of this committee, and chairman of another committee of twenty-five which will act as a "strategy committee" for the whole group.

The Committee of Twenty-five held its first meeting this afternoon, and the Committee of 500 will meet tomorrow. It was said that some of the city's most prominent and influential citizens would be enlisted in this group.

It was generally believed that the Committee of 500 would be a new "vigilantes" organization which would be ready, if necessary, to emulate the action of prominent Englishmen in driving and guarding trucks loaded with milk and other foodstuffs during the general strike in London in 1926.

Federal authorities were watching the situation closely tonight and redoubling their efforts to bring about a peaceful settlement. General Hugh S. Johnson arrived in San Francisco by airplane from Portland, Ore., but it was understood in well-informed circles that he had not decided how far personally he would try a hand in the situation.

President Roosevelt's National Longshoremen's Board issued a statement declaring that public peace and safety were the paramount issues at present, and repeating its earlier offers of mediation of the two-month-old strike of the longshoremen, in sympathy with whom the general strike was called.

Meantime, the army, navy and marine corps were reported ready for action if they should be called upon, at the Presidio, headquarters of the Ninth Army Corps area, Fort Baker, and the Mare Island Navy Yard.

Despite the efforts of the Federal authorities to bring about peace, it was admitted in these quarters that they feared both sides in this industrial warfare were determined upon a fight to a finish.

In well-informed Federal circles, the main issue is seen as having transcended the original dispute between the International Longshoremen's Association and the Waterfront Employers Association, into a bitter struggle between virtually all organized labor here and the powerful local industrial association, as to whether San Francisco is to become a "closed shop" city.

Some Federal authorities believe that both labor and capital have made up their minds in favor of a show-down on this issue at the present time. Labor wants complete union recognition and collective bargaining, and is willing to risk destruction of its existing union structure for the sake of fighting for these objectives, it was said, whereas the employers see the attainment of such ends by labor as tantamount to the closed shop, and are equally determined on a finish fight.

In these same well-informed Federal quarters the widespread belief in local official and business circles that the general strike is a revolutionary, communistic attempt is not accepted. Although these Federal officials regard some of the most active strike leaders as extremely radical, they do not consider them Communists, but, on the contrary, regard their struggle as strictly a labor dispute.

It is too early yet to determine what the predominant public opinion, which is usually the deciding factor in the success or failure of a general strike, will be in the present situation. There is very strong opposition to the strikers in business circles, but opinion seems to be widely divided among the general public. Support for the strikers strictly on the issue of labor unionism is reported to be surprisingly strong in some quarters which a few years ago probably would have been counted as definitely opposed to the mere idea of a general strike.

At the same time, it is generally believed in practically all circles, liberal and radical as well as conservative, that the strikers will rapidly lose their share of the public's favorable sentiment if they indulge in violence, or try to use their picket lines to starve the city into submission to their demands.

So far, everything indicates that the strike leaders themselves adopt this view and follow this policy. Besides their actions tonight to ease the strain of the general strike on the public, they have exempted milk deliveries from strike restrictions from the beginning and have taken precautions to insure deliveries of all necessaries to hospitals and other public institutions.

What conservative elements now really fear most, from the standpoint of violence, is that, in case the present more or less conservative trend of the general strike policy fails, and the unions begin to fear the loss of their struggle, extremists may seize control, or radical rank-and-file unionists may get out of hand.

Such a fear was widely manifest in the heart of the city this morning, at the time the general strike went into effect. There was an unmistakable feeling of tenseness in the air. This feeling wore off somewhat during the day, as no serious violence or looting occurred, but some of it remains tonight.

One factor that softened the effect of the general strike upon the public was that it did not come all at once and suddenly. The longshoremen's strike and the sympathetic strike of the maritime unions have tied up shipping in the port, and the movement of goods from the piers for weeks. Moreover, the teamsters' sympathetic strike, declared last week, had already partly paralyzed the commerce of the city before today's general strike became effective.

Therefore, the chief effect of today's walk-outs was to inconvenience the average citizen by making it hard or impossible for him to get to his office, factory or shop, to get foodstuffs beyond the bare necessaries of life, to eat in restaurants, drink in bars, have his laundry done or his suit pressed, go to the movies, and so on.

General Strike Called Off by San Francisco Unions

by Russell B. Porter

SAN FRANCISCO, JULY 19.

THE GENERAL strike was called off this afternoon and most of the 50,000 union men and women who have been out for the last four days returned to work or prepared to get back on the job tomorrow morning.

Across San Francisco Bay, in Oakland and in other parts of the East Bay section, the unions acted likewise, so that almost all of the 100,000 workers who laid down their tools in the metropolitan district have picked them up again.

The order calling off the general tie-up, which began at 8 o'clock Monday morning, did not end the longshoremen's strike, which began more than two months ago, or the walk-out of the marine unions, which started soon afterward as the first of those ordered out in sympathy with the dock workers.

The chances were, however, that the longshore and marine disputes would be submitted for arbitration to President Roosevelt's recently formed National Longshoremen's Board. Pending this the men in these unions may or may not return to work.

The San Francisco Teamsters' Union tonight voted to take a secret ballot at 7 o'clock tomorrow morning on the question of ending their strike. If the teamsters vote to end their strike, the most important, although not the most spectacular, factor in paralyzing commerce, industry and shipping of this great seaport has been removed.

Since the teamsters started their sympathetic walk-out last week, before the general strike was declared, goods have not been trucked from warehouses except with special permission of the unions, with the result that many factories, stores and other businesses have had to shut down for lack of materials and for lack of egress for their finished products.

Incidentally, members of the teamsters' union, together with a few longshoremen unsympathetic with their radical leadership, are understood to have composed the "viligante" squads which raided Communist and other radical headquarters day before yesterday, beating radical agitators, breaking windows, and smashing office equipment, while the police followed them with the arrest of more than 300 as Reds.

Within an hour after the vote to abandon the general strike was taken, the entire picture changed in San Francisco. Late this afternoon, for the first time in days, the streets were clogged with trucks hauling foodstuffs, big kegs of beer, gasoline and oil, and other goods of various types; with taxicabs carrying passengers of all kinds, many of them erstwhile strikers celebrating the end of their four-day socio-economic spree; and with happy, merry-making pedestrians stepping into movie theaters, hotels, restaurants, bars, confectionery stores, and other places that had been closed.

Tonight San Francisco once more had snapped back into its normal place as one of the liveliest, pleasantest, most exhilarating cities on the American Continent, instead of what appeared almost like a city of the dead at the zero hour on Monday morning, when nobody knew whether revolution, looting, rioting or what not was to be the outcome, and instead of the half-alive, half-dead community that has seen the general strike gradually disintegrate during its four-day life and finally crumble to pieces.

The whole city, labor and capital, strikers and non-strikers alike, breathed a collective sigh of relief when the news was announced that the general strike was over.

The only exceptions were the comparatively small group of radical agitators who have followed the regular Communist tactics and tried to prevent a settlement and to stir up continual trouble, and the likewise relatively small group of die-hard employers who wanted to seize the opportunity for a showdown today to have martial law employed, break the long-continued strength of union labor here, and make San Francisco a more or less completely "open-shop town."

Practically everybody else was happy, and thousands swarmed down town into the hotels, restaurants, clubs and streets to celebrate the event. They were tickled to death that there was to be no more interference with their food and transportation, with their laundry, tailor and barber shops, with their drinking and night club going, with their trips to the movies and the theatre, and with all the other activities of their customary way of life.

More than this, those who understood the significance of a general strike were deeply relieved and showed it plainly at the end of a threat to government and organized society, of a danger of civil war and of a possibility of bloodshed and destruction which has kept every well-informed person in a state of high nervous tension here for days.

Business men gave thanks that once more the city and the Port of San Francisco could be opened to trade, ending the daily loss of untold millions in business transactions, salaries and wages; Federal, State and city officials that a potential insurrection against constituted authority had subsided; and the average middle-class householder and rent payer, that he or she and their children could get fresh meat, vegetables and fruit again instead of living largely on canned foods.

This feeling of thanksgiving spread very obviously to the larger part of union labor circles also. The conservative old-line labor leaders who had been forced into the general strike because younger and more radical leaders had swayed a strongly articulate minority of the rank-and-file into a reckless demand for direct action, were delighted that they had been able to bring the general strike to a quick end, without turning public opinion definitely against the organized labor movement.

The great majority of the rank-and-file of the strikers also were delighted. Most of them had let their leaders vote them into the general strike, and had gone out without understanding the suffering it might bring upon them and their families, as well as upon the general public, and without the slightest idea of the implications of a general strike as a revolutionary movement against the existing political, economic and social system.

They did not want to overthrow the government or to establish Soviets and were as shocked as anybody else when it was revealed that some of the agitators who had been working with them did have some such aims.

For the most part, the strikers were characterized merely by a general feeling of unrest growing out of their experiences in the depression, and merely wanted to show their sympathy with the striking longshoremen and maritime workers in a way that they rather vaguely hoped would "better conditions" for those men.

That such was the predominant attitude of the great mass of the rank-and-file was clearly shown by the alacrity and good nature with which all classes of workers went back this afternoon. Teamsters, taxicab drivers, street car and bus men, waiters, bartenders, everybody with whom the public came into contact, said and showed by their actions that they were glad to be back at work and that they wanted everybody to understand that they were not Bolsheviki or radicals, but just as good Americans as anybody else.

Before the settlement which made such good feeling possible could be reached, great pressure had to be brought to bear on extremist elements on both sides of the controversy. General Hugh S. Johnson, spokesman and special representative of President Roosevelt's National Longshoremen's Board; the members of that board—Archbishop Edward J. Hanna, Assistant Secretary of Labor Edward F. McGrady and O. K. Cushing, San Francisco attorney—and moderate elements in the ranks of both labor and capital, worked most of last night and all morning today at one conference after another in the effort to bring about peace.

General Johnson resorted to the threat of "the crack-down" on the extremists on each side before the settlement was reached. He warned the labor unions in a public statement that they could not expect any Federal aid in arbitrating the longshore and marine disputes until the general strike was lifted. Then he warned the "die-hards" in the employers' ranks that they could not expect any aid from him in the strike situation if they went ahead with their plan to have martial law declared here today.

The demand for the declaration of martial law was made upon Mayor Angelo J. Rossi in a stormy conference at City Hall early this morning by leaders of the Committee of 500 appointed by the Mayor on Monday to help the constituted authorities in case of necessity.

Mayor Rossi is reliably reported to have refused in the most angry terms to declare martial law, asserting that he did not intend to submit to dictation by any one element in the community and pointing out that such an official action, at the very moment when conservative labor leaders were about to bring the general strike to an end, might break the whole thing wide open again and possibly result in serious trouble and bloodshed.

In an address over the radio the Mayor asserted that the crushing of the general strike, while it showed that San Francisco would not tolerate communistic or any other interference with constituted authority, "must not be construed to mean that San Francisco either desires or will tolerate any attempt to destroy union labor or invade its rights."

General Johnson sent a radio message to President Roosevelt aboard the cruiser Houston announcing the end of the general strike and predicted that the whole situation would be settled within twenty-four hours. He told reporters that he hoped to have the longshoremen and marine workers' strikes before the President's National Longshoremen's Board for arbitration tomorrow.

Assistant Secretary of Labor McGrady said:

"It certainly was the right thing to do and what this board has urged right along. The action of the general strike committee was sane, sensible and American."

Mr. Cushing characterized the end of the general strike as "a move in the right direction."

The decision to end the general strike came after a long meeting of the general strike committee, consisting of delegates of each of the striking unions, at the Labor Temple. It was a stormy meeting, indicating the unrest still smoldering in labor ranks, and the resolution to go back to work was carried by only seventeen ballots. The vote was 191 to 174.

Edward D. Vandeleur, chairman of the general strike committee, president of the Central Labor Council and president of the municipal carmen's union, announced the adoption of the resolution. It revealed that the strike committee based its action upon "a crisis threatening the community with a disastrous result attendant upon the breaking down of civil government when superseded by martial law," and upon the action of the National Longshoremen's Board in announcing a plan for the arbitration of the longshore and marine workers' grievances in accordance with the wishes of the general strike committee.

The resolution made the ending of the strike conditional upon the acceptance of the board's arbitration plan by the ship owners and the Waterfront Employers Association, but this was regarded as a mere formality, as workers of all unions were flocking back to work by the thousand within an hour after the resolution was adopted.

The resolution also pledged continual moral and financial support of organized labor here for the aid of the longshore and marine workers' strikes.

The executive committee of the general strike committee will continue in existence formally for the time being, it was said, but may be dissolved at will on the call of Mr. Vandeleur as chairman.

A separate resolution empowered Mr. Vandeleur to recall the general committee "if he so desires in behalf of organized labor and their interests."

Another resolution asked Governor Frank F. Merriam to remove all National Guard troops, now numbering about 4,500, from the city, "in the interests of peace and good-will of all citizens of our metropolitan area."

No word has been received here from Governor Merriam as to what he intends to do about the troops. It was indicated that the soldiers would remain on the waterfront until all danger of further clashes between the dock and ship strikers and strike-breakers, who have been unloading ships and taking trucks from the piers to warehouses, has been removed.

The only discordant note in San Francisco's chorus of jubilation over the end of the general strike came from Harry R. Bridges, militant and radical Australian leader of the striking longshoremen and chairman of the joint marine strike committee. Bridges asserted that the striking longshoremen would never return to work unless they received control of the "hiring halls" without arbitration and that the striking marine workers' union would remain out with the longshoremen.

It is in the hiring halls—restaurants, saloons and other places where the longshoremen gather waiting for work—that jobs are handed out when a ship comes in and when goods have to be moved off the piers. Hitherto the employers have controlled these halls and distributed the jobs through their "straw bosses."

The main issue in the original longshoremen's strike, which started all the trouble early in May, was the longshoremen's demand for union recognition and collective bargaining under the NRA, which they construed as meaning union control of the hiring halls and consequent distribution of the work. The employers rejected this on the ground that it meant a "closed shop."

The end of the general strike brought with it the end of the "permit" system whereby the general strike committee issued or denied permits to business men to run milk, ice and food trucks through the city streets or into the city from outlying areas, to open restaurants, to feed guests in hotels and clubs, and so on. No other single feature of the general strike so infuriated business men.

Fifty Are Shot in Minneapolis as Police Fire on Strikers

MINNEAPOLIS, JULY 20.

ABOUT FIFTY persons were wounded by bullets and twenty others were injured by beatings when police opened fire in a battle with striking truck drivers near the market section here today. The fight started as pickets attempted to halt a wholesale grocery truck moving under guard from the area.

National Guardsmen already in the city hurried into the section and took command after the encounter, and 3,400 others were immediately ordered to Minneapolis by Adjt. Gen. Ellard A. Walsh.

Governor Olson considered declaring martial law as a tense situation prevailed.

First reports that a striker had been killed in the rioting could not be verified late tonight.

Of the wounded, several were reported to be in a critical condition and one was believed to be dying.

In the battle, the police, under orders to shoot into the strikers if necessary, used shotguns and pistols. Most of the wounded, several of whom were merely onlookers, were shot in the arms and legs.

The two wounded policemen were Sergeant August Brannon, 58, who was slugged, and Patrolman John Green, who was shot in the leg.

During the morning two food trucks had moved out of the district under police guard and had made deliveries to retail stores without molestation from a growing crowd of pickets. By afternoon 150 patrolmen had been sent to the scene to keep the throng in check.

Shortly after 2 P.M. a third food truck moved out from a wholesale house. It was followed by twelve squad cars, each carrying four policemen, all armed with shotguns.

The truck turned onto Third Street North; another truck loaded with strike pickets cut in ahead of it. Policemen quickly lined the street, but the strikers plowed through the cordon and drove directly into the front of the truck. Police rushed from the convoy cars and opened fire with shotguns on the pickets' truck. Two pickets fell off, wounded, but the truck continued up the street, being fired on from both sides of the street.

Sergeant Brannon jumped on the running board, attempting to halt the pickets' truck, but was battered over the head and hurled to the street badly injured.

During this clash more than a dozen were wounded.

Meanwhile, more pickets had poured into the area, breaking through the police lines. Other patrolmen rushed up and forced them back. Then the strikers rallied and began a new charge. The police again opened fire, aiming for the most part in the air and at the sidewalks, but some of the bullets ricocheted and many more in the crowd were wounded. By this time the pickets' truck had run the gauntlet of gunfire and disappeared through the crowds.

At this point four truckloads of National Guardsmen, who had been held in readiness at the armory, arrived at the scene in trucks along with ambulances. Only four wounded strikers were picked up by the City General Hospital ambulances, however. The others had been rushed in private cars to an emergency hospital at strike headquarters, a vacant garage in the Loop district.

With the arrival of the troops the fighting died down.

Thirty minutes later the district had been cleared of pickets and the food truck continued on its way to make deliveries. Meanwhile private ambulances rolled up to the guarded strike headquarters and carried the wounded to regular hospitals.

None except truck union members was permitted to enter the headquarters, and when John Warren, reporter for The Minneapolis Daily Star, remonstrated with the guards he was severely beaten, later being taken to General Hospital.

Word of the fighting reached Governor Olson in St. Paul quickly and he summoned General Walsh to his office. After a brief conference two regiments were ordered to proceed at once from Camp Ripley, a National Guard camp 100 miles north of here. The troops started here aboard special train.

Governor Olson came to Minneapolis to view the situation. He said he would determine after a survey whether martial law was required. The governor went into a new conference with representatives of the employers tonight.

Immediately after the police-striker battle, taxis quit running in the streets of Minneapolis, as the drivers went on a sympathy strike, and there were reports that union oil truck drivers who had been on the "exempt" list also were planning a walkout.

Hopes for an early and peaceful settlement of the truck drivers' strike faded as a result of today's developments, although the Rev. Francis J. Haas, Federal conciliator, continued his efforts throughout the day. Meeting with the employers' advisory committee during the morning, he presented what was described as a tentative skeleton for peace. He then asked the employers to submit a plan of their own, built around his suggestions.

Father Haas's plan was twofold, relating to produce commission firms in one group and all other industries in the other. The plan would give the union the right to represent inside workers, described as "all employes who are not drivers, loaders or office or sales help," in collective bargaining with employers, if those workers wished the union to do so. The plan also calls for definite wage provisions, though no figures have been set up so far.

Minneapolis Is Put Under Martial Law in Strike Deadlock

MINNEAPOLIS, JULY 26.

THIS CITY was under a military dictatorship tonight as the result of failure on both sides to get together in a settlement of the truck strike which has crippled commercial transportation for nine days.

Governor Olson declared martial law after noon when he was informed that the employers refused to accept in full the revised settlement terms proposed by the Rev. Francis J. Haas and E. H. Dunnigan, Federal mediators.

The members of the striking truck drivers' and helpers' union, meanwhile, had voted complete acceptance of the plan by 1,866 to 147. The Governor had given both sides twenty-four hours to accept the peace plan, with martial law as the alternative..

In declaring the military dictatorship Governor Olson placed Brig. Gen. Ellard A. Walsh in command of the martial law area, which includes Minneapolis, all of Hennepin County and a section of St. Paul embracing the State Fair Grounds, where 4,000 guardsmen have been quartered since Saturday.

From the *New York Times*, July 27, 1934, copyright © 1934, 1962 by The New York Times Company.

Troops Move into City

General Walsh immediately set up headquarters in the Minneapolis armory and late in the day troops began moving into the city to take control. Military officers were also dispatched to the various city and county courts to inform the officials to continue in their present capacity in the usual manner.

By the Governor's order, however, the Police Department and the Sheriff's office became subject to General Walsh's orders and they were told to continue their customary duties pending further orders. A provost marshal is to be appointed to rule these two departments.

General Walsh drew up regulations to govern both private and business conduct during the military rule. Regulations concerning trucks declare that military passes shall be necessary for movement except in certain instances.

Trucks carrying common necessities may move without permits, as may vehicles owned and operated by farmers and carrying farm products, vehicles carrying passengers, trucks carrying merchandise in interstate commerce, government vehicles and cars carrying merchandise for personal use of the driver or his dependants.

Permits for movement of any other vehicles must be obtained from the troop commander's office.

Other regulations order all places of amusement to close by midnight. Gatherings of more than 100 persons out of doors must have approval.

Military Courts Planned

Military courts will be set up to act on violations of military rule.

The regulations order all non-residents having no legitimate business or reason for being in the city to leave forthwith. Citizens are warned to refrain from visiting riot areas.

In proclaiming martial law, Governor Olson said:

"The intervention of military rule was conditioned entirely on the settlement and ending of the strike.

"That necessitated complete acceptance of the proposed settlement by both sides. The employer group having refused to accept results in continuation of the strike and the probable continuance of disturbances in the city of Minneapolis.

"In order to protect the citizens of Minneapolis, therefore, it is imperative that martial law be declared.

"I hope the strike negotiations will continue and that a settlement may be arranged by Father Haas and E. H. Dunnigan at the earliest possible moment."

Replying to the proposed settlement plan, the employers' advisory committee, which represents 166 truck fleet owners, asked modifications in three of the six provisions and absolutely rejected the sixth.

This provided that the "arbitration award should in no event provide for a wage scale of less than 42½ cents per hour for inside workers, helpers and platform men and 52½ cents per hour for truck drivers."

"It is ridiculous and out of all reason," the reply on this point said, "to suggest an arbitration of wage scales by a stipulation that arbitration must start with a minimum scale that is an increase of the existing minimum scale. This is contrary to all principles of fair arbitration."

Before the employers announced this decision the advisory committee issued a statement attacking the Governor for his threat of martial law.

Quick to reply, the Governor attacked the Citizens Alliance, "of which you are members," as being "dominated by a small clique of men who hate all organized labor and are determined to crush it."

One Killed, Twenty Hurt as Deputies Crush Kohler Strike Riot

KOHLER, WIS.

ONE MAN was killed and more than twenty were wounded tonight in a savage battle between 400 special deputies and a mob of some 1,500 strikers and sympathizers who stormed the Kohler Manufacturing Company plant, hurling bricks, stones and clubs.

The dead man was identified as Lee Wakefield of Sheboygan. He died of gunshot wounds. Among those wounded by gunfire, all from Sheboygan, were Tony Knaus, Walter Busse and August Tasche.

Alex Weinert, another of the wounded, is not expected to recover.

The battle, a climax to several disturbances earlier in the day, saw the demonstrators hurling missiles through windows and plate-glass doors in the pottery, the employment office, the administration building, and even the infirmary of the plant.

Women and children were in the ranks of the besiegers, and their presence kept the deputies, stationed inside the plant grounds, from using tear gas, stench bombs and guns until it became apparent that this was the only recourse.

Warning of impending trouble came in the morning, when the deputies, then numbering only about 100, crashed through lines of pickets to escort a car of coal, which had previously been turned back.

Following that clash, some 300 additional deputies were recruited under the command of E. R. Scheulke, a captain of the National Guard who lives in Kohler.

This small army was stationed in the American Club and around other parts of the grounds of the plumbing equipment plant, which has been in a state of siege since a strike was called here about two weeks ago.

The pickets outside countered by calling for aid from Sheboygan and other surrounding towns. As a result, a steady stream of men has been coming into Kohler all day.

The first hint of trouble tonight came when the besiegers began gathering near the pottery building on the south end of the company grounds.

Inside the administration building, on the opposite end of the grounds, were former Governor Walter J. Kohler, president of the company; Sheriff Ernst Ziehm, who had rushed to the scene from Sheboygan, some thirteen miles away, and other officials of the plant.

At first the demonstrators contented themselves with booing the special police and shouting imprecations at plant officials. Then some one threw a brick which crashed through a window.

That was the signal for the entire mob to seize stones and every other available missile to bombard the building. Then they moved north toward the employment office and the infirmary, which suffered similar treatment. Still the deputies made no move.

As the rioters reached the administration building rocks soon began to crash through its windows. Reports which came from the besieged structure by telephone were that there was not a whole pane of glass left on either the first or second floor.

A set of double glass doors at the front was shattered, and missiles described by those inside as "stones as big as grapefruit" went hurtling along the corridors. Two telephone girls on the first floor maintained their posts, however, and kept the plant officials in touch with outside authorities.

Finally, when the attack reached its height, the deputies sallied forth. Tear gas and stench bombs filled High Street, on which the infirmary fronts. The police went into action with nightsticks, and the demonstrators met them with sticks and clubs.

Although it was said not all of the deputies were armed with guns, shots began to ring out. It was impossible to tell whether only one or both sides were firing.

After two hours of battle the crowd finally yielded to the superior armament of the deputies.

As soon as the gas had dissipated, however, the mob formed again, but was again driven back, this time forming just outside the city limits. Police in squad cars kept the thoroughfares clear of people, and at 9 P.M., Anton Brotz, village president, ordered all residents to go to their homes.

Sporadic trouble continued, however, and the mob at the city limits threw stones and rocks at police whenever they came near. Newspaper camera men were driven away and their cameras broken.

The fighting early in the day broke out when pickets turned back a car load of coal coming to the plant, which maintains the light and power for the town. The train crew hauled the car back to Sheboygan. The deputies were then mobilized.

Escorting the car, they charged the picket lines, dispersing the besiegers and tearing down barricades and field headquarters established by the strikers.

Mr. Kohler had declared that the residents of the village would face a shortage of water if the coal supply was interrupted, and said that the pickets had broken both the law and their promise not to interfere with the delivery of coal.

Henry Ohl Jr., president of the Wisconsin State Federation of Labor, issued a statement tonight saying martial law actually prevailed at Kohler without being proclaimed by the Governor.

He described the situation as a case of men being hired to come in and defeat the purposes of the strike, as well as the aims of the union. Maude McCreery, labor leader of Sheboygan, expressed similar sentiments.

Mr. Kohler's assertion that the besiegers of the plant were mostly agitators who had infested the village was supported by a petition signed by 1,500 Kohler employes, and presented to the village president.

It declared that the signers wanted to work for the company under the terms now in effect. It asserted that "an organized group, not from Kohler Village," was forcibly and riotously interfering with business at the plant.

Proposal for Better Industrial Relations

by Robert F. Wagner

The company union has become a focal point in the industrial relations problem that confronts the nation. It was under vigorous debate during the NRA hearings last week and it is dealt with in a bill, designed to eliminate strife between labor and industry, introduced in Congress by Senator Wagner, who has served as chairman of the National Labor Board since that body came into existence. The subject, together with other phases of the problem, is discussed in the following article.

DESPITE THE emergency language in which it is cloaked, the recovery program embodies principles of reform as well as revival. The statistical indicia of revival are not to be denied, but the need for reform is still acute. And there is substantial agreement as to the path that reform must take if we are to achieve any approximation to social justice and avoid the recurrence of cataclysmic depressions. The fruits of industry must be distributed more bounteously among the masses of wage-earners who create the bulk of consumer demand.

This central problem has been envisaged broadly by the National Recovery Administration, led by General Johnson and ever subject to the dynamic personality and brilliant intelligence of President Roosevelt. But despite their best efforts, the major portion of the problem remains unsolved. While re-employment has swelled the total volume of wage payments, the real earnings of the individual working full time are slightly less than they were last March.

Some of the minimum-wage provisions under the codes are lower than the standards actually prevailing in industry and in most of the upper wage brackets there have been reductions in hours without corresponding rises in hourly rates of pay. Despite the ameliorative features of a share-the-work movement, it is hardly the road to prosperity.

The reasons for the present difficulty are not hidden. The constant readjustments necessary to strike a fair balance between industry and labor cannot be accomplished simply by code revisions or by general exhortations. They can be accomplished only by cooperation between employers and employes, which rests upon equality of bargaining power and the freedom of either party from restraints imposed by the other.

Congress recognized this when it enacted Section 7 (a) of the Recovery Act, restating the right of employes to deal collectively through representatives of their own choosing. But ambiguities of language and the absence of enforcement powers have enabled a minority of employers to deviate from the clear intent of the law and to threaten our entire program with destruction. Therefore, I have introduced a bill to clarify and fortify the provisions of Section 7 (a), and I am sure that it will meet with the support of the vast majority of people interested in economic welfare.

Company Unions

At the present time genuine collective bargaining is being thwarted immeasurably by the proliferation of company unions. Let me state at the outset that by the term "company union" I do not refer to all independent labor organizations whose membership lists embrace only the employes of a single employer. I allude rather to the employer-dominated union, generally initiated by the employer, which arbitrarily restricts employee cooperation to a single employer unit, and which habitually allows workers to deal with their employer only through representatives chosen from among his employees.

In the fall of 1933 a thoroughly reliable study was made which covered more than one-fourth of the total number of wage-earners engaged in mining and manufacturing. An inquiry of this magnitude may be accepted as a fair sample of conditions in industry at large. It showed that only 9.3 per cent of employes are dealing with employers through trade unions, while 45.7 per cent are bargaining on an individual basis and 45 per cent are enlisted in company unions. Less than 14 per cent of the employers embraced by the study are recognizing trade unions.

It is worthy of note that company unions are most prevalent in the largest plants. This means that in the very cases where the bargaining power of the employer is strongest, the worker is least free to improve his own position by unhampered affiliation with others of his kind.

It is also true that these unions have multiplied most rapidly since the enactment of the law which was intended to guarantee to the worker the fullest freedom of organization. The number of employes covered by company unions rose from 432,000 in 1932 to 1,164,000 in 1933, representing a gain of 169 per cent. More than 69 per cent of the company-union schemes now in existence have been inaugurated in the brief period since the passage of the Recovery Act.

The company union, as I have defined it, runs antithetical to the very core of the New Deal philosophy. Businessmen are being allowed to pool their information and experience in vast trade associations in order to make a concerted drive against the evil features of modern industrialism. They have been permitted to recognize the values of unity and the destructive tendencies of discrete activities, and to act accordingly. If employees are denied similar privileges they not only are unable to uphold their end of the labor bargain; in addition they cannot cope with any problems that transcend the boundaries of a single business.

The company union has improved personal relations, group welfare activities, discipline and the other matters which may be handled on a local basis. But it has failed dismally to standardize or improve wage levels, for the wage question is a general one whose sweep embraces whole industries, or States, or even the nation. Without wider areas of cooperation among employees there can be no protection against the nibbling tactics of the unfair employer or of the worker who is willing to degrade standards by serving for a pittance.

The inability of employes to unite in larger groups has not only limited their efforts to secure a just share of the national wealth. It has interfered with their attempts to provide insurance against sickness and old age, and to exert an effective influence upon salutary labor legislation. It has hampered the efforts of labor to preserve order within its own ranks, or to restrain the untimely and wayward acts of irresponsible groups. In this latter aspect, its unfavorable effect upon employers as well as workers stands clearly forth.

Even when dealing with problems that may without injury be delimited to the single company, the worker under company unionism suffers two fatal handicaps. In the first place, he has only slight knowledge of the labor market or of general business conditions. His trade is tending a machine. If forbidden to hire an expert in industrial relationships, he is entirely ineffectual in his attempts to take advantage of legitimate opportunities.

Secondly, only representatives who are not subservient to the employer with whom they deal can act freely in the interest of employees. Simple common sense tells us that a man does not possess this freedom when he bargains with those who control his source of livelihood.

I am well aware that many employer-dominated organizations now permit their employees to choose outside representatives, and the National Labor Board has affirmed this policy in a recent case. But this right is a mockery when the presence of a company union firmly entrenched in a plant enables an employer to exercise a compelling force over the collective activities of his workers. Freedom must begin with the removal of obstacles to its exercise.

Major questions of self-expression and democracy are involved. At a time when politics is becoming impersonalized and when the average worker is remote from the processes of government, it is more imperative than ever before that industry should afford him real opportunities to participate in the determination of economic issues.

The company union is generally initiated by the employer; it exists by his sufferance; its decisions are subject to his unimpeachable veto. Most impartial students of industrial problems agree that the highest degree of cooperation between industry and labor is possible only when either side is free to act or to withdraw, and that the best records of mutual respect and mutual accomplishment have been made by employers dealing with independent labor organizations.

The principal argument advanced by the proponents of company unionism is that it promotes industrial harmony and peace without subjecting the individual company to the intrusion of outside labor groups who have no interest in the company's practices. Of course, in our complicated economy the interests of all employers and all employees are inextricably intertwined, and the assumption that outside workers have no valid interest in the labor standards prevailing within a plant is demonstrably false. Besides, a tranquil relationship between employer and employee, while eminently desirable, is not a sole desideratum. It all depends upon the basis of tranquillity. The slave system of the old South was as tranquil as a summer's day, but that is no reason for perpetuating in modern industry any of the aspects of a master-servant relationship.

As a matter of fact, the company union cannot sustain even the claim that it tends to insure industrial peace. Men versed in the tenets of freedom become restive when not allowed to be free. The sharp outbreaks of economic warfare in various parts of the country at the present time have been caused more by the failure of employers to observe the spirit of Section 7 (a) of the Recovery Act than by any other single factor. It has been my observation that industrial strife is most violent when company unionism enters into the situation, and that the company-union line of organization is least likely to bring forth the restraint of irresponsible employees by others of their own group.

The implications of what I have just said are clear. If the employer-dominated union is not checked, there are only two likely results. One is that the employer will have to maintain his dominance by force, and thus swing us directly into industrial fascism and the destruction of our most-cherished American ideals; the other is that employees will revolt, with widespread violence and unpredictable conclusions.

The final argument advanced for company unionism is that it should be allowed to compete against trade unionism in an open field. If by company unionism one means simply the right of employees to confine their activities to a single employer unit when they wish to do so, I do not object to that principle in the slightest and there is nothing contrary to it in the bill which I have introduced. But if by company unionism one includes the right of employers to obstruct the development of a more widespread employee cooperation, such a policy cannot be allowed to continue if we intend to pursue the philosophy of the new era.

The New Bill

The new bill forbids any employer to influence any organization which deals with problems such as wages, grievances and hours. They should be covered by a genuine labor union. At the same time, the bill does not prevent employers from forming or assisting associations which exist to promote the health and general welfare of workers or to provide group insurance, or for similar purposes. Employer-controlled organizations should be allowed to serve their proper functions of supplementing trade unionism, but they should not be allowed to supplant or destroy it.

Failure to meet the company-union challenge has not been the only defect of Section 7 (a) of the Recovery Act. This section provides that employees shall be free to choose their own representatives. It has been interpreted repeatedly to mean that any employee at any time may elect to deal individually with his employer, even if the overwhelming majority of his co-workers desire a collective agreement covering all. Such an interpretation is detrimental to the practice and contrary to the theory of collective bargaining. It permits an unscrupulous employer to divide his employees against themselves by dealing with innumerable small groups or with individuals.

In my opinion, Congress certainly did not intend that the law should operate to place employees in a more unfavorable position than they were before the Recovery Act was passed.

The proposed legislation does not resolve the question of the closed-union shop. Such issues should be worked out by labor and industry in the course of experience. But the bill, if enacted, would make it clear that Congress has not intended to foreclose the issue by illegalizing the closed-union shop or by placing any other obstacles in the way of making collective bargaining a working reality.

The third major defect of Section 7 (a) is that, while it guarantees to employees the right to organize, it does not state explicitly the right to receive recognition through their representatives. This explains why company unionism has increased so rapidly despite the fact that other labor organizations have added 2,000,000 to their membership during the past year. Employees have been assured of their right to join whatever unions they prefer, but they have been forced to bargain either individually or through company unions.

This refusal of employers to deal with properly chosen representatives has been the cause of more than 70 per cent of the disputes coming before the National Labor Board. The new bill is designed to remedy this evil. It is modeled upon the successful experience of the Railway Labor Act, which provides that employers shall actually recognize duly chosen representatives and make a reasonable effort to deal with them and to reach satisfactory collective agreements.

When the factual situation that confronts us is analyzed carefully and comprehended fully, I am sure that employers as well as employees will favor the proposed measure. Fair-minded employers who are now allowed to band together in huge trade associations do not desire to deny analogous rights to their workers. Fair-minded employers do not relish the pretense that industry and labor are upon an equal footing, when in fact industry controls both sides by dominating the strategic points in the areas of controversy.

Most important of all, far-sighted and broad-visioned employers who recognize the certainty of economic discord and the threat to our entire economic program that is implicit in the present status of labor relations will join wholeheartedly in this proposal for improvement.

There always will be an unfair minority who are amenable only to coercion. For this reason the National Labor Board, under the new bill, would be vested with statutory sanctions and given actual powers of investigation and restraint similar to those exercised by the Federal Trade Commission in cases of unfair competition. It would be composed of seven members, including two representatives of employers, two of employees, and three of the general public, and it would be empowered to set up regional or local boards.

The present National Labor Board, set up by executive order, has carried on its activities for half a year. In that short time, it has helped 650,000 employees, who were engaged in disputes, to return to work or to remain at work, upon terms satisfactory to all interested parties and promising durable peace. The chief function of the new board would not be to act as policeman or judge, but to mediate and conciliate industrial disputes, and to offer its services as arbitrator when the parties so desired. Aside from its power to prevent the specific unfair practices that would be forbidden by the law, it would not have the slightest flavor of compulsion. It would have no kinship to compulsory arbitration. It would continue to promote peace rather than strife and to appeal to the better judgment and good intentions of industry and labor.

When this board is established and bolstered by adequate sanctions and a clarification of the substantive law, it will help to solve the thorniest problem confronting us today, and be one of the chief bulwarks of our future economic prosperity and social justice.

Debunks company unionism

Lewis Quits Office in the Federation

WASHINGTON.

BRINGING TO a climax a long fight between industrial and craft unionism within the ranks of the American Federation of Labor, John L. Lewis, president of the United Mine Workers, resigned today as vice-president of the federation.

His resignation, which automatically carries with it withdrawal from the Federation Executive Council, was contained in this curt letter to William Green, president of the federation:

> Dear Sir and Brother:
>
> Effective this date, I resign as a vice president of the American Federation of Labor.
>
> Yours truly,
>
> John L. Lewis.

Mr. Lewis's resignation is understood to have been provoked by a rebuke received from Mr. Green and the executive council for his stand at the recent convention of the federation in Atlantic City, at which he advocated the establishment of vertical unions, embracing all workers connected with a particular industry, such as automobile manufacturing, as opposed to craft unions of specialized workers, even though these various craft unions might all be employed in the same industry.

Only twelve hours before he resigned, it is reported, Mr. Lewis received from Mr. Green a long letter which the mine workers' official is said to feel questions the good faith of his views.

The executive council, all but one of whose seventeen members is a craft union official, opposed Mr. Lewis's views and disputed his contention that craft unions are no longer effective in a formal report made public several days ago to the convention.

Mr. Lewis does not wish to take the United Mine Workers, admittedly one of the strongest unions in the country, out of the federation at this time, it is reported authoritatively, but will open a campaign within a few days for the establishment of vertical unions in new trades and the resignation of five members of the executive council who have particularly combated his moves.

Labor officials here foresee one of the most serious and spectacular of the many internecine conflicts since the organization of the federation and speculation is current as to whether Secretary Perkins will feel it advisable to use her offices in an attempt to restore peace.

Mr. Lewis nominated Mr. Green, who was secretary of the United Mine Workers, to succeed the late Samuel Gompers as federation president in 1925, and has nominated and supported him in every convention since that time. Now that the split has occurred, those close to labor affairs here see looming a titanic struggle which they expect to be carried to the convention of the federation in Tampa in November, 1936.

Mr. Lewis, it is understood, will campaign for the defeat for reelection to the executive council of J. C. Hutcheson of the Carpenters Union, O. A. Wharton of the Machinists, G. M. Bugniazet of the Electricians, Daniel J. Tobin of the International Brotherhood of Teamsters and John P. Frey of the Metal Trades Council. So far as could be learned today, he will not oppose Mr. Green personally.

In union circles here, it was felt that, if the expected struggle develops, Mr. Lewis can count upon the support of Sidney Hill-

man of the Amalgamated Clothing Workers, David Dubinsky of
the International Garment Workers, Thomas H. Brown of the
Mine, Mill and Smelter Workers, and Joseph Obergfell of the
Brewery Workers Union.

All of these men supported him in the Atlantic City convention, where the dispute developed such feeling that Mr. Lewis
engaged in fisticuffs with Mr. Hutcheson on the floor.

The resignation was not a surprise in labor circles, for it was
known that in the last year Mr. Lewis found himself in a hopeless minority on the question of industrial union against craft
unionism.

For years he has fought at conventions to have the federation
go on record as favoring the organization of mass production
industries along industrial lines and to have the executive council
enlarged, so that "new blood" might be "injected into the old
guard."

On both points he won a victory at the San Francisco convention in October, 1934. With the enlargement of the council
he also won a place on that body. But after a year of experience
he found that the policies he advocated were anathema to most
of the older members of the council. Usually the vote against
him was fifteen to two or fourteen to three.

Unable to make any headway in the council, Mr. Lewis carried
his fight to the floor of the convention in Atlantic City. The industrial unionists were beaten on roll-call votes by approximately
11,000 to 8,000.

Two weeks ago the chiefs of the unions interested in industrial
unionism met in Washington and formed the Committee on Industrial Organization. The new committee, it was announced,
was designed to assist the organization of unions in the unorganized mass production industries. John Brophy, of the United
Mine Workers of America, was placed in charge and offices were
opened.

The unions which formed the committee were the United Mine
Workers, the Amalgamated Clothing Workers of America, the
International Ladies' Garment Workers' Union, the International
Typographical Union, the Oil Field Gas and Refinery Workers
and the Cloth Hat, Cap and Millinery Workers.

Mr. Lewis's power in union affairs has grown steadily ever since he was elected acting president of the United Mine Workers in 1919 and president in 1920. He succeeded Frank J. Hayes.

Resignations from the executive council because of disagreement are not unprecedented, but in most previous cases they have not been over such fundamental questions. Mr. Tobin resigned several years ago because of a dispute, but is now a member again.

Mr. Lewis is expected to make known his precise plans at a press conference scheduled for Monday morning. The resignation must be formally accepted by Mr. Green before it can become effective, but Mr. Lewis's associates expressed no doubt that it would be.

The Split in the A. F. of L.

by Louis Stark

WASHINGTON.

LABOR DAY, 1936, finds organized labor in the midst of its gravest crisis in a half century. Fighting an unprecedented cleavage in its own ranks, labor in this campaign year is also waging an important political struggle. The stakes are enormous.

The future of the labor movement—the direction and rapidity of its growth and the extent of its power—is in the balance. On the outcome of the political struggle may depend labor's participation in a possible political realignment of workingmen, farmers and middle-class groups.

As a result of the internal strife, adherents of the two wings of the American Federation of Labor are almost at each other's throats. Even the nominal unity which leaders sought to preserve is no longer possible, for the long internal battle for change in structure and policy is almost at an end. For good or evil that fight is now apparently to be transferred to two separate organizations, the American Federation of Labor and a rival organization which is about to be born.

The air is already filled with charges and countercharges.

From the *New York Times Magazine,* September 6, 1936, copyright © 1936, 1964 by The New York Times Company.

Craft union leaders may soon issue orders to their supporters in the thousands of local unions, city labor bodies and State labor federations to "give no quarter" to the "dual" unionists, to smite them hip and thigh. In that case industrial unionists, through the Committee for Industrial Organization—the American Federation of Labor's young rival—or its successor, will fight back.

The war will be fought as all wars are, by the enlisted men, the rank and file. Carried on today in the union labor halls, the rivalry may well be extended tomorrow to the job, to the building in the course of construction, to the factory and the mine. In some places employers will be confronted by rival labor unions, each insistent on "recognition." Where one group clearly controls the situation the other group may seek to insert a wedge that will upset such control.

There are now approximately 4,000,000 workers in labor organizations, the vast majority—about 3,500,000—being in the A. F. of L. The remainder comprise the railway brotherhoods, and other independent unions in the radio, shipbuilding, shoe and leather industries, in the government and various miscellaneous enterprises.

Approximately 2,500,000 workers are covered by employe representation plans. Thus, out of approximately 25,000,000 industrial and "white-collar" employes, 6,500,000 are enrolled in some form of plan or organization.

Formed fifty years ago as a protest against the all-inclusive policy of the Knights of Labor, that mixture of sprawling groups which barred only saloon-keepers, bankers and lawyers, the A. F. of L., under the guidance of Samuel Gompers and his associates, concentrated on welding a tight, compact group of skilled workmen. These "aristocrats" of labor, dominating certain key positions in industry, fought doggedly against great odds to build and maintain their unions, to win collective contracts from employers. These unions became the keystone of labor's temple, and their officials were the high priests, conducting all rites and ceremonies.

As small-scale industry gave way to the processes of mass production, skill broke down before the onslaught of the assembly line. The new development, bringing with it multitudes of simple processes, tended to "robotize" the work of skilled operatives.

As a "commoner" in labor, the unskilled worker at the turn of the century was timid, scarcely organized and filled with a sense of inferiority. Twenty years later, stirred by the growth and immensity of the great industries which he had helped to build, he surveyed his handiwork. He saw the new motor car which could not have existed without mass production, the vastly improved rubber tire on which the car rolled to its destination and other new and better products. Craft pride gave way to industry pride.

The "commoner" then knocked at the gate of the labor temple and demanded a place in the ritual commensurate with his importance. Rebuffed by the high priests, he found, with other discontented, a congregation of his own on which the high priests, alarmed by the formation of what they deemed a rival "sect," formally pronounced anathema.

The new "sect" comprises ten national and international unions and the major division of an eleventh—more than 1,000,000 members, a third of the A. F. of L.—which maintain that the federation has been too slow to change its structure, that it has delayed too long in organizing the workers in mass-production industries. Uniting last November as the Committee for Industrial Organization, these unions began an active campaign to organize the workers in mass-production factories on an industry-wide basis.

The A. F. of L.'s craft union leaders were not opposed to the organization of mass-production workers, but insisted that specialized tradesmen employed in these factories be segregated for membership in the craft unions. Men on the assembly line in an automobile plant, for example, could belong to the mass-production union, but electrical workers and machinists were to join the unions of electrical workers and machinists.

Despite the split on policy and the more obviously destructive aspects of the internal conflict, net gains are being made by the two wings of the labor movement. Thus the Steel Workers Organizing Committee, operating under the direction of the C. I. O. and the steel union—in defiance of the A. F. of L.'s council—have already enrolled, so the officers claim, several thousand workers. Nearly 200 organizers are operating in the steel centers, appealing to the nearly 500,000 steel workers to enter union ranks.

About 35,000 rubber workers have been unionized, and their organization, in affiliation with the C. I. O., of which John L. Lewis is chairman, is seeking members among the remaining 85,000 outside the union fold.

At the next A. F. of L. convention the carpenters will report an increase of 100,000 members, making a total of 300,000. Gains have also been announced by machinists, electrical and radio workers, men's and women's garment workers.

In the heart of the nation's basic industries a ferment is at work. There is a vast seething and stirring in the ranks of those who wear the blue denim of labor's regiments, the men who process steel, build rubber tires, radios and electrical equipment, tend the nation's textile looms, fashion its machine tools and mix its chemicals.

"Organize," is the message of the union leaders to these several million workers. "Market your services cooperatively."

But the average worker, deeply affected by the depression, is bewildered. He wonders what will happen if he joins a union. What good will it do him? "Suppose I am fired," he mused. "What would my family do?"

He is inclined to be moderate in his hopes and expectations and very patient, however aroused he may become by what he deems to be injustice. Then, too, the comparative sense of security which he had before 1929 is gone. In those days he could "chuck up a job" without much thought for the next one. But that is not possible today and under the impact of the depression, the average worker has come to value, above all else, security. He wants tenure of job, for he is no longer the happy-go-lucky individual who wandered into new pastures in more prosperous years whenever he felt the urge. He sees the job as his investment and his wage as the return on that investment. He resents being turned out by a straw boss or petty foreman for inadequate reasons. When "lack of orders" is assigned for a lay-off, his resentment tends to turn to management, the employer and society for not arranging things better.

But security for the average workman does not stop at job

security, it has come to mean social security as well. Security is his chief topic of conversation. On economic matters his viewpoint is usually bounded by the horizons of his experience. Having seen skill subordinated to the automatic machine, he hopes that some way may be found to guide the machine—not to suppress it—so that there will be plenty of shoes, clothing, radios and automobiles for all.

Individual opportunity and social advantage—these are the poles toward which the average laboring man is moved at one time or another. Until the business indices began to climb, his eyes turned for help to the only sources which were able to give it, the Federal, State and local governments.

If the worker is one of those who have found employment in recent months, he is again interested in "good wages." He has less confidence in keeping a steady job, because "things are changing so fast," and for that reason, if for no other, he wants a higher wage. But there are other reasons. As prosperity returns and prices go up, these men will ask for more wages to offset living costs. They want more than that. Labor used to ask for a "living" wage, then a "comfort-level" wage; now the demand is for a wage that brings with it some of the luxuries of life.

There is also the question of working hours. Formerly the steel worker was employed twelve hours, but now he and his fellows have the eight-hour day. In many industries the forty-hour week prevails. Since the NRA some have had the thirty-five and others the thirty-six hour week. This shorter work day has been made possible by technological advances, by increased efficiency in production. Progress continues in science and industry through the improvement in machinery and technical processes of production. But unemployment also continues.

One of labor's chief objectives, therefore, is the shortening of the work day and work week so that employment may be spread. The demand now is for the six-hour day and five-day week.

Conservative in its social and economic outlook, labor leadership has also been conservative politically, although frequently the rank and file have demanded more radical action than the union officials were willing to take. That is what is happening today on the economic and political fronts.

Usually the labor vote is divided between the candidates of the Republican and Democratic parties; the Socialist and Communist parties appeal only to the minority of class-conscious workers. In former campaigns anybody who attempted to "deliver" the labor vote as a whole was regarded with suspicion. Despite the promises of labor leaders, made to one or the other of the leading parties, the labor forces had a way of dividing in about the same way as other elements in the population.

There was a reason for this division. When the nascent labor movement was struggling for existence Gompers feared it would be irretrievably damaged if it entered politics as had the British and European labor movements. Out of this fear grew the "nonpartisan policy," to "reward our friends and punish our enemies."

But the present campaign is witnessing a dramatic break with the past. A. F. of L. leaders have formed Labor's Nonpartisan League, a body outside the official sanction of the federation, and have departed from precedent by endorsing a Presidential candidate, Mr. Roosevelt, "for 1936." They have not endorsed the Democratic party, for two significant reasons: *First,* the league includes Republicans, Democrats and Socialists; *second,* such endorsement would interfere with the league's other objective— its maintenance after 1936 as a "permanent" institution, free from the leading-strings of a political party and ready for a possible realignment.

To what purpose? League members do not profess to read the future, but they answer this question frankly. They say that if a liberal party becomes necessary in 1940 they wish to be ready for it. In such a realignment, they feel, labor will need a machine to support its economic policies, to protect the workers of the nation, organized and unorganized.

"Protection from what?" one asks.

"From economic royalists," is the reply. "From reactionary employers who refuse us the legal right of organization and collective bargaining. From the danger of what happened in Germany and Italy when the trade unions were smashed. It must not happen here."

Out of the league's work has already come a Labor party in New York State. If this touches off similar action in other

States the stage will be set for an American Labor or Liberal party on a national scale in 1940. Toilers in labor's political vineyard envision farmers, sympathetic middle-class groups, intellectuals and labor's millions marching shoulder to shoulder toward a new social, economic and political order.

Twenty-four Hurt in Flint Strike Riot

FLINT, MICHIGAN.

AFTER MORE than five hours of hand-to-hand fighting with the police, in which at least twenty-four persons were injured by bullets, stones, clubs, knives and tear-gas bombs, a siege was on this morning at the Fisher Body plant No. 2, where "sit-down" strikers are defying the courts and the State authorities.

Governor Murphy, who rushed to Flint by automobile, was in conference at the Hotel Durant on steps to be taken to end the fighting. Under his orders a company of the 125th Regiment of the Michigan National Guard was mobilizing for riot duty at the Flint armory, prepared to prevent further bloodshed and rioting.

In addition it was reported that forty State policemen, in response to appeals by Flint officials for aid, would soon arrive to enter the fray.

The police meanwhile could do little more than hold their lines against some 800 strikers, pickets and sympathizers who were being directed by the broadcasting apparatus of a sound truck parked near the plant gate. The truck was surrounded by the automobiles of strikers as a barricade to prevent the police from approaching.

Virtually every window in the two-story factory building appeared to have been broken. The street before the plant, which is opposite the Chevrolet factory in Chevrolet Avenue, was littered with debris.

Rioters had torn up stretches of the asphalt pavement to obtain missiles to hurl at the police. At another point along the avenue the curb stones had been pried up and had been broken into pieces by the strikers.

That some of the strikers were armed was held certain, because at one point a message was shouted from the sound truck:

"Go home and get your guns and come back again."

The wounded, however, were believed to have been injured mostly by fragments of exploding tear-gas shells fired by the police, and by missiles, rather than by gunfire.

Of those hurt twenty persons were taken to hospitals, among them five policemen.

One of the strikers, Earl de Long of Flint, described as a driver, was said at the hospital to be in a serious condition, with a wound in the abdomen.

Most of the others were reported wounded about the legs, as if by fragments of tear-gas grenades that had exploded near them.

Three of the injured refused hospital aid. The twenty-fourth of the known casualties was a Detroit newspaper photographer, who was slashed on the hand when he attempted to obtain pictures of the rioters in action.

Two other photographers, employed by The Flint Journal, were beaten by rioters, but not seriously hurt, and it was believed that others who approached too close to the front line of battle had also been roughly handled.

Governor Murphy arrived shortly after 1 A.M. with Adjutant General John Bersey, commanding the National Guard; Oscar Olander, commandant of the State police; Caesar J. Scarvada, captain of the State police, and Edward Kemp, Assistant Attorney General, who acted as legal adviser to the Governor.

The party, which had traveled by automobile from Lansing,

met immediately with City Manager John M. Barrinber and Chief of Police James B. Wills.

At that time the number of policemen who had been dispatched to the Fisher Body factory numbered about 100. There were, besides, some twenty deputies from the office of Sheriff Thomas W. Wolcott.

Police Held Back From Plant

The police had established a line about 100 feet from the main gate to the Fisher plant, but could not approach nearer because of the barrage of missiles laid down by the rioters.

Some three thousand persons, including many women who appeared to be hysterical and were believed to be relatives of the strikers in the besieged plant, were gathered to view the fighting, plainly visible in the glare of the street lights and by the illumination that streamed from the windows of the factory.

Machine Guns Held Ready

The police had virtually exhausted their supply of tear-gas bombs in an attempt to dislodge those of the 800 rioters who remained inside the plant. An appeal to Detroit for more gas had resulted in a reply that none was available.

Inside the plant some two-thirds of the strikers were concentrated. Outside about a third managed to block the advance of the police.

Machine guns, brought from police headquarters, were held ready for action and a number of the police and sheriffs carried riot guns. These would not be used, however, the authorities said, unless the rioters opened fire.

Police Driven Back by Water

The trouble began when about 400 "sit-downers," who have been occupying the second floor of the plant since Dec. 30, swarmed suddenly from their positions and overpowered the plant policemen, taking possession of the entire building.

As the disturbance spread, a riot call was sounded, bringing the city policemen to the plant. The first officers arrived with supplies of tear-gas bombs, hoping to quell the disorder with these.

Streams from the fire hoses brought into play by the rioters drove the policemen back from the windows, however, so that the gas bombs were ineffective.

Meanwhile a crowd of about 200 strikers, who were outside the plant, charged the gates, overcame police resistance, and joined their comrades inside.

About 200 more strikers or sympathizers then appeared outside the plant. A group of about equal size ran out from the plant, broke through the police lines, and joined the crowd in the street in hand-to-hand fighting with the policemen.

The police, according to first accounts, could do little more than hold their ground and protect themselves as well as they could from injury.

It was at this point, witnesses said, that police patrol cars began to arrive with reinforcements.

The rioters seized and overturned the cars, swarming around them so densely that the police could not disperse the crowds.

The police reported that, despite the odds against them, they had not yet used their revolvers.

Troops Surround Plants Following Riots in Flint

by Russell B. Porter

FLINT, MICHIGAN.

MARCHING ORDERS issued at midnight to troops mobilizing over the State will concentrate the full National Guard strength of 4,000 soldiers today in Flint where a regiment took over last night an area in which new rioting in the General Motors strike occurred in the afternoon.

Despite the troop movement martial law was not declared.

The 126th Infantry, including machine gun detachments, about 1,200 strong, with rifles, bayonets and steel helmets, started for the scene under Colonel William Haze just before 8:45 P.M., moving in motor trucks to all sides of the sit-down besieged Fisher Body plant No. 2 and the Chevrolet plant No. 4, across the street.

Although occupation of the latter factory by sit-downers began the day's trouble, the most serious fighting took place at Chevrolet plant No. 9, half a mile away.

Just before midnight troops had control of hills atop both ends of Chevrolet Avenue, covering the Flint River Valley, in which Fisher No. 2 plant is located. Machine guns were set up on both sides a short distance from the plant.

At that time union organizers in a sound car were exhorting

a crowd estimated at 500 to 1,000 union men and sympathizers gathered in front of Fisher No. 2, on the site of the battle of Jan. 11.

Fisher No. 2 is about 100 yards from Chevrolet No. 4, across the street and on the other side of the river. Before the troops arrived many occupants of Fisher No. 2 had moved into Chevrolet No. 4.

The Military Intelligence Service reported that 1,150 men were in the occupied Chevrolet No. 4, of whom 250 were sit-down strikers, 700 outsiders and 200 "loyal" workers who would like to get out but could not.

At 1 A.M. the crowd inside the National Guard lines had dwindled to about 200, but the troops had still not tried to clear the sector in front of Fisher No. 2. No one who left was permitted to return.

The remaining pickets included a number of women belonging to the "Women's Emergency Brigade," who rested and got food at a restaurant inside the lines. They had brought packing boxes and cardboard with them, with which they made shelters. They had salamanders for heat. They announced that they intended to stay all night in the picket line.

When the Chevrolet night shift went off duty at 1 A.M., the "loyal" workers left the zone without molestation.

Because of the cold, the troops went inside all Chevrolet plants except No. 4, using them as barracks from which patrols were sent out.

Colonel George L. Olsen, second in command of the troops here, said at midnight that unless the orders were countermanded no one would be allowed to pass through the lines with food for the sit-downers, or for the purpose of going to work in any of the Chevrolet plants.

Union officials said that they had asked Governor Murphy to permit food for the sit-down strikers to pass through but no reply had been received.

According to the union, the company notified Governor Murphy Sunday night that it considered the strike "at an end," and intended to reopen all its plants today, including those seized by sit-downers, following the expected issuance of an injunction.

Union men made it plain that this belief on their part, plus alleged discrimination against union men at Chevrolet, precipitated the riot. The union said that twelve union men had been discharged at Chevrolet last week, and two yesterday. According to the union, "hired thugs" aided the company police in the day's riot.

No troops were sent into Chevrolet plant No. 4 or the Fisher plant No. 2, which are held by the sit-down strikers, but sentries with fixed bayonets were stationed in front of these plants.

The troops threw their cordon progressively around all sides of the Chevrolet plant as their first action and had it surrounded by a ring of bayonets by 10 o'clock. Then they began encircling the Fisher Body plant No. 2, across the street. State Police entered the area behind the troops. No resistance was reported.

No one was allowed inside the National Guard lines without a military pass.

Although the troops have orders not to enter the buildings held by the union or to try to evict the sit-downers forcibly, their cordon prevented any food or supplies from getting into the plants. The sit-downers in the Fisher Body plant have laid in a supply of canned goods, but the men in Chevrolet No. 4 have no food. It is only a matter of time before they are starved out unless the situation changes.

Fisher Body plant No. 1, which is several miles from Fisher Body plant No. 2, was not involved in today's trouble, and was not included in the military zone established by the troops. About 700 sit-downers are said to be inside Fisher No. 1, and about 200 in Fisher No. 2.

Orders for the troop movement were received at National Guard headquarters in the Flint Armory from Colonel Joseph H. Lewis, commander of the 2,300 troops in the city.

Colonel Lewis spent the afternoon and evening in Detroit conferring with Governor Frank Murphy of Michigan and State Police officials. The Guard was called out by Governor Murphy after repeated requests from the city and county authorities, who told him they could not control the situation.

Mayor Harold Bradshaw of Flint and Sheriff Thomas Wolcott of Genesee County asked the Governor to come here personally to investigate the situation as well as to send troops to the danger zone.

They Mayor sent the following telegram to Governor Murphy:

"Confirming our telephone conversation, I join Sheriff Wolcott in requesting use of the National Guard to take care of strike situation in city of Flint, the city police and the Sheriff's office being inadequate to insure maintenance of law and order, particularly as the number of unruly persons from out of town is increasing rapidly. The situation demands immediate action."

The reference to "unruly persons" was to union "shock troops," said to be several hundred strong, sent here by unions among the Ohio rubber workers, Pennsylvania steel and coal workers, and Detroit automobile workers affiliated with John L. Lewis's Committee for Industrial Organization.

Between 200 and 300 members of the United Automobile Workers of America took full possession of the ground floor of the Chevrolet No. 4 plant (a motor assembly plant) yesterday. They held both front and back gates, which they barricaded, while company police barricaded themselves on the second floor. Three company policemen were thrown over the fence near the main gate.

Company police held the adjoining plant No. 5 behind barricades. Men were working on the night shift in No. 5 as well as in all other Chevrolet plants except No. 4.

The score injured in the afternoon rioting included strikers, non-union workers and company police. Three were taken to Hurley Hospital. Eleven were treated at the Chevrolet plant hospital and the others at the plant first-aid stations.

The rioting started at about 3:30 o'clock, when the day shift was leaving and the night shift was coming on. It began during the court hearing which was held on the company's petition to compel the union to evacuate Fisher Body plants Nos. 1 and 2 and to stop picketing them.

Union sound-cars sped through the streets calling all union men to union headquarters at 2 P.M., ostensibly for a demonstration on the court house lawn against the use of injunctions in labor disputes.

Instead, the union supporters, including a group of about

twenty women with red berets and red armbands, known as the "Women's Emergency Brigade" of the U.A.W., descended on Chevrolet plant No. 9 at the same time as union men inside the plant staged sit-downs in several different units.

Several hundred strike sympathizers, including the women's brigade, attempted to keep non-union workers from entering the gates of No. 9 plant, about one-half mile from No. 4. Company police rushed to the gates to defend the men, and a battle ensued.

Simultaneously, fights started in various units of the factory, as company police and loyal workers tried to eject the sit-downers.

The worst of the fighting took place at the gates in front of Chevrolet No. 9, which is a motor parts plant. An organizer in one of the union's sound-cars directed the battle through loud speakers. The union men were armed with heavy clubs and blackjacks. The women also used clubs, with which they smashed windows in the plant, while their leader, carrying an American flag, rallied them on.

Company police and non-union workers used clubs and blackjacks in the struggle at the factory gate, and also inside of No. 9 plant, where several hundred non-strikers attacked a group of fifteen or twenty-five sit-downers.

Most of the injured received their wounds in the battle at No. 9. For the greater part the injuries were not serious, but were inflicted by blows from clubs or in fist fights.

Sheriff Wolcott, with a group of deputies, and Captain Edwin Hughes of the city with about twenty men, quelled the disturbance at No. 9 when they arrived on the scene swinging their clubs. One tear gas bomb was thrown into the milling mob in the plant, but the union men quickly dispersed after the arrival of the police.

Fighting continued at other plants of the Chevrolet company, however, and it was an hour and a half before peace was established. Then it was discovered that the strikers had effected a strategic move while the police attention was diverted to No. 9 plant.

About 300 of the 1,900 men working in Plant 4 stayed in the plant at the end of the afternoon shift and seized the ground floor when most of the non-union men left. They kept the night shift from entering the place, except for recruits from the union ranks, and took over the floor before the company police assigned to it realized what was going on.

There was fist fighting inside No. 4 plant between the union men, on one side, and company police and "loyal workers" on the other side, but the union supporters proved to be in an over-whelming majority at that time and place. The few non-union men still in the plant retreated through the gates, and the company police took refuge on the second floor.

In five other Chevrolet plants where union men attempted to stage sit-downs, non-union workers joined company police in expelling them. There were brief encounters, mostly fist fights, in those plants.

Thousands of spectators were attracted to the vicinity during the battle. They remained until the union sound-cars left the field to return to headquarters in a downtown office building, calling all union men to a mass meeting. Then the crowd drifted away, but it returned to the sector at night when news spread that the strikers had made good their seizure of the Chevrolet No. 4 unit.

Before the troops occupied the Chevrolet-Fisher sector, several hundred union men, together with women wearing the red and white "EB" armbands, returned in automobiles and on foot. Some of the men carried clubs. They congregated in the vicinity of Chevrolet No. 4, and some climbed over the fence to join their comrades inside.

Until the National Guard arrived the police threw as many as possible of their 120 men, together with some Sheriff's deputies, into the zone. The police were armed with tear gas guns and pistols, but it was apparent that they could not cope with the union men and their sympathizers.

After the local authorities began their requests to the Governor for National Guard action, the Governor ordered an investigation by State Police. The result was reported by telephone to Oscar Olander, head of the State Police, who was conferring with the Governor and Colonel Lewis in Detroit.

A statement issued last night by Robert C. Travis, chief local organizer for the U.A.W., gave the union's side of the riot, its reason and its inception as follows:

"The sequence of events in today's occurrences at the Chevrolet plants in Flint that recently resumed operation was:

"1. Last Sunday evening I called Plant Manager Arnold Lenz, suggesting a conference for today (Monday) to reach an amicable settlement regarding disputes over union discrimination on the part of the management at the Chevrolet plants in operation.

"2. Mr. Lenz at first tentatively agreed, but this morning when I phoned him at his suggestion he refused to proceed with the conference and gave no reason. Finally he said he could not meet me until Tuesday, again without stating a reason.

"3. Discrimination against union men seeking to work at their customary jobs continued today (Monday) and one man with twenty years seniority was fired, apparently for wearing his union button.

"4. Feeling among the men ran so high that the shop stewards met. Soon after 3 o'clock a protest movement on the part of the workers began in various plants, and in half an hour the word had spread from plant to plant till seven plants were experiencing sit-down protest strikes. About 7,000 workers were involved.

"5. Then company police and hundreds of thugs, armed with tear gas pistols, tear gas bombs, blackjacks and clubs manufactured in the Chevrolet woodshop, attacked all workers in Plant No. 9, using floods of tear gas. It was a clear case, apparently, of company thugs against the workers, since all the injured workers were found in the plants and no one was injured on the outside of the company property. City police do not seem to have been involved.

"6. The battle lasted an hour and a half, and to judge by the line-up about 90 per cent of the workers are with the union against the company and its murderous thugs.

"7. It is rumored that large bodies of armed thugs are still within easy attacking distance of Plant No. 4, now in possession of the sit-downers, and other plants.

"8. The workers intend to keep sitting down until the vicious and illegal discrimination against union men by General Motors, and the clubbing of American citizens by private armies of the corporation, is ended once for all."

The police denied Mr. Travis's statement that no police took part in the battle. In company circles it was denied that any "hired thugs" were used by the company. All the fighting against the union men, it was said, was done by the local authorities, the regular company police, and non-union men who had become outraged because of being kept from work by the strike.

It was also denied in company circles that 7,000 men at the Chevrolet plants joined the strike. The company said that only a few hundred men took part in the new sit-downs and that the overwhelming majority of the 6,000 men on the day shift and the 6,000 on the night shift remained "loyal" to the company.

The company also denied that Mr. Lenz had refused to talk with Mr. Travis about alleged discrimination. It said that Mr. Lenz was too busy to talk with him, but agreed to do so tomorrow afternoon. Then, according to the company, Mr. Travis hung up the telephone. The riot followed.

The company said that Mr. Travis asked Mr. Lenz on Sunday for a meeting to discuss the alleged dismissal of three or four men for union activity since the reopening of the Chevrolet plant. It said that Mr. Lenz agreed to a meeting and asked Mr. Travis to telephone him later to fix a time. The only reason that Mr. Lenz wanted to postpone it until tomorrow, it was said, was that he had no time yesterday.

According to the company there was no discrimination against the union in the firing of the men referred to. The company said that all the dismissals were in line with an agreement made before the reopening by Mr. Lenz with Mr. Travis and other union officials.

The men were fired, it was said, for wearing union buttons and soliciting union members in the plant and for picking fights with non-union men during working hours. According to the company, the union had agreed on these offenses as just cause for dismissal.

The Buick plant here reopened today with 2,000 of its 15,000 men back on part-time jobs. There was no trouble. Before the end of the week the Buick company plans to have 6,000 men back on a part-time basis, unless today's events change the situation.

The Broad Challenge
of the Sit-Down

by Russell B. Porter

DETROIT.

IN THE past few months the country has been brought face to face
in sudden and dramatic fashion with a deep and underlying social
problem, the inner significance of which the general public is just
beginning to comprehend.

The new labor technique of the sit-down strike on a scale of
great magnitude has aroused an outburst of enthusiasm (or hysteria) among the rank and file of hitherto unorganized labor, has
bewildered employers and has forced the nation to consider
whether this new weapon is simply a passing fad or whether it
presages something in the nature of an economic revolution, with
political changes as well.

The major sit-downs have been ended, at least temporarily, by
Governor Murphy's settlement of the General Motors strike and
by his success in persuading the Chrysler strikers to evacuate the
plants in advance of a settlement. Governor Murphy believes that
he has "outlawed" the sit-down in the form in which it has become alarmingly familiar to the public recently, but it remains
for the future to show whether his hopes are justified. So long as

From the *New York Times Magazine,* April 4, 1937, copyright © 1937,
1965 by The New York Times Company.

hundreds of thousands of men and women in the mass-production industries and the service trades remain in their present social ferment the issue remains critical, as shown by the debates in the Congress, the press and public meetings throughout the land and by the continued sit-downs even in plants where they have been barred by agreement.

President Roosevelt's decision not to intervene is interpreted as an indication that he believes the situation is improving. But there are many who predict more sit-down trouble and fear it may call for Federal action sooner or later if something is not done to remove the causes of the present wave of unrest and at the same time to curb this means of relieving the distress of the workers.

This wave of tremendous force, rising from the submerged depths of workers who regard themselves as underpaid, over-worked and badly treated, has swept the country, but nowhere has it broken with greater force than here in the sit-down capital of the nation. Hotels, department stores, five-and-ten-cent stores, many varieties of retail stores and small manufacturing plants, and even public relief offices, as well as the mammoth automobile factories which dominate the center of the motor industry, have been seized in whole or in part by the workers and have been forced to close.

The sit-down is unquestionably the easiest and most effective method organized labor has ever devised to stop production and force business and industry to meet its demands or at least nego-tiate. Against the background of the New Deal, of proposed changes in the Supreme Court and in Federal labor legislation, and of the world-wide economic breakdown and social unrest since the World War and the depression, it stands out as the most im-portant development, for good or evil, in the social history of our industrial civilization. What does it mean? Where did it come from, how is it operated, and what does it portend?

The history of the movement shows that there are two kinds of sit-down strikes—"quickies" and stay-ins. In a quickie, the workers simply stop work and production temporarily without seizing possession of the plant. The dispute is settled, the men return to work and production is resumed within a few hours.

If such a strike lasts overnight, it becomes a real sit-down or stay-in. The men take complete possession of the company's property, sometimes even of its executive offices and files, drive out the plant policemen and watchmen, sleep and eat there, and set up their own "self-governing community."

Quick sit-downs formerly were known as stoppages. They have been common for some years in the coal industry and garment trades, which form the backbone of John L. Lewis's Committee for Industrial Organization, the American labor group chiefly identified with the sit-down strike. The stoppages did not attract much public attention because they ended so quickly.

Real sit-down strikes began during the depression in a sporadic way in Great Britain and various European countries. Scottish, Welsh, French, Polish, Hungarian and Yugoslav coal miners, Spanish copper miners, Polish rubber workers, Grecian tobacco workers and Indian textile workers engaged in stay-in strikes, sometimes coupled with hunger strikes.

Sit-down strikes were first "popularized" in this country by the Akron rubber workers in 1935 and 1936. These were mostly quickies, but one led to the big Goodyear strike early last year. The United Rubber Workers is a C.I.O. union.

The world's first sit-down strike on a grand scale was the series of stay-ins in France which ushered in Premier Blum's Socialist government last May. At one time 1,000,000 French workers held possession of plants in various cities, industries and trades.

The first overnight stay-in strike in the American automobile industry took place in the Bendix parts plant at South Bend last November. It started as a quickie to protest company-union practices, but shifted gears to a stay-in after the company ordered the men out of the plant.

According to the men, they feared a lockout and decided to stay in to protect their jobs. The experience of the United Automobile Workers of America, a C. I. O. affiliate, which conducted the Bendix strike, served to perfect the technique which has been followed in the recent large-scale automobile strikes.

One of the most essential parts of the technique of the sit-down is the element of surprise. If carefully planned in advance, the sit-down usually is scheduled to begin at the time the men change shifts. Thus the union can draw men from both shifts to stay in the plant. If the union is not thoroughly organized, only the union members on the day shift are notified that a sit-down will be called when the night shift comes on at 3:30 P.M. Then the union men from the day shift hang around, let the non-union men go home, and sit down with the unionists on the late shift.

When the stay-in strikes first came into use it was the theory that every striker should stay in the plant all the time. Gradually the technique has been changed, so that now many are sent home, leaving a minority to hold the fort. This simplifies the problems of food, sanitation and recreation.

The organization of self-discipline within a sit-down plant is an important factor. Under a general shop committee there must be special committees to police the plant, watch for stool-pigeons, keep out liquor and other contraband, prevent smoking except in washrooms, keep up the fire protection and sanitation systems, clean up the floors, protect the machinery from sabotage, hold "kangaroo courts" to punish violators of rules, maintain food supplies and so on.

The problem of maintaining living quarters in a building designated for manufacturing is complicated. Sometimes the sit-downers can be fed from the company kitchens and cafeteria, but almost always food has to be brought into the plant from outside. This means an outside picket line to guard the gates and windows, arrangements with near-by restaurants and a woman's auxiliary to help prepare and serve the food.

Mass picketing goes hand-in-hand with the stay-in strike, because the men holding the plant need the support of large and militant reserves on the outside to help ward off attacks by the police or by company guards. There is also a large additional outside staff for messenger service, information, publicity, legal aid and other support for the strikers.

Especially important psychologically is the problem of recreation and entertainment. The morale of the men has to be kept up. There are union bands, orchestras, singers, reading groups and educational classes. Sometimes moving pictures are shown in the plant cafeteria. Setting-up exercises are held at regular hours, and baseball, basketball, hockey, wrestling and boxing are staged.

Radios and phonographs having records of labor songs, such as "Solidarity Forever," are played, and there are games of ping-pong, checkers and cards.

Nearly always amplifying systems are set up throughout the plant so that strikers in remote departments can be notified when visitors appear for them at the main gate, and the men can be rallied from all sections to meet the threat of an attack at any particular point.

In a military sense the technique of the sit-down has been well developed. Each plant has what might be called a "department of defense." A special committee surveys the plants for weak points and takes special pains to guard them against invasion. Barricades are put up wherever needed. Weapons are gathered from the company's stock of fire hoses and extinguishers, acid cans, door hinges, wrenches, nuts, bolts and other missiles.

An army organization is established, with the chairman of the shop committee as the "general," his committee as the general staff and the shop stewards and other union officers as commissioned and non-commissioned officers. Sentries are posted, regular watches served and alarm systems set up. Outside organizers skilled in military tactics are sent inside the plants to help strengthen the defenses.

In case of battle with police or company guards, outside pickets are counted on to counter-attack, and the women's emergency brigade to break windows to let tear gas out of the plant. The unions maintain sound cars, with amplifiers mounted atop automobiles, from which crowds are harangued and battles directed.

The technique is aggressively organized in advance. The procedure is laid down in a set of rules carefully studied by union organizers, in classes in labor tactics at special labor colleges and in educational classes at union headquarters.

The issues raised by the sit-down strike have usually been discussed in terms of the conflicting interests of industry and labor. From this point of view the main problem is that of property rights.

As industry sees it, the sit-down involves a clear and simple seizure of property in open violation of law. The C. I. O. no longer attempts to defend the legality of the sit-down, but tries to justify the use of an admittedly illegal technique on moral and ethical grounds. It holds that the end justifies the means—the end being the improvement of the workers' wages, hours and working conditions against the refusal of industry to grant collective bargaining in the manner demanded by the union. Human rights are paramount, and supersede property rights, according to this viewpoint.

So far management has not found an effective solution to the problem of how to keep its plants open in face of the new technique.

Many companies, however, are strengthening their plant protection systems, organizing their "loyal" workers and revising their method of production in efforts to minimize the threat of the sit-down. Industry is also supporting new legislation to make it a felony to organize or participate in a sit-down.

In the long run labor may find itself faced with as many problems as industry, or more, as a result of the growth of the sit-down. It has begun to discuss the prospect of new measures to legalize the sit-down and it is considering the organization of a new political party to seek such legislation on the basis of a changed conception of property rights in which the worker's right to protect his job against lockouts and strike-breakers would be superior to the company's right to control its property and in which the worker, having invested his life in the plant, would have a right to share in the management of industrial problems, such as the speed-up, which affect the conditions under which he works.

Labor is already facing the boomerang consequences of the spirit of lawlessness encouraged by the sit-down. The promiscuous use of sit-down strikes recently has led to abuses in which racketeers and ex-convicts have taken over labor unions and seized plants with outside strong-arm men never employed by the plant or store involved. These in turn have provoked a reaction in which police raids on sit-downers have been conducted without writs or warrants, and threats of vigilantes to take the law into their own hands have been made.

Small rebellious groups of workers who take advantage of the ease of the sit-down technique in order to stop production over some petty grievance in a strike unauthorized by the union are also causing embarrassment to labor leaders who desire to build up a reputation for responsibility in carrying out contracts and agreements made in collective bargaining.

The demonstration of how effective a minority may be in such a strike has also created a problem for labor, which may be faced some day with sit-downs called by a militant minority of Communists or others seeking to take over control of the union leadership as a means toward seizing power in the government. C. I. O. unions believe that the solution of such problems lies in complete organization, which they say will enable responsible labor leaders to prevent abuses.

Varied and complicated as may be the problems which the sit-down poses for industry and labor, the issues it raises for the public interest are much more vital and fundamental. The sit-down is regarded by many as not only an illegal trespass on company property but a ruthless exercise of economic power, in which the strikers defy the local police and Sheriff, the Governor and Mayor, the courts and the great body of public opinion which desires to go on living and working under an organized system of society and government.

These critics see the sit-down as a challenge to all constituted authority, threatening, if carried to a logical conclusion, the breakdown of democratic government and the development of chaos, anarchy, mob rule and dictatorship in successive steps; as a potential invitation to revolution conducted by a militant minority in a position to stop industrial production and thus paralyze the nation. They hold that the sit-down is definitely a left-wing weapon, whether the majority of workers who are using it so enthusiastically today realize it or not.

So far, although some Communists and other radicals have been helping behind the scenes, the sit-down movement has apparently been mainly a revolt of workers, skillfully organized and led, to correct the abuses of the old economic order and to gain the "more abundant life" that was promised to them in the New Deal.

They have not tried to operate the factories, as did the Italian workers in the Communist move which preceded Mussolini's March on Rome, nor have they used the sit-down directly for political purposes, as did the French workers who refused to evacuate the seized plants last year until the Blum government promised them new labor legislation and social reforms.

But those who hold grave fears of the consequences of the sit-down are not reassured. They think they can foresee the possibilities of violence and a decidedly revolutionary turn if the situation is allowed to drift. They call for some constructive, far-reaching plan that will remove both the threat of the sit-down and the causes of social unrest and labor disputes. Michigan seems to be the laboratory in which a solution is being sought by the trial and error method.

The C.I.O.

by Russell B. Porter

DETROIT.

ORGANIZED LABOR as represented by the Committee for Industrial Organization today is Big Business and its leaders are becoming Big Business Men. They have millions of dollars at their command through the collection of initiation fees, dues and special assessments from hundreds of thousands of workers in mass industries and they use these vast resources of capital to expand into one industry after another.

With political allies in Federal and State governments, they are exercising an economic power in the country which would have been deemed impossible a few years ago—before the depression —and they are leading the way to what some believe will be in effect a social revolution. Even such a traditional stronghold of the open shop as this capital of the automobile industry has been swept by the prevailing wave of enthusiasm for organization under the banner of this new school of labor leadership.

These C.I.O. leaders are a different kind of men from the old school, illiterate or semi-literate, pot-bellied type of labor leader, with his big cigar eternally in his mouth, with his tough way of talking and acting, and with his union offices in some crowded,

From the *New York Times Magazine,* March 28, 1937, copyright © 1937, 1965 by The New York Times Company.

dirty and smelly hole-in-the-wall. They are intelligent, well-educated men who can deal with industrialists and business men on terms of intellectual equality.

They use airplanes to fly back and forth across the country, they rent the most expensive suites in the best hotels for conferences and they sometimes occupy offices in the most modern and comfortable office buildings, as does the Steel Workers Organizing Committee in Pittsburgh and Chicago—offices which are even more pretentious than those of the employers.

They have copied the most up-to-date methods of industry. Their organization is as streamlined in a business sense as that of the most Taylorized corporation. At the top they have chosen leaders from related fields to serve just like a board of directors which has this and that financial and business interest represented on it.

They have a diversified group of leaders—hard-boiled, hard-bitten veterans of the labor movement like John L. Lewis himself, practical labor politicians, "self-made intellectuals" who have risen through the ranks from mines and steel mills, and young college-bred intellectuals who are embracing a career in the labor movement which probably never would have appealed to them had not the depression curtailed the opportunities in industry.

They have an educational department in which these college graduates give courses for ambitious workers in trade-union organization, the history of the labor movement, strike tactics, labor economics and labor conditions in Russia, Japan, China and other foreign countries. Some of the organizers have taken special courses at the Brookwood Labor College. One is a Harvard graduate, and also a veteran coal miner and union organizer. Another is a 1933 graduate of Michigan State, now research director for the automobile workers here. The local organizational director for the automobile workers is a Dayton University graduate, who wears a gold football on his watch chain. Homer Martin, president of the United Automobile Workers of America, is a former Baptist preacher and former national A.A.U. champion in the hop, skip and jump.

At Pittsburgh the chief organizer looks, acts and talks more like an English actor than the conventional type of American labor leader. Most of the men of this new type of labor leader are young, either in their late twenties or early thirties. But even the battle-scarred veterans like Mr. Lewis and his old comrades from the United Mine Workers, the International Ladies' Garment Workers and the Amalgamated Clothing Workers, who form the "brain trust" of the C.I.O., are men who have read widely, thought deeply on industrial questions and might be characterized in many cases as "intellectuals."

A comparatively small group of practical men and intellectuals working together smoothly, they are "selling" the idea of the C.I.O. to great masses of workers by the same methods as the most efficient sales department of a big corporation adopts in advertising its products. They are using all the latest devices of mass psychology—the press, the radio, the newsreel, the moving picture and even the sound car with its loud-speaker over which gifted orators sway thousands of workers at a time.

Representing a membership of 1,000,000, about half in the United Mine Workers, when it was organized, the C.I.O. now claims another million workers added in the past year, including 300,000 in the automobile industry and 200,000 in steel. It has used the economic power inherent in the organization of such masses of workers with ruthless and daring militancy.

Seizing plants by sit-down strikes regardless of their legality and massing thousands of pickets from other C.I.O. unions in other cities and States in front of the gates, it has defied the police and the courts to dislodge them and return the property to the owners until their demands are met.

Leaders of the C.I.O. are as realistic as the most domineering financier or industrial baron was in the days when gigantic battles were fought to control the railroads and industries of the country. Now the fight is over the control of the workers in the mass production industries. The C.I.O. is challenging the employers for control, and is organizing on lines parallel to those of modern business and industrial corporations in order that it may be able to fight management on its own ground, with the same weapons as management uses.

It is the theory of the C.I.O. that the structure of mass production industries is such as to call for a corresponding structure of labor organization. In industries like steel, automobiles, glass, oil and textiles large numbers of workers are concentrated together, rather than scattered all over the country in small numbers as in other trades. It sees the tendency of labor in industry moving away from skills and toward mechanization and leveling out.

The workers in any mass production industry have the same problems to face. There is an industry-wide uniformity of working conditions. When a big corporation controls sixty or seventy plants, as does General Motors, there is a uniform labor policy. The individual counts for less. There is an impersonal relationship between him and his bosses, especially if the ownership is absentee. The worker finds that he cannot get any satisfaction for his grievances, as an individual, according to the C.I.O., which then steps in to sell him the idea of collective action in one big union.

It is argued by C.I.O. leaders that the structure of labor organization must conform to the structure of industry if it is to succeed. If an industry is organized on a craft basis, they say, labor organization should be on a craft basis. But if it is organized on a mass production basis, like steel and automobiles, with the general policy of the corporation determined and directed from a central point, industrial or vertical unionism is necessary. The more highly integrated an industry, the more highly integrated must be the type of labor organization.

Thus the C.I.O. has a much more centralized form of organization than the American Federation of Labor, with its autonomy for separate unions, ever had. The C.I.O. is a closely knit organization with a centralized policy, originating in one point, and that point is C.I.O. headquarters in Washington.

This set-up enables the C.I.O. to bring all its resources of men, money and machines to bear upon any given situation. It has a huge war chest, made up chiefly from special assessments levied upon the members of the United Mine Workers through the check-off system which goes with the closed shop in the soft-coal industry. From this bulging treasury came the $500,000 appropriated to organize the steel workers, the financial support of the General Motors strike at the rate of $625,000 a month, and the funds to carry on the Chrysler strike.

The same resources enable it to hire intelligent, well-paid organizers, to send experienced men from the United Mine Workers wherever they may be needed, now in the automobile field, now in steel, now in rubber, today in oil, tomorrow in textiles, and to organize "flying squadrons" and "shock troops" in one city, State and industry, and send them in fast automobile cavalcade to any place where mass picketing is necessary to help one of the C.I.O. unions.

From the same source come the funds for the machinery of twentieth-century labor organization—the rent of commodious offices and hotel suites, the purchase of sound cars which go from place to place to arouse the enthusiasm of the workers in organization drives and strikes, and so on.

Here again, the C.I.O. leaders argue, they are merely following in the footsteps of Big Business. They say that the Morgans, the Du Ponts and other great financial interests have concentrated control of the mass production industries in Wall Street, so that the automobile workers, the steel workers, the rubber workers, the oil workers, the glass workers, the textile workers are all working for the same people. Thus it is perfectly natural for them to create a "united front" of labor to offset the "united front" of capital, according to the C.I.O.

Another appeal the C.I.O. is making to labor is based upon its theory that the worker, with the economic frontier gone, so that he can no longer "escape" from unfavorable working conditions by going West or getting a job in another industry, is now looking within the industry itself to see how his conditions can be improved. He is thinking about the process of manufacture in relation to himself as well as about wages and hours. Analyzing things, he has become concerned with the economic structure of the industry, the speed of production, the development of technological improvements and labor-saving machinery, the system of pay, whether straight wages, piece work or bonus.

Thus demands of the C.I.O. are not merely for higher wages and shorter hours; it wants a voice in determining the conditions under which men work, and under which steel, glass, oil and automobiles are produced. It desires to assist in deciding how fast the conveyor lines shall move in the automobile plants, how grievances shall be handled, how seniority rules shall operate.

A characteristic of modern business which the C.I.O. has adopted with effective results is the principle of the division of labor. Besides its leaders and organizational directors, it has specialists in different kinds of organization. From the coal, steel and rubber districts, for example, groups of well-trained men come into the automobile field.

There are certain men for secret, "underground" campaigns, where the attitude of the company is such that the workers cannot be approached openly, but have to be seen in house-to-house canvasses. Others are skilled in the emotional appeal necessary for arousing crowds in places where public meetings can be held. Still others have experience in the strategy and tactics of strike organization and are called upon when something in the nature of "military" knowledge is needed for offensive and defensive purposes in seizing and holding plants in sit-down strikes.

It also has skilled technicians in various fields. Clever lawyers in New York, Washington, Detroit, Chicago, Pittsburgh and elsewhere give it the same sort of advice corporations always have received as to how to get around embarrassing laws, and how to act so that if there is any violation of law in a sit-down strike it will be hard to prove that the union or its leaders ordered the men to seize somebody else's property or to defy a court injunction.

Labor has gone a long way when it has research departments which compare in statistical knowledge with those of big corporations. The C.I.O. unions, like steel and automobiles, hire bright young men out of the colleges to study the economic structure of the corporation they are dealing with.

These research men have to be able to analyze a corporation's financial statement, keep track of its financial condition, its profits, losses, assets and liabilities. They follow the trade publications, the reports of the Departments of Labor and Commerce, and the financial and business pages of the daily newspapers to see which way the trade winds are blowing.

Consequently, when the union goes into conference with the management, its negotiators are able to meet the company's men on their own ground. When the company says it has not the money to do what the union asks, the union committee comes right back with some pertinent observations made by its research department.

In propaganda, a field in which big corporations have been accused of having a monopoly in past labor disputes, the C.I.O. is at least holding its own, and some observers believe that it has had the edge on management in recent troubles. Experienced newspaper men have been employed by the C.I.O. unions and they are doing a good job.

These labor press agents go out of their way to maintain cordial relations with all sections of the press, whether it is pro-labor, anti-labor, or impartial. They telephone to reporters that the union is doing this or that, or that it might be well to go to a certain place at a certain time; they send messenger boys out with copies of press releases, and they try to keep rambunctious rank-and-file members from interfering with reporters and photographers in the pursuit of their duties. They get out remarkably well edited newspapers of their own.

They persuade union leaders to meet reporters in press conferences and talk as candidly as possible, just as public relations men for big corporations long ago got their employers to abandon the old "the-public-be-damned" attitude. That attitude used to be just as prevalent in union as in company circles, particularly in times of industrial strife.

In addition, the unions employ technicians in other branches of promotional activity—radio, movies and the like. They make special appeals to groups and to group leaders, including war veterans, church congregations, women's clubs, and racial and national organizations. They bring out bands to keep up the morale of sit-downers and pickets, have their war veterans wear uniforms and overseas caps in picket lines, and in all ways get the most out of the latest knowledge of mass psychology.

The U.A.W. began the drive against General Motors last September, when the research department sent out questionnaires to all local unions, asking for information as to wages, hours, whether there was a speed-up in a given plant, what type of seniority they had and what they wanted, the average length of the lay-off period before the production of new models begins, and other conditions.

Research men familiar with the industry also made a study of the economic structure of the corporation, learning what plants fed other plants and therefore were to be considered "key" or "bottleneck" plants, which would halt all company production if occupied by sit-down strikers.

The union then concentrated its organization efforts on the "key" plants, chiefly the Fisher Body plants in Flint and in Cleveland and the Chevrolet engine plant in Flint. It seized all these plants with sit-down strikes, and without bodies and engines G. M. had to close down practically all its other automobile plants.

At the Chevrolet plant the anti-union defenses of the company were so well organized that the union had to use "underground" methods remarkably similar to those employed by the A.B.C. and student secret societies in the anti-Machado revolution in Cuba. In other G. M. plants the results of the November elections, with the widespread belief that Federal and State authorities would be sympathetic toward labor organizations and the consequent lessening of workers' fear of joining unions, permitted open meetings and organization.

In both the automobile and steel drives the C.I.O. has been confronted with company defenses based on espionage systems. It attacked these systems by using spies of its own, and managed to expose many company spies among union members and among the workers in the plants. In addition it helped start a back-fire against the companies and professional agencies of espionage through the La Follette committee's investigation at Washington.

The union had less difficulty in organizing the Chrysler Corporation. Apparently the fact that G. M. had paid less attention to company unions than Chrysler helped the former and hurt the latter. The union was unable to enroll more than a "militant minority" of G. M. workers, although it stopped production by striking key plants, but it has organized a majority of Chrysler employes. It was aided in doing this by capturing 103 out of 120 positions as employe representatives in the company union set-up at January elections.

In the steel drive, the C.I.O. also made a special campaign to enlist company union representatives, and succeeded in adding about 20 per cent of them to its payroll as organizers, who brought in many of their constituents to sign union cards.

The whole picture, as seen in retrospect of the automobile and steel situations, appears to be one of a highly articulate and intelligent combination of practical labor leaders and intellectuals. heading a mass of inarticulate but militant production workers in a left-wing movement the consequences of which to the future of the country cannot yet be seen.

John L. Lewis and His Plan

by S. J. Woolf

WASHINGTON.

OUT OF the strife of the past year between capital and labor, and between two labor groups differing on methods of unionization, John L. Lewis has emerged as an outstanding figure. The unions composing his Committee for Industrial Organization have pressed the idea of one union per industry and have been suspended by the American Federation of Labor. They have gone on to enlist many thousands of workers behind their theory, and have won collective bargaining in such rock-ribbed industries as motors, steel and electric manufacturing. Now they are seeking to consolidate their gains in these fields and go on to others.

To Mr. Lewis, directing these efforts from his oak-paneled office in Washington, the progress of the C.I.O. comes as no surprise. He expressed firm belief that at last the time has arrived when the laborer will have been proved "worthy of his hire."

He is a big man, Lewis, burly and intense. There is an evangelical fervor about him that brings to mind the old-time circuit rider who, with a pistol in his saddlebag, carried the gospel to the outposts of civilization.

Something in the appearance of this spokesman for labor reminds one of Senator Borah. Both men have an abundance of flowing hair, long upper lips and small noses, and keen eyes peering out from beneath bushy eyebrows. But Mr. Lewis is younger and thinner, more rugged and less suave than the Idaho Senator. About the Senator there clings the urbanity of legislative halls; about John L. Lewis there is the atmosphere of sooty mine and factory towns.

Well-made clothes and a magnificent office have not dispelled the feeling that here is a worker, one who has groveled in the darkness of coal mines to scrape out a meager sustenance. A dignity which requires that his daughter, who is his secretary, address him as Mr. Lewis seems strangely out of the picture.

When I asked Mr. Lewis what he thought labor should have, he leaned back in his red leather chair and carefully unwrapped a large cigar. Lighting it deliberately, he replied:

"Labor wants the right to organize. It wants the right to participate through collective bargaining in the increased productive efficiency of modern industry; to benefit and not suffer through the improvements brought about through the genius of our inventors and our technological experts.

"It demands as its legal as well as its moral right freedom, freedom in political expression, which in many cases has heretofore been restricted."

He paused for a moment to let the words soak in. There is a strong sense of the dramatic about Mr. Lewis. Neither in private nor in public does he ever lose a chance to produce an effect.

"For too long," he continued, "labor has been bargained for and purchased in the open market in the same way that steel and iron and other raw materials have been bought. Wages have been fixed by the discredited law of supply and demand instead of with a regard for human standards of living. Employers have got the most possible out of their employes and given them as little as possible in return. When business has slowed down no concern has been felt for the workers; they have been ruthlessly discharged."

His left elbow rested upon his glass-topped desk as he spoke, and in his right hand was his cigar, the end of which he had already bitten ragged.

"Starting from a basic guarantee of the rights to organize and bargain collectively," he went on to explain, "labor demands shorter hours, the prohibition of child labor, equal pay for men and women doing substantially the same kind of work. It also insists that all who are able to work and willing shall have the opportunity for steady employment."

At this point the theory behind the C.I.O. was referred to by Mr. Lewis.

"Of course I do not have to tell you," he said, "that these objectives of labor can be won only through industrial unionism. The craft unions have shown they could not bring these conditions about. They are a survival of a past era of our economic development. When they were organized industrial enterprises were small, and inventive genius and modern engineering research had not developed the machines or the methods which are now employed.

"Today individual owners have given way to corporations, management is separate from ownership and business policies are determined by banking houses. Human skill and training have been subordinated to machines and only a small proportion of the workers are craftsmen. Machine operators can be trained in a short time and they, together with unskilled workmen for whom there is no place in the craft unions, constitute more than three-quarters of all the workers. For a union to function today it must represent all, not only skilled labor.

"Raise the valleys and the peaks will also rise. The wages of skilled labor will be increased proportionately when the unskilled workers—those in the lowest grades of occupation—receive adequate minimum rates of pay."

"A living wage?" I put in.

He pounded his huge fist upon his desk. "No," he roared, "not a living wage! We ask more than that. We demand for the unskilled workers a wage that will enable them to maintain themselves and their families in health and modern comfort, to purchase their own homes, to enable their children to obtain at least a high-school education and to provide against sickness, disability and death."

Mr. Lewis then went on to speak of the difficulties which labor encountered when it was refused the right to organize. He pointed out that under these circumstances the industrial worker must accept whatever terms are offered and he emphasized that it was futile for one employe to attempt to bargain with a billion-dollar corporation. With no organization behind him he must accept the dictum of the employer as to pay, hours of work and the conditions of employment.

"But this is not all," he continued. "The industrial octopus is not satisfied with these things. It also determines not only everything of consequence to the worker but also everything of consequence to his family; when the man shall work, how he and his family shall live, the kind of clothes they shall wear, the degree of education the children can have. In other words, there has been a higher power set above the worker which has fixed his social status and that of those dependent upon him."

Mr. Lewis himself has felt the weight of this "higher power." Perhaps it is memories of his boyhood days in Lucas, Iowa, where he was born fifty-seven years ago, that have spurred him on in his work. He was the son of Welsh immigrants, whose ancestors for generations had been miners. His father joined a union, a dangerous thing to do in those days. After leaving school young Lewis worked in his father's trade. Then he suddenly left Iowa and for a dozen years roamed the country.

When he was 27 he married Myrta Edith Bell, a school teacher in his native town. He already had an acquaintance with the Bible, but Mrs. Lewis introduced him to the beauties of Shakespeare and Plato, and her influence is felt in his speeches, which often contain classical allusions.

Within two years of his marriage Mr. Lewis met Samuel Gompers. The little English cigar-maker who headed American labor in those days was struck by the forceful personality of the young miner and put his talents to use. No two men could have been more unlike than the president of the federation and his protégé. One small, bald, almost retiring, always dressed formally in frock coat, high collar and white bow tie; the other big, vociferous, with a shock of hair and careless of his appearance. Still, what one attained by suavity, the other achieves by force.

Lewis rose rapidly. By 1919 he was president of the United Mine Workers, organized on the industrial-union principle. A few years ago he determined that craft unionism could not bring about the organization of the mass-production industries and in November, 1935, he formed the C.I.O. to do the job.

Although often described as a radical, Mr. Lewis has time and again fought left-wing blocs in his own union. When they have attacked him in miners' meetings, filling the air with cat-calls and boos, he has tossed back his rebellious mane and answered them in his bull-like voice, which fairly shakes the rafters. He cannot be shouted down, nor do threats affect him. He thunders forth his dictates and bellows out his principles. In his conferences with employers his manner, though more subdued, is no less positive.

He ascribes the antagonism between capital and labor to the wrongs which labor has endured.

"Considering the things that have happened," he said, "is it any wonder that a feeling of bitterness and injustice has sprung up among the workers? The employers have had the power not only to fix the economic and social standing of the worker but also to interfere with his political status and his political rights. The worker has a right in the realms of logic, philosophy and morality to exercise his own freedom of choice in banding together with others to bargain with his employer—likewise organized."

Mr. Lewis took the position that labor unions fight only because they are forced to and that up to now they would have been unable to achieve their gains in any other way. He declared that they must be constantly on the defensive against attacks by employers, and he expressed the conviction that if employers would be compelled by law to recognize the rights of labor to organize, then true equality of bargaining would ensue and employers and labor unions would be free to turn to more constructive objects.

"I think most people have come to realize," he said, "that we cannot progress industrially without real cooperation between workers and management, and this can only be brought about by equality in strength and bargaining power of labor and management.

"Labor is sincere in its desire to help. It looks forward to an industrial procedure which will increase productive efficiency and lower prices to the consumer."

Mr. Lewis does not hold that invested capital or management

should not receive a reasonable and generous return, but beyond these limits the productive gains, he maintains, should be passed on to the workers in the form of higher wages and improved working conditions. By such means, he says, there would be created a new mass purchasing power.

"Labor," he insists, "does not ask for more than its fair share of profits, but it objects to excessive profits accruing to a few while the workers are forced to get along on a bare subsistence."

As to the attitude of capital, Mr. Lewis was inclined to be optimistic. "I am beginning to hope," he said, "although we still have fights on our hands, that the industrial and financial autocracy which has flourished in this country for the last thirty years and which subordinated to its anti-social and anti-democratic activities not only our industrial but also our political institutions, will begin to see the light.

"The action of steel's leaders is encouraging. Perhaps others will appreciate the futility of fighting against a changing world. I hope that the day has at last begun to dawn when it will no longer be possible to exploit labor and to regiment all classes of our citizens.

"Labor must have the right to participate in the future of the nation, economically, socially and politically. I put 'economically' first because the other two will naturally be achieved when the first comes about.

"The great social and political questions which rock the country today arise from economic maladjustments. Political participation is a by-product of improved economic conditions.

"We all know that democracy in this country has been on trial. In order for it to survive we must have an industrial democracy as well as a political one. Political action by organized labor is increasingly necessary to safeguard the rights and principles of industrial democracy and also to secure legislative and even constitutional sanctions for its economic program. We have got to recognize the fact that the rights of those who work for a living are equal to those who profit from the labor of those who do the work.

"I was brought up with the idea that under our form of government all men were equal before the law and had equal opportunities. As I grew to manhood I saw that this was not so. Our democracy was not functioning in a way that preserved this equality of opportunity and parity of privilege before the law.

"I am convinced that the organization of the workers in the mass-production industries to a point where they may become articulate in voicing their grievances and stating their ideals and their objectives is the greatest contribution toward the preservation of political democracy in this country. This is the best insurance that we can take out against communism.

"Give more Americans the right to participate in the government and in the increased productivity of our industrial establishment, give them the opportunity to share in the fruits of the genius of our men of science and distribute our wealth more broadly, and we shall have a greater Americanism which will have no foes to fear."

Battle in Chicago

CHICAGO, MAY 30.

FOUR MEN were killed and eighty-four persons went to hospitals with gunshot wounds, cracked heads, broken limbs or other injuries received in a battle late this afternoon between police and steel strikers at the gates of the Republic Steel Corporation plant in South Chicago.

One of the dead was identified as Earl Hanley, 37, of Indiana Harbor, Ind. He died tonight in the Burnside Hospital of a fractured skull.

Twenty-nine of the injured were victims of gunfire. Twenty-three were policemen, all hit by missiles.

The clash occurred when about 1,000 strikers tried to approach the Republic company's plant, the only mill of the three large independent steel manufacturers in this area attempting to continue production. About 22,000 steel workers are on strike in the Chicago district.

The union demonstrators were armed with clubs, slingshots, cranks and gear-shift levers from cars, bricks, steel bolts and other missiles. Police charged that some of the men also carried firearms.

After their repulse in the march, which began at 4 P.M., the

From the *New York Times,* May 31, 1937, copyright © 1937, 1965 by The New York Times Company.

strikers tried to reassemble for another attack on the plant, but gave it up with the arrival of police reinforcements.

The police said they stood their ground but made no effort to harm the invaders until showered with bricks and bolts. The police then used tear gas. When the rioters resorted to firearms, the police said, they were forced to draw their revolvers to protect themselves. Even then, the police declared, they first fired into the air as a final warning.

At a late hour three of the dead were still unidentified. Police interpreted this as a confirmation of reports that outside agitators had played a leading part in the raid on the plant.

Governor Horner arrived from Springfield shortly after the battle, accompanied by Adj. Gen. Carlos E. Black. He left the Congress Hotel with General Black and said he was going into conference with both sides.

"Are you going to call out the military?" the Governor was asked.

"I can't determine what I shall do until I know what the situation is," he replied.

It was understood that he was hoping to arrange a conference with James P. Allman, Police Commissioner, and Van A. Bittner, regional director of the Steel Workers Organizing Committee of the John L. Lewis Committee for Industrial Organization. It is the S.W.O.C. that ordered the strike which has thrown 70,000 steel workers out of work in five states.

Informed of the riot, Mayor Kelly, at his summer home at Eagle River, Wis., attributed it to "outside mobs who came into Chicago to make trouble."

He expressed confidence that "the well-disciplined police" would fulfill its duty to "protect life and property" and added that "we can settle our troubles if we are left alone."

Joseph Weber, field representative of the S.W.O.C. and chairman of the meeting which preceded the riot, telephoned a report of the riot to Mr. Lewis.

Several women and several boys were among the injured. Some of these were mere observers.

The injured were taken to half a dozen hospitals on the South

Side. Many of the less seriously injured were arrested after being treated.

The riot grew out of a meeting held by steel-mill strikers in protest against the action of police, who turned them back Friday night when they attempted to approach the Republic plant.

The march was organized at this meeting held outside C.I.O. headquarters at 113th Street and Green Bay Avenue, three blocks from the plant. The strikers said they were going to march through the main gate entrance in an effort to force closing of the mill.

Heading the march were strikers from the Youngstown Sheet and Tube Company and Inland Steel Company plants in the Calumet district. They had been invited to the mass meeting and had volunteered to lead the march on the Republic plant, where about 1,400 workers were said to be still on job.

The union men chose a time when the police were changing shifts, hoping, the police said, to catch them disorganized. But Captain James L. Mooney, Captain Thomas Kilroy and Lieutenant Healy, expecting trouble, kept all their 160 men on hand.

Carrying banners and chanting "C.I.O., C.I.O.," the strikers drew within a block and a half of the gate to find the police lined up awaiting them. Captain Kilroy stepped forward and asked the crowd to disperse.

"You can't get through here," he declared. "We must do our duty."

Jeers greeted his words. Then the demonstrators began hurling bricks, stones and bolts.

The police replied with tear gas. The crowd fell back for a moment, choking, and then, the police say, began firing at the officers. The officers fired warning shots and, when, according to police, the strikers continued firing, they returned it.

Men began dropping on both sides. The strikers fell back before the police bullets and swinging police clubs.

Police wagons then raced onto the field and began picking up the injured. Some were taken to the Republic plant's emergency hospital, some to the South Chicago Hospital and some to the Bridewell Hospital.

The strikers retired to a position a block away and began trying to reorganize their ranks.

Most of the policemen who were injured were struck by steel bolts hurled by the strikers or shot from their slings.

The most seriously wounded of the policemen was Bryant McMahon. At the steel company's emergency hospital it was found that his head had been deeply gashed and that he would have to be removed to another hospital.

Other policemen treated at the emergency hospital were Peter Cleary, John Hooley, Henry Lawson and John Prescott.

Cleary saw a brother officer beaten to the ground by one of the crowd wielding a metal rod. The striker was disarming the prostrate officer when Cleary went to the rescue. He saved his fellow-officer, but his glasses were shattered in his eyes by a blow from the striker's weapon.

Harry Harper, whose occupation was not immediately learned, had an eye gouged out during the battle. Victor Anderson, 44, who is not a steel worker but had accompanied the mob out of curiosity, fell wounded by a bullet.

A boy of 11, Nicholas Leurich, received a bullet wound in the ankle. A boy of 9, who identified himself only as James, was shot in the leg.

The battle was watched from the plant windows by the nonstriking workers. Wives and other relatives and friends of many of them had called for a Sunday visit and had been permitted inside the gates just before the attack. They fled in terror.

John Prendergast, chief of the uniformed policemen, closed all roads leading to the plant late tonight. Guards permitted only those with business in the district to pass.

Soon afterward the union pickets, on duty at the plant since the strike began Wednesday, were withdrawn. There was no explanation.

The mass meeting preceding the advance was addressed by Leo Krzycki, regional director for the Steel Workers Organizing Committee of the C.I.O., and Nicholas Fontecchi, field director.

Mr. Fontecchi said that the C.I.O. had no intention of permitting the police to protect law violators, an insinuation, it was believed, that some companies were not complying with the Labor Relations Act.

In view of today's violence, police looked forward with anxiety to the gigantic mass meeting of all C.I.O. sympathizers which has been called for tomorrow afternoon in Kosciusko Park.

Legal action, involving the expected placing of formal charges against the Republic company by the Steel Workers Organizing Committee, must wait until after the holiday week-end.

C.I.O. legal experts, led by Mr. Bittner, may go to United States Attorney Michael L. Igoe with the formal charges that Republic has violated the Wagner Labor Act by refusing collective bargaining and sanctioning interference with legal picketing.

Whether the steel company's law experts plan to make a surprise move and "beat the union to the bench" would not be affirmed today by Frank L. Auerman, Republic spokesman.

Avowedly the union meeting tomorrow is to map the drive to close the Republic plant and make 100 per cent effective the Chicago area strike against the independent producers.

Inside the plant, J. L. Hyland, vice president of the Republic Corporation, addressed the loyal workers today. He said:

"I imagine you men are interested in how long this plant will operate. I am here to tell you that it will continue to produce steel just as long as you men want to work."

He declared that men who had gone on strike were returning to their jobs daily. This was denied by Mr. Bittner and other C.I.O. leaders, who asserted that more and more of the men inside the plant were deserting to join the strike.

While the company asserted that there were 1,400 workers in the plant, strike leaders insisted there were fewer than 700.

Over the holiday week-end the workers in the plant, who are still under a state of actual siege, held baseball games and a minstrel show.

A new strike here today closed the Valley Mould and Iron Corporation plant at 108th Street and the Calumet River, where 260 men are employed.

The strike at the Valley plant was orderly. The night shift of ninety marched out two hours before the usual quitting time, after giving notice of their intention to J. L. Pickering, foreman. He closed the plant at once.

Charles E. Swab, in charge of the foundry, said the men had given no previous intimation of their intention to strike. They had demanded C.I.O. recognition, he reported, and he had told them he would have to take the matter up with the main offices of the company at Hubbard, Ohio. The company was still considering the matter, he said, when the strike came.

Nine Hundred Chicago Police Guard Strike Area as Riots Are Hinted

by F. Raymond Daniell

CHICAGO, JUNE 1.

A MASS funeral for the victims of Sunday night's rioting in front of the Republic Steel Corporation plant in South Chicago, where pickets clashed with police guarding company property, was being planned tonight as the death list rose to six, with more than thirty still in hospitals.

Van A. Bittner, regional director of the Steel Workers Organizing Committee, making his first visit to the scene of the Memorial Day battle tonight, said that delegations from all unions affiliated with the C.I.O. in the Chicago area would attend the funeral Thursday afternoon in Eagles Hall. There the bodies will lie in state from 4 A.M. until the hour of the funeral.

He said he expected 25,000 unionists to attend and participate in a parade to follow.

Meanwhile, an inquest convened by Coroner Frank Walsh into the deaths of the first five pickets to die, sat long enough to establish the identity of four of the dead as employes of the

Inland Steel Company plant across the line in Indiana, and of the fifth as an active member of the Communist party, who was employed by the WPA.

Then, at the suggestion of Alexander J. Napoli, Assistant State's Attorney, and over the protest of attorneys representing the union and the C.I.O., Coroner Walsh continued the proceedings until June 15 to permit the police and prosecuting authorities time to investigate further their suspicion that the fatal riot was precipitated by agents provocateurs brought in from outside.

Later formal charges of conspiracy to commit an illegal act were filed against sixty-five of the rioters, who are either under guard in hospitals or in police station cells. The charges were filed on orders of Captain John Prendergast, chief of the uniformed force. Those who were able were ordered arraigned tomorrow morning in felony court. Conviction may mean a maximum punishment of five years in prison and a $2,000 fine.

Nothing was said at the inquest about the manner in which the pickets were killed, but an inspection of the records at the morgue established that every one of the five whose deaths the coroner was investigating, was killed by bullet wounds, presumably from police guns.

None of the policemen who were injured was shot and leaders of the strike insist that their pickets were not armed when the police charged the line.

The police, on the other hand, insist that the strikers after listening to inflammatory harangues by their leaders started a march on the company's property, armed with brickbats, clubs and gear shift handles. The police fired only after it became apparent that tear gas and clubs could not prevail against the strikers, the officials said.

All efforts to bring about a settlement of the strike at the Republic plant seemed to have bogged down after Governor Henry Horner's futile effort to compose the differences between the company and its striking workmen, whose leaders vow they will not return to work until the company signs a contract recognizing the S.W.O.C. as the sole bargaining agency for the men.

This the company will not do, even though the S.W.O.C. should establish in an election that it has a majority of the employes, James L. Hyland, its Western manager, has told the Governor and the union leaders. Efforts of Leonard Bjork, regional director of the National Labor Relations Board, and of Robert Pilkington, Federal labor conciliator, have failed to budge the company from this position or induce the union leaders to ask for less.

Frank L. Lauerman, in charge of the company's industrial relations, issued the following statement setting forth the position of the corporation, the only one of the independents in the Chicago area which has tried to maintain operations in the face of the strike:

"We are continuing to operate plants in Warren, Canton, Buffalo, Niles and Chicago because thousands of men in these plants want to continue at their jobs. These men had ample opportunity to leave the plant when the strike started, but they chose to stay in. They are free to leave at any time they please.

"We are not going to let them down now simply because outsiders are seeking by force to close these plants and put these men off the payroll. Moreover, we have large orders on the books and customers are demanding steel.

"In spite of the strike the corporation is now operating at over 40 per cent of its steel-making capacity. During May, in Buffalo, the company actually broke all previous records in blast furnace and blooming mill production and equaled its former high record in open-hearth steel production.

"We are making every possible effort to avoid circumstances that might lead to violence: In Warren and Niles, for instance, we have been flying food into the plant so that it would not involve any clashes with pickets at the gates; in Warren the food planes are being shot at by gunmen in the picket lines and one of our men unloading food from the plane inside the plant was struck by a bullet.

"The extent to which picketing has taken on the form of a military invasion is illustrated by the fact that practically all of the picketers involved in Sunday's riot in Chicago were not and never had been employed by Republic.

"To shut these plants down and send these men home in order

to avoid any possible clashes in picket lines would be like turning your house over to robbers because you were afraid if they tried to get in one of the robbers might get hurt.

"Every principle of law and decency demands that the thousands of men working today in our picketed plants be given full support in their determination to keep on working and get paid."

Mr. Lauerman took a group of newspaper men through the South Chicago plant in the forenoon to substantiate his statement that production was being maintained on a respectable scale. About half the blast furnaces were going, and scattered through the great, sprawling factory some 300-odd men could be seen doing odd chores. It was said that as many more employed on the night shift were sleeping, but these were not visible.

In unused parts of the plant an improvised recreation room had been set up with ping pong tables, a piano and a dozen or more checker boards for the amusement of the employes who chose to remain at work when the strike began last week. A laundry and pressing service was maintained by the company.

Spokesmen for the Republic Corporation denied that the loyal workers were receiving any bonus for remaining on the job, but admitted that a special food allowance of $1.50 a day was provided in addition to the regular mess.

The one positive result of the Governor's conference with strike leaders, officials and company representatives was a clarification of the rules of picketing. According to Mr. Bittner, the strikers won the right to picket the plant in unlimited numbers so long as the picketing was peaceful and the pickets were unarmed.

Despite this the picket line, after Sunday night's riot, was pretty slim until nightfall, when more than sixty strikers arrived in automobiles and took up their regular march before the gates. Mr. Bittner said that the number would grow steadily until more than 1,000 men were on the line.

Twice during the day the police received word that the strikers were planning a new march upon the gates to attempt to drag out the loyal workers by force if necessary. No outbreak occurred at any time, however, and the pickets trudged their weary elliptical course before the gates without interference from the 100-odd police on duty.

The police, fearful that the strikers, augmented by sympathizers from other mills, might try to storm the plant, took elaborate precautions to prevent any such invasion of the company property.

John Prendergast, chief of the uniformed force, ordered a guard of 900 policemen to stand watch over the plant in three eight-hour shifts. As an emergency measure, Chief Prendergast ordered 200 reserves held at the Hyde Park station, ready for instant duty.

While the coroner's inquest ostensibly was called to fix responsibility for the fatal Memorial Day shooting which Mr. Bittner characterized in a formal statement as "one of the most disgraceful affairs that has ever taken place in the annals of our country," this afternoon's session in the morgue was devoted entirely to identifying the victims as "outsiders."

Soon after the inquest was adjourned Anthony Tagliere, 26, an employe of the Republic Corporation, died in a hospital of gunshot wounds, bringing the total of dead to six. He was the first of the victims of the shooting to be identified as an employe of the company before whose gates the riot took place.

Four of the others were identified as Kenneth Reed, Joseph Rothmund, Alfred Causey and Earl J. Handley. The fifth, listed during the inquiry as "unidentified white man," was identified tentatively as Sam Popovich, address unknown.

With the exception of Rothmund, whose wife, Margaret, admitted he was not a steel worker but a Communist employed on the WPA, the others, with the possible exception of Popovich, were identified as striking employes of the Inland Steel Company, in Indiana.

Mrs. Rothmund, a middle-aged woman, who said she and her husband had come here from Alabama only six months ago, told the coroner and the jury of six that her husband had left home to help out with a picnic that was being given by a fraternal order of which he was a member.

Under the questioning of James J. Whalen, deputy assistant coroner, she conceded that the "fraternal order" was the International Workers Alliance, of which she said her husband was a member.

Her husband was a baker by trade, Mrs. Rothmund said, but for the past few months he had been employed by the government on the WPA. She knew from his own statements, she said, that he was a Communist and she had been told he belonged to the C.I.O.

Under questioning by Hart E. Baker, David J. Bentall and Ben Meyers, lawyers representing the union, Mrs. Rothmund said she had no direct knowledge of her husband's connection with the C.I.O.

Mrs. Rothmund said she had three grown children, aged 24, 22 and 18 years. Mrs. Gladys Causey, another widowed by the rioting, said she had two daughters aged 11 and 18, and a son who was "just turned 16."

Most tragic of all was the testimony of Ervin Shesler, brother-in-law of Kenneth Reed, who said that his sister was left with one child 19 months and another just 3 weeks old. Reed was 25, he said.

The Assistant State's Attorney moved for an adjournment for "a couple of weeks," just after Captain Thomas Kilroy of the Chicago Police Department took the witness stand. All three of the union attorneys objected, but Coroner Walsh said that nobody's interests would be injured by delay, whereupon Mr. Meyers said there was one party to the issue that would be injured and that was "the public."

"You don't represent the public," said Mr. Napoli, and Mr. Walsh promptly shut off further argument by setting June 15 at 9:30 A.M. for a resumption of the hearing.

Meanwhile, Wilbert F. Crowley, First Assistant State's Attorney, beginning an investigation into the shooting, said he was convinced that "outsiders" were to blame. There was enough evidence in his hands now, he said, to bring riot conspiracy charges against some of those involved in the rioting.

It might even be strong enough before he finishes, he said, to justify warrants for conspiracy to commit murder. Neither he nor any other officials showed any interest in the strikers' charges that the police were at fault.

Mr. Crowley, who took charge of the investigation without waiting for the return of State's Attorney Thomas J. Courtney, who is out of town, issued the following statement:

"The law will be enforced; property rights will be protected.

"We will track down those responsible for this riot and punish them to the full extent of the law.

"I am informed that many of them were outside agitators.

"I am particularly concerned as to who spoke at the meeting which preceded the riot and what those speakers said."

The meeting was held at the union's headquarters in South Chicago, not far from the plant which, while within the corporate limits of Chicago, is more than fourteen miles from the Loop. Many leaders of the strike addressed the gathering, denouncing the "scabs" who remained at their jobs.

Mr. Bittner, the field marshal of the steel strikers' army here, made public a telegram he had received from Philip Murray, national chairman of the S.W.O.C., from his office in Pittsburgh. Declaring that he was "shocked at the almost indescribable horror," Mr. Murray pledged the moral and financial support of the organization to bring the guilty ones to justice. He added:

"There is a growing feeling that there is definite collusion between Chicago police and Republic Steel Corporation. Evidences of this corporation's flagrant violations of the law are to be found on every hand."

On his own account, Mr. Bittner issued the following statement:

"The strike situation at the plants of the Inland Steel Company, the Youngstown Sheet and Tube Company and the Republic Steel Corporation is very satisfactory. The action of the police in South Chicago in shooting down defenseless men, women and children was one of the most disgraceful affairs that has ever taken place in the annals of our country.

"These people were peacefully marching along a public highway and in accordance with the statement issued by Mayor Kelly they were asserting their rights to peacefully picket the plant of the Republic Steel Corporation.

"The fact that not a single policeman was shot is a demonstration that our people were not armed and were only shot down because they desired to picket the plant of the Republic Steel Corporation.

"The blood of the men, women and children who were shot

is on the hands of those officers of the Republic Steel Corporation who were responsible for having the police officers on the ground to prevent peaceful picketing at any cost.

"The shooting of our people at South Chicago has not discouraged the strikers. On the other hand, our people have dedicated their lives to the proposition that these men have not died in vain and that the Republic Steel Corporation must sign a wage agreement with the steel workers' union.

"It is the purpose of the Steel Workers Organizing Committee to bring the men who were responsible for this shooting into court charged with the murder of our defenseless victims. We shall bury our dead and take care of their families.

"This sad affair in South Chicago Sunday afternoon was the spark that kindled the flame of unionism from one end of our country to the other. Every trade unionist in America is determined that the Steel Workers Organizing Committee must win this strike.

"The conferences with Governor Horner came to naught because of the attitude of the steel barons who control Republic Steel Corporation. The Governor did all he could to bring about a constructive and lasting settlement of the strike. The Steel Workers Organizing Committee offered two constructive, peaceful methods of ending the strike at the plants of the Republic Steel Corporation.

"First, we offered that a vote be taken under the supervision and direction of the National Labor Relations Board to determine who should be the collective bargaining agency for all the employes of that company, and if the Steel Workers Organizing Committee won the election, which we would by an overwhelming majority, that the Republic Steel Corporation sign a contract with our union. This the representatives of the Republic Steel Corporation flatly refused to do.

"Second, we offered to submit the entire matter to President Roosevelt and be bound by whatever decision he, or his representatives, might render. Again the representatives of the Republic Steel Corporation said no.

"We arranged with Mr. Prendergast, Chief of Police, to continue picketing the plant of the Republic Steel Corporation. The chief agreed that we could have any number of pickets we desire. This program will be put into effect immediately."

While the leaders were trying to round up strikers for the picket line before the Republic gates, twenty-two women, wives of strikers, appeared at City Hall and began marching up and down outside with placards denouncing the police, and calling upon Mayor Kelly to "wipe the blood off your hands."

Despite the effort of a passer-by to snatch a placard from one of the women marchers, they picketed for about two hours and then disappeared.

Part 2

WAR AND PEACE: 1940–1960

DURING WORLD WAR II, Walter Reuther of the United Auto Workers became one of the better known and more influential of the younger generation of American labor leaders. Among the reasons for his rise to prominence was his fertile and imaginative mind. Willing to consider ideas deemed impractical by other trade unionists, and to express them in public, Reuther was able to catch the public imagination. His article included in the selections below illustrates how he conceived of the war emergency as an opportunity to enlarge the worker's voice in industry and to strengthen the power of trade unionism. Reuther pledged to maintain labor peace and high productivity in return for giving workers, through their union, a voice in management. Was this an attempt to accommodate employers within the existing corporate order or an effort to restructure American society and alter radically the existing distribution of wealth, income, and power?

Perhaps more important for the nation's future than Reuther's ideas and proposals were the changes that the war emergency wrought in the composition and aspirations of the working class. R. L. Duffus' article on Detroit suggests how the war altered that city's population mix, how it affected the worker's relation to his job, and how it released new forms of tension. The news story on the Detroit race riot of June 1943 gives substance to some of the social and economic tensions that Duffus six months earlier could only imagine.

The end of world war in 1945 only served to introduce an era of Cold War in which Soviet Russia replaced Nazi Germany as the enemy. No sooner was the war against Germany over than many trade unionists who over the years had been fighting communism in the labor movement resumed their anti-red offensive. David Dubinsky, long one of the labor movement's leading anti-communists, reveals in his article of 1946 labor's quite early enlistment in the postwar red scare. One can only wonder after reading Dubinsky's essay whether such sentiments as he expounded cultivated the ground for the bitter harvest later reaped by Senator Joseph McCarthy, or whether, as Dubinsky constantly asserted, if other Americans had been aware of the "red menace" as early as he and had acted against it, there would have been no Age of McCarthyism. The reader may judge for himself.

The struggle against communism and corruption in the labor movement, and the coming to power in 1953 of a Republican administration which was reputedly anti-labor, brought the divided American labor movement back together. In 1955 the AFL and the CIO merged into a new united national labor federation, choosing George Meany, long-time AFL secretary-treasurer and president of that organization since November 1952, as chief executive of the AFL-CIO. Meany's article presents his vision of the role of the American labor movement and his suggestions concerning what trade unions should seek in the future. This selection allows the reader to compare Meany's 1955 visions and proposals with those of John L. Lewis in the 1930's and Walter Reuther in the 1940's.

James Riddle Hoffa quickly became the most notorious labor leader of the 1950's. No trade unionist seemed a better symbol of the affluence and complacency associated with the decade. Rising to power in what had become the nation's largest union (the Teamsters), in the wake of Dave Beck's fall from grace as a result of his corrupt union practices, Hoffa paid himself a remark-

ably high salary, invested union pension funds in plush Miami
Beach and Las Vegas real estate developments, and presented
a mind singularly devoid of ideas. Yet the rank-and-file Teamsters
cheered Hoffa and supported him in the face of all manner of
adversity, including the McClellan Committee's uncovering of a
variety of sordid practices in the union and the Kennedy administration's series of federal trials that eventually put Hoffa behind
bars. A. H. Raskin's article probes the roots of Hoffa's support
among Teamsters and is, in effect, a scathing commentary on the
nature and values of American trade unionism during the Eisenhower years.

Labor's Place in
the War Pattern

by Walter P. Reuther

THE TITANIC effort which alone can bring our nation victory over
the Axis war machines cannot be the responsibility of any single
group in America. Our major home-front factors—labor, management and agriculture, and government representing all three—
each has its specific responsibilities, but none can function fully
and effectively except as part of a team.

No group may evade its own obligations by harping on the
deficiencies, real or fancied, of the others, yet it is reasonable that
all should expect the cooperation and integration which alone
can make it possible for our armed forces to match and eventually
crush the might of our enemies.

The war prescribes an essential new pattern for all of America;
the disastrous alternative to victory calls for an end to both
business-as-usual and unionism-as-usual. This new pattern is already being followed to an extent. It will have to be observed to
the full as the increasing size and gravity of our military operations bring the issue of victory or defeat closer to a decision.

For American labor, as for all our people, the war holds in its

From the *New York Times Magazine,* December 13, 1942, copyright ©
1942, 1970 by The New York Times Company.

balance the precious gains of centuries of patient, costly struggle.

When Pearl Harbor sounded the end of a period of peace, labor had not obtained universal security. There were still dark spots, particularly in the South, where poverty was the rule for millions of our people. We had not yet related production and distribution to the needs of all workers. Nevertheless, American labor had advanced to the most favorable position it has known in our history. American labor had achieved a status in America, as individuals and as an organized group, which appeared to doom for all time a return to the exploitation, the long hours, the speed-up and the low wages which obtained in many industries only a generation ago. Collective bargaining had been accepted in the steel and automobile industries, the greatest citadels, in other years, of anti-unionism. The general acceptance of collective bargaining among American employers and the maturing labor movement in the mass-production industries promised much for equity and peace in industrial relations. Not all problems were solved, but there were emerging patterns and mechanisms for solutions without the bitterness and violence of earlier decades.

Labor's new status in America and its hopes for further progress could not survive an Axis triumph. Even the most casual observer of nazism and fascism must know that the first victims of these satanic twins have been the working people and their organizations. Freedom of speech, of press and of organization, foundation stones of labor's efforts for security, are denied those workers who come under the sway of totalitarianism. The Nazi counter-revolution is accomplished by systematic murder and annihilation of the labor movement.

A recent survey published by the Inter-Allied Information Center graphically illustrates the fate of working people who fall prey to the power of the Axis. Fully 6,000,000 non-German workers are now in involuntary servitude in the Reich. They are chained to arms and munitions factories where they must forge the weapons for the continued slavery of their families and their countrymen. Hitler has demanded that Laval send 150,000 French workers into forced labor in Germany. More than 300,000 Belgian workers, once members of proud and strong labor unions, are already in enforced labor in Germany. Hundreds of them have been deported for work in Norway. Mass deportation of Greek workers to Germany has taken place. Some 80,000 Slovak workers and 60,000 Czechs have likewise been placed in slavery in Hitler's German workshops. Food ration cards were withdrawn from Dutch workers who would not "voluntarily" go to Germany. Fully 450,000 Hollanders, who also once knew the strength and protection of labor unions, have thus been driven into slavery in a country not their own. The Polish Ministry of Information in London estimates that 1,500,000 Polish workers have met a similar fate.

The Japanese have made forced labor their policy in the conquered territories of China. During the last five years the Japanese have rounded up 5,000,000 Chinese laborers and have deported them for labor in the northeastern provinces and in Japan.

These tragic realities must compel American labor to an appreciation of its obligations as a major member of America's war team. Labor's place in the new pattern that war has forced on America is clear.

Labor's first obligation is to realize that we are not now producing solely to provide our population with their everyday needs, but that we are producing primarily to protect our freedom, our nation and our homes from destruction.

Labor must face the challenge of the war as it would a forest fire or a flood that menaced the home town. The promise of labor's spokesmen that strikes will be abandoned for the duration of the war, a pledge which has been underwritten by labor's organizations in conventions, must be honored.

Actually there are far fewer strikes than anti-labor propagandists would have us believe. A recent article in a national magazine declared there have been 700 strikes in Detroit since Pearl Harbor. The United States Bureau of Labor Statistics reveals, however, that from Dec. 7, 1941, to Aug. 1, 1942, there were but 170 strikes, involving 66,400 workers in all of Michigan. The idleness amounted to seven one-hundredths of 1 per cent of available working time, and not all of it was in defense plants.

Nevertheless, these few strikes should not have occurred; they should not be repeated. Those responsible for the strikes—and they are not, in all cases, the workers—have left the entire labor movement open to serious injury in the public mind.

Grievances in many cases are sound ones. Our Federal machinery for adjusting individual grievances, as well as group or corporation-wide grievances, has operated at far too leisurely a pace. The answer to this is not to be found in an irresponsible defiance of these agencies by unauthorized strikes; "pulling the pin" these days means "pulling the pin" on our marines, sailors and soldiers in the Solomons, as well as on the employers. The answer lies in the formulation and vigorous prosecution by labor of plans for speedier adjustment of grievances, both through governmental agencies and through provision for impartial umpires.

The experience of industries where labor-management relations have functioned most harmoniously points to establishment of impartial umpire systems as the fairest and most effective way of airing and adjusting the many individual or small-group grievances which arise in the shops. Many of these differences cannot be adjusted in direct negotiation between union and management. Where there is no arbiter whose decision is binding on both parties these grievances hang fire for months. Where they are not settled they are lasting sources of discontent. Workers who have agreed not to exercise their right to strike feel frustrated and grow resentful.

Labor's proper course under the circumstances should be insistence that the National War Labor Board create a series of courts manned by impartial umpires. These might be geographic or industry-wide in their scope. Obviously the hundreds of grievances which arise in a single area or in a large corporation within a week cannot be handled by the War Labor Board in Washington. They should be turned over to industrial arbiters who would have the obligation of rendering a decision within two or three weeks at the outside. These impartial umpires are not needed in plants or industries where collective agreements already provide for such a system. They should supplement those labor-management contracts which do not provide for an umpire system.

In a war the winning of which depends so much upon the mass

production of war materials in the shortest possible time, labor has a solemn obligation to produce at maximum speed and capacity. Given the assurance that additional production from increased individual effort and sweat will not mean exorbitant corporation profits and periodic unemployment because of material shortages or unbalanced production schedules, labor should be eager to produce to the fullest extent possible without injury to the health of the worker or to the quality of the product.

Neither the government nor efficient management will insist upon a speed-up that is unsafe or beyond human endurance. Such a policy is uneconomic and leads inevitably to large-scale absences and eventual dissipation of our manpower.

Labor's insistence on maintenance of forty-hour work-week standards reflects more than a desire to maintain economic advantages. Labor feels that maintenance of forty-hour work-week standards constitutes a most effective safeguard against the reckless use of our manpower.

Our manpower resources are our most valuable asset, on both the fighting and production fronts. They should not be dissipated by continuation of lack of planning and coordination.

The absence of intelligent manpower allocation and failure to achieve proper balance in production scheduling have created overemployment side by side with unemployment. Owing to our failure to meet skilled manpower requirements by proper allocation and adequate upgrading and training programs, skilled war workers in many vital plants are being burned out by ten- and twelve-hour shifts, six and seven days a week.

If overemployment and unemployment have been permitted to develop at a time when the forty-hour work-week standards place a penalty of increased labor costs on work over forty hours per week, it is logical to expect even greater dissipation of our manpower resources if the forty-hour work-week standards are relaxed.

The eight-hour day and the forty-hour work week are among organized labor's most cherished possessions, won through tremendous sacrifice and struggle over many years. To abrogate them after organized labor has voluntarily given up premium pay for Saturdays and Sundays as such, would constitute a severe blow to labor morale.

Insistence on maintenance of the eight-hour day and forty-hour work-week standards does not mean that a longer workday or work week should not be worked. Even with the proper allocation of manpower, the war cannot be won by a forty-hour work week. It may require a fifty- or sixty-hour work week. No matter what is required, labor has the obligation to work with maximum effort as many hours per day and per week as are necessary to achieve total production.

In addition to insisting on maintenance of forty-hour work-week standards and intelligent use and allocation of manpower, it is labor's responsibility to insist on and to cooperate in the development and enforcement of campaigns to reduce loss of man-hours due to accidents and illness.

A recent report of the National Safety Council stated that "Casualties to United States armed forces from Pearl Harbor to Nov. 15, 1942, excluding the African campaign, have been 5,694 dead, 3,435 wounded, 39,827 missing or prisoners—a total of 48,956. Casualties to American workers through accident in the same period have been 44,500 dead and 3,800,000 wounded."

The millions of man-hours lost through sickness and industrial accidents is many times greater than the hours lost through strikes. To conserve our manpower resources and to reduce to a minimum our loss in man-hours, labor, management and government must meet the challenge of the increasing number of industrial accidents and sickness with determination equal to that with which they face the strike problem.

Labor's obligation to increase war production does not end with the maximum effort and sweat on the part of the individual worker. Labor's years of experience in manning the workshops that make up the arsenal of democracy have equipped labor to assume a broader responsibility. The millions of workers who make up the membership of organized labor constitute a tremendous reservoir of creative and technical knowledge. To facilitate the making of its maximum contribution labor has been urging that it be given representation on the top war-production planning and policy-making agencies. It was in the discharge of this broad responsibility that labor urged the early conversion of peacetime industry to war production. From its experience labor understood the need for, and urged the creation of, a supreme economic high command to organize and give over-all direction to our war economy.

Labor was performing its high obligation when it constructively pointed out that we could not mobilize our material and human resources for total war unless we had an over-all, coordinated and planned production program under which the allocation of materials, men and machines was made by relating one to the other.

Labor again was meeting one of its broad responsibilities when it proposed that the production of tanks and planes and other war materials could in many cases be doubled and trebled through the creation of tank production pools, aircraft production pools, etc. The maximum utilization of production machinery and plant facilities could be achieved only on the basis of organizing production on an industry-wide basis without regard to corporation lines or consideration of post-war competitive positions of a given industry.

The lack of over-all direction and coordination in our war production effort has created a manpower problem which daily becomes more threatening, an acute material shortage and an unbalanced production schedule, necessitating a serious curtailment of vital production in many plants.

A beginning has been made in the establishment of labor-management production committees in some 1,500 of our 10,000 war plants, and these groups present an opportunity for channeling labor's creative ideas into the war effort.

Labor must make it clear, in promoting these joint committees and in asking for a voice in the policy, planning and administrative war agencies, that it is not seeking power but rather an opportunity to participate as a democratic partner in the advancement of our war effort.

Labor must make it plain that it is not interested in "control" of industry, that it does not seek to use the war emergency and our nation's dependence on labor to seek reorganization of the fundamental basis of American economic society. Labor need not approach its opportunity to make a creative contribution as a means of building its prestige and its influence. Results will talk louder than any blueprint or theoretical formulations on labor's new role in America. Let labor give earnestly and without thought of self-gain to the war effort. By the results of such a course labor will have earned its right to the confidence and the further trust of the entire nation; if labor fails to make this creative contribution, it will, conversely, lose status both in war time and post-war America.

Labor has demanded a place in the top councils of our war-production agency. In a people's war, labor has a rightful claim to such a place. It can and will sustain that claim only by acceptance of the obligation to make the utmost contribution to production and by refusing to use its power for advancement of interests which are not calculated to advance the war effort.

Under the leadership of President Roosevelt, representatives of the Congress of Industrial Organizations and the American Federation of Labor have just begun peace negotiations. In these negotiations labor faces a solemn obligation to the nation and to itself. The nation and the rank and file of labor have a right to expect that the participants in the negotiations demonstrate a capacity of labor statesmanship and an ability to rise above minor considerations in the interest of broader issues. The many resolutions adopted at labor conventions urging "labor peace" must now be translated into a practical program of joint cooperation which will best advance the interest of the worker and the nation.

Organic unity is not to be expected overnight, but it is necessary at once to achieve the cooperative relationship requisite to labor's maximum participation in the war effort. A step in the right direction would be the creation of a top labor council, composed of representatives of the C.I.O., A. F. of L. and the railroad brotherhoods, whose purpose would be to work out practical machinery and methods to achieve maximum war production, to adjust organizational problems and to eliminate jurisdictional disputes.

Similar subcouncils could be set up by unions having overlapping or similar jurisdictions, to perform a comparable function on a lower organizational level. The top labor council should establish a court of arbitration to which all unresolved questions of jurisdiction could be referred in an orderly manner for final disposition, all parties agreeing in advance to be bound by its decisions.

The prospects for peace would be enhanced, and the war effort would certainly be served if, pending the reaching of a complete accord, rival unions in single industries could work out a cooperative, nonaggression pact. A labor court of arbitration to settle all jurisdictional disputes which cannot otherwise be adjusted is in order without further delay. Those who refuse arbitration of jurisdictional disputes and who permit such disputes to lead to strikes in war plants lay themselves open to the charge of treason to their country and to the best interests of the labor movement.

A further major obligation that labor must meet is the building of high labor morale. Contrary to the belief of many people, high labor morale cannot be purchased by a 5 or 10 cent an hour wage increase. Labor morale must be developed and must flow from a conscious understanding of the fundamental issues involved in the winning of the war. The worker's morale, his mental attitude when he steps to his machine or his work post each morning, in many cases is the decisive factor in determining his production, both as to quantity and quality.

To date, an adequate job has not been done on the morale front. Some of the fault lies in the difficulty of labor organizations adjusting themselves to the new wartime problems. However, one of the major obstacles in the building of labor morale is uncertainty of the future and fear of a repetition of the economic chaos, unemployment and insecurity that followed the last war. In meeting after meeting of industrial workers this question is most often raised by the workers.

The answer must be a clarification of our war aims. The high-sounding principles of the Atlantic Charter must be translated into concrete, commonplace, everyday things that the great mass of workers can grasp and understand. We cannot fully release the tremendous energy stored within the millions of American workers unless we demonstrate that we are determined to win the peace as well as the war. We must plan now and with determination for the full mobilization of our human and material resources to meet the problems of the post-war period. The fight against unemployment, poverty and insecurity cannot be won by half-way or half-hearted measures. The war against human insecurity, like the war against the Axis, must also be a total war. A meaningful pledge and program for such a war is a fundamental requisite for the total mobilization of labor behind our drive for victory.

A City That Forges Thunderbolts

by R. L. Duffus

DETROIT.

WITHIN THE past twelve months the city of Detroit has changed
its occupation. It has beaten its plowshare into a sword. In three
or four months more it will reach the crest of the greatest flood of
potential mechanical violence from any comparable area in all
history.

Guadalcanal, Tunisia, the Aleutians and the Russian front have
already received goods made by the hard-working people of Detroit. The market is not satiated. The tempo of production rises.
What of the city and the people under this new dispensation of
war? Is this like the war boom of twenty-five years ago, or has
something new entered into the picture and into the people's
minds?

The visitor who has spent a week in the city's war plants, streets
and public places and who has talked to some of those who fre-
quent them may still be puzzled. He is likely to see past, present
and future in a jumble almost as chaotic as the sprawling pattern
of the city itself, where towers testify to a peacetime grandeur,
new factories to a present strength and determination, miles of

From the *New York Times Magazine,* January 10, 1943, copyright © 1943,
1971 by The New York Times Company.

jerry-built houses and thousands of families crowded into small rooms, shacks and trailer camps to an inability to solve a great problem over night, and acres of untenanted prairie to possibilities not yet realized.

Detroit, as they say, has changed over. The expression is not quite correct. Apart from what is going on in the plants there is still some surprise and confusion in the city itself, as people try to adjust themselves to a new congestion, new habits of working and living, and new problems of human relations.

There is no precedent for a thing quite like this happening to a city like Detroit. For that matter, there is no city like Detroit. There are no accustomed symptoms to look for. What one expected would happen has not happened. What one didn't expect has taken place.

The re-visiting traveler, descending from his train, doesn't get the full impact at once. The outward and visible downtown city hasn't altered much. Uniforms in the street crowds, American, Canadian, Australian, tell of the war, but so do they in every city nowadays. Motor cars, despite gas rationing, still move in comparatively greater numbers and with greater speed than they do in New York City. Neither the sternness of war nor the effervescence of a frantic prosperity is at first noticeable in Detroit.

These things are there, but you do have to look for them. You look for them in your hotel. You find that the bellboy who carries your bags is from Atlanta and has been on his job for two days. You know that within a month or so he will be in the Army or in a war factory. You find that the middle-aged woman who cleans your room would like to work in a factory, but has been told she can't because she has only her first citizenship papers. You learn that the room itself is under Army lease and that you can be turned out if the Army wishes to move in. The Army doesn't move in, but you feel precarious.

You hear that there are 20,000 newly arrived Federal employes in Detroit, and more on the way—representatives of a consumer who intends to receive just what he ordered. You become acquainted with a bartender, who tells you that munitions workers drink "shots and shells"—a double shot of rye whiskey and a shell of beer.

You hear all sorts of tall stories about "Hill Billies" (this term is said to include every one who has migrated into Detroit from south of the Michigan line, and hence might even, because of the way the line runs around Detroit, take in a few Canadians), who are not accustomed to wearing shoes, and whose wives buy them boxes of three-for-fifty cigars. Your taxi driver says he knows for a fact that one new arrival mailed a letter in a fire-alarm box before he had been in town half an hour.

You hear stories, but perhaps they tell more about the old settlers than about the new arrivals. You look for the reality. You don't find it at a theatre where a musical comedy is being shown. There are a few males in sweaters and with no ties in the orchestra, but half the seats are empty. You don't find much of it in saloons, expensive restaurants or the obvious night spots. You get a sense of it in a downtown drugstore, where you have to fight your way to get to the refreshment counter at midnight; in advertisements for help wanted; in department store crowds; in your inability to get a messenger to run an errand for you; in the recorded fact that one Detroit toolmaker reached the dizzy height of $2.75 an hour for his straight time, time and a half for overtime and double for the seventh day, and didn't mind working long hours; in a 30 per cent increase in trucking accidents, ascribed to green drivers replacing experienced men who had gone into the factories; in sixty-nine trucks out of one firm's fleet of 450 tied up on a Saturday night, not by a strike, but by lack of drivers.

If you simmer down what you see and what you hear and believe you begin to understand what has happened to Detroit. The great war migration into the city is a fact. Within two years, by Census Bureau estimates, the metropolitan area of Detroit has added 336,000 people to its population, to make a total of more than 600,000 engaged there in the war industries.

This is something, but it isn't enough. Detroit not only has to deal with existing congestion. It has to decide how much more congestion it can stand without having people stepping on each other's toes all over the place. Some authorities say that 100,000 more workers will be needed from outside the area, in addition to at least 40,000 Detroit women who have said they would take war jobs. Others say that immigration into the area will have to be discouraged because there will not be enough beds for the newcomers to sleep in or enough street cars, buses and automobiles (or gas) to carry them to and from their work.

There is one other contradiction in the Detroit picture. The area has about 200,000 Negroes. Negro leaders say their labor has not been fully utilized, and that those employed are often working below the level of their skills. "Idle Negro workers here," said one reliable spokesman, "are baffled by talk of a manpower shortage." There are some signs that necessity will take care of this situation.

High wages are a statistical fact. A union contract signed last August with a typical war materials company lists more than 130 jobs, of which the highest pays $1.88 an hour for tool and die workers, the lowest 75 cents an hour for some of the women. The unskilled worker under that contract gets 85 cents an hour.

Some shops run an average payroll of $80 to $90 a week. The average working week is close to fifty hours and would be higher if it were not pulled down by individual absenteeism, shortage of materials, changes in production plants, such as the current shift from tanks, guns and ammunition to planes and ships, and the unavoidable delays of the not quite complete changeover. It will surely run higher as the new production lines get rid of their "bugs." The average Detroit war worker now gets something like $50 in his weekly pay envelope, and when he works longer he will naturally get more.

This isn't hay. Neither is it fantastic wealth for those accustomed to the automobile industry. The fantastic element is introduced when this much money comes into the hands of rural newcomers who have been accustomed neither to much income nor to large cities. The veterans trot along about as they always did when times were good. They live, by and large, where they have always lived.

It is the late arrivals who change Detroit and are changed by it. Add to their numbers the regiments of newly employed women and of men drifting in from other occupations and you have something to think about. Inject into the situation the tension between white migrants from the South and the new and old Negro workers (there were about 25,000 in the automobile and allied industries at the peak of civilian production), and there is more to think about.

This tension is felt in the shops. When you visit the plants you usually see Negroes working by themselves, or engaged in pushing, hauling or lifting occupations which differentiate them from the whites. The Negro forms about 10 per cent of the population of Detroit. The problem isn't simple for him, nor for those who wish him well. It ties in with housing, because he has always been the worst housed in Detroit.

There are trailer camps—maybe miles of them altogether. They are pretty well organized. One such camp has a trailer with a front porch, very neat, permanent-looking and homelike. This camp also has an air-raid shelter. Across the road, a few hundred feet away, were houses which looked as though they had cost between $15,000 and $25,000. Outlying Detroit is pretty well scrambled—no doubt about it.

Rows and rows of little houses, mostly white-painted or unpainted wood, but sometimes faced with brick, bloom at intervals over the flatlands. Between the groups are occasional farmhouses and fields where corn grew last Summer.

You see signs urging you to buy a share in America at so much down and so much ever after. Some of these signs are new. The little houses don't cure the housing shortage. The plan to turn vacant stores into apartments holds out some promise. Another proposal is to make use of country clubs.

Linked to housing is transportation. Many a Detroit worker is accustomed to driving from ten to as much as twenty-five miles to work, alone or in company. The great parking lots around the larger plants are astounding, even with gas rationing in force. If the worker falls back on street car or bus lines he finds scant remedy. The city-owned Detroit street railways are carrying nearly a third more passengers than they did a year ago, which means that 200,000 new passengers are making round trips daily.

But even bad housing and congested public vehicles and all the other troubles that are intensified when a city has to take care of 15 per cent more people than it is equipped for are endurable when there is full employment, and a stir of something worth working for.

Detroit's working population tastes the joys of being very much wanted. The first effect of this state of affairs, especially on the new residents, was to cause a good deal of restless shopping around for the ideal job among all the jobs offered. The labor turnover in many instances has been remarkable. One Detroit manufacturing corporation hired 2,700 employes in a recent month. It lost 2,000 for various reasons, chief among them the lure of other jobs, although dislike of city life, dissatisfaction with working hours, and "vacations" also figured. A 10 per cent turnover monthly has been no rarity. It may be too early to determine how much the stabilization order of Manpower Director Paul V. McNutt will do to relieve this situation. Some action of the kind was undeniably needed.

The old hands don't shift. They know what seniority means in slack times, and they know what slack times have meant in the past and can mean in the future. But the drifters, the new hands, are not necessarily idlers. They have been shopping, as often as not, for more work and longer shifts—for more overtime.

The whistles blow, by day and by night, and the crowds come surging out. Some are dog-tired. You get that way in a long shift. They want food and sleep. If they seek amusement they are likely to turn to neighborhood movie houses, beer saloons, dance halls. The Southern whites have brought the square dances with them. Halls where these can be performed are crowded, with waiting lines stamping feet to the music within.

What does this army of workers think about? Is it aware of the great issue it is helping to determine? It probably does think about that issue, and it is probably as serious about it as the men who are doing the fighting. Soldiers think and talk about their personal affairs, their relatives, their girls, their food, and so do workers in munitions factories. They are embarrassed by heroic generalities. When they talk about the war they are likely to mention their own buddies who are in it. Or they scrawl something about Hitler and Tojo on a tank and let it go at that. Generally they appear to give more attention to the Japanese than to the Germans.

But they do want to get on with the job. They may stop working for a minute or two when visitors appear, especially if one of the visitors carries a camera and seems about to use it, but they want that overhead crane brought over, they want that forging—quick. They lean over precise machines, with something like affection in their eyes. And they complain of things which stop or interrupt the work—not of the work itself. There is no oratory in their natures. They do want to get the stuff out.

Against the night sky are the chimneys of great factories. Lights blaze. Machinery roars and thunders. A democracy at war has its troubles and its weaknesses. But the work gets done. It does get done. And this is Detroit at the beginning of 1943—a city amazed and often confused, but a miraculous city, a city forging thunderbolts.

Detroit Race Riot

DETROIT, JUNE 21.

FEDERAL TROOPS in full battle regalia, with jeeps, trucks and armored cars, moved into Detroit tonight to help city police, home guards and State troops restore order in the country's worst race riots since the East St. Louis (Ill.) disturbances in the first World War.

[After Federal troops arrived and President Roosevelt's proclamation calling for peace had been received, rioters dispersed and quiet was restored, according to The Associated Press. Mayor Edward J. Jeffries stated at midnight that the situation was much improved.]

The death toll at 10:20 P.M. had reached twenty-three, including twenty Negroes and three white persons. The injured, overflowing hospitals, numbered at least 600 and the number arrested and taken to jails and prisons exceeded that number.

With Detroit and its metropolitan-area population of about 2,500,000 persons—tens of thousands of them employed in Detroit's many war factories—under a state of emergency, Federal troops came from Fort Wayne, Ind., and Mt. Clemens, Mich., near Detroit.

They augmented two battalions of military police from Fort

Custer and River Rouge Park as the shootings, beatings and pillaging continued unabated.

Late tonight local and State police pumped more than 1,000 rounds of ammunition and dozens of tear gas bombs into an apartment house to rout Negroes sniping from upper windows.

The siege had begun at 9:15 P.M., a few minutes after several Negroes were seen to run into the building with shotguns and revolvers.

The police first used the tear gas, which drove out most of the tenants on the lower floors, but the besieged group held out.

The police began to return fire with fire and the neighborhood rang with shots for more than two hours, the battle ending with the surrender of the Negroes. Two of them had been killed and a policeman, Lawrence Adams, was wounded seriously.

The Federal troops did not take part in the apartment house siege, but assisted other police in patrolling the riot areas, mostly in the downtown Negro section.

The Federal soldiers rode down Woodward Avenue, Detroit's major thoroughfare. They had orders to "clear the streets." With 1,110 assigned here, 1,200 others were held in reserve at Fort Wayne.

Only Workers Escape Curfew

All persons, except those going to and from their jobs in war plants, already had been ordered to stay in their homes under the 10 P.M. to 6 A.M. curfew ordered by Gov. Harry F. Kelly when he declared that a state of emergency existed.

Brig. Gen. William E. Guthner, in charge of military police for the Army's Sixth Service Command, announced that he had been authorized by his headquarters at Chicago to "cooperate with State and city police."

General Guthner said the request for Federal troops was made by Governor Kelly after the mobs had ignored his emergency proclamation. It was learned that 2,000 additional troops would arrive in Detroit tomorrow.

Shootings, stabbings and hundreds of street fights throughout the metropolitan area had led Governor Kelly to declare the state of emergency.

Detroit's municipally owned Receiving Hospital, whose chief surgeon, Dr. Austin Z. Howard, described the riots "as the worst calamity in Detroit's history," overflowed with injured. It was necessary to borrow blood plasma from the Red Cross to treat seriously injured victims.

Of the dead, twelve succumbed at Receiving Hospital. Others died in ambulances en route to the hospitals, and several were found dead in the streets. One white man was found shot to death in the Negro section and a Negro was found dead in a theatre with six bullet wounds. The injured included a policeman who had been shot six times.

A Warning Against Communists in Unions

by David Dubinsky

WHAT COMMUNISTS do in the trade unions of any country vitally affects the welfare and security of its entire people, and not merely its organized labor movement.

No organization in American life has been immune from Communist penetration. Obedient to centralized direction, Communists have bored within church bodies, educational institutions, women's clubs, scientific groups and, believe it or not, business men's associations.

But the labor unions have been their special target. Without control of the trade unions the Communists would be lost. The unions form their economic base. Without direction of the key workers' groups, their other "transmission belts" would be useless. The workers' organizations are the largest and most vital nongovernmental body in the community. They are primarily dedicated to improving working conditions, to raising living standards. They are part of a delicate mechanism of modern life, the core of "human engineering." The influence of organized labor reaches far beyond its 13,000,000 members or their families.

For this reason the significance of Communist operations in

From the *New York Times Magazine,* May 11, 1947, copyright © 1947 by The New York Times Company.

trade unions can scarcely be exaggerated. Like termites, they bore into the "house of labor," but are not an integral part of the structure because the spirit and aims of totalitarian communism are totally distinct from and hostile to the ideals and policies of free trade unionism.

Free trade unionism may have its faults, but they can be remedied because essentially the processes of these unions are democratic, even though, at times, they may fall short of the ideal.

But communism, in unions and other organizations, is conspiratorial. It is based on the elimination of majority rule. It aims to establish the one-party state as the sole power over all groups. The unions, they are convinced, are the stepping stones to this goal.

The Communist technique is simple. The party agent forms the acquaintance of a member of a union which is marked for capture. They form a "cell" or "fraction" of a few like-minded members. With the help of the party agent a program is prepared. Naturally, it follows the Communist party line.

At the outset, the party representative's choice falls on a unionist who knows something about parliamentary procedure. Then the stage is set. The innocent is introduced to an important party functionary or well-known party speaker; he is taken to cocktail parties and dances and no time is lost in introducing him to attractive partners.

The next scene is at the union meeting. Hardly is the gathering called to order before the Communist "fraction" starts to work. A member or, better still, a stooge or "innocent" makes a motion. The debate is on. It may and frequently does last long into the night. Slowly the members who want some sleep slip out of the room. As they do, the Communist tide rises. A vote may be taken at 1 or 2 o'clock in the morning. The party-liners win.

Sounds simple, does it not? It is simple. And yet that is the way the followers of Stalin have captured trade unions. The same procedure used at national conventions results in the Communist capture or control of the larger units.

The Communists cannot act singlehanded. They must have help. They must be part of a crowd, of a "united front" or a "popular front," whatever the name may be. Because they know what they want, because they are skilled in parliamentary tactics, and use any methods or weapons and because they reject no trick or device, they make headway.

But the Communist "fraction" does not always plant its own member in the union president's office. This place is often reserved for the ambitious opportunist who is ready to "play along." The "fraction" may even seek out a pliable promising non-Communist party man to bear the the title of president and thus serve as a good cover for the actual party control of the union. If he stands for the party program, that is enough. Of course the real job, such as secretary-treasurer and organizational director, must go to strict party men.

The whole Communist apparatus is highly centralized—"democratic centralism" is the phrase. But forget the "democratic." That's camouflage. The machinery is geared for quick action, for when the party line is "handed down" it must be obeyed with blind military discipline. There is no time for debate, only for "discussion and approval."

The Communists refer to themselves as the "vanguard" of labor. Nothing could be further from the truth. They have disrupted many unions with their factional quarrels and have left in their wake many saddened and disillusioned members, destroyed businesses and blasted hopes. Far from being "progressive," as they claim, they are really "dynamic reactionaries," as someone has called them.

To them ethics and morality are "bourgeois" virtues. Therefore, in the unions, as elsewhere, they will support a conservative or reactionary if he should oblige them by favoring a pro-Soviet or pro-party line.

Many cases are at hand to prove this assertion. Indeed, we can show examples of union leaders who have dipped into their organizations' treasuries and grossly mismanaged union affairs without any condemnation by the Communists. In such cases the Communists have jumped hard on anyone who has tried to unseat the financially delinquent and incompetent non-Communist "friend of the Soviet Union."

As self-constituted champions of the Negro race the Communists have never faltered in praise of their alleged attitude on race

discrimination. Yet they have never criticized the head of one of
the nation's important unions who is known to be largely responsible for drawing the color line in his own organization.

Why? This union official, though not a Communist, has, out
of vanity, or ignorance perhaps, permitted his name to be used as
a sponsor of Soviet "front" outfits.

In another important union the national president has winked
at Communist domination of local activities in two important
metropolitan areas. By this concession he has bought off criticism
of his administration of union affairs. This officer even sits at
labor conventions with men he knows are Communist leaders of
his affiliates.

It is evident that vanity and lack of principle by non-Communist unionists have a bearing on the reasons why pro-Communist
elements make headway in the mass workers' units. Opportunism
is a quality that is found everywhere.

Even in our own international union any local officer, no
matter how conservative or incompetent, can avoid criticism by
Communists and even obtain their support by merely endorsing
some resolution favoring Russian foreign policy or the party line.

To Communists the yardstick of a union leader's "progressiv-
ism" is not the soundness of his labor policies but his readiness
to approve Kremlin policy. That is why I consider them totalitarian reactionaries.

The fact is that real progressive unionists are the foremost
targets of these Leftists while conservative unionists are quite safe
from their onslaughts. The reason is simple. The liberal unionist
knows the score. He is wise to Communist machinations. He can
find his way through the jungle of double talk raised by the
"saviors of the working class." This will explain why the ILGWU
has been the butt of bitter Communist assaults for so many years.

Although our union is free of the Communist menace today,
it was not always so. In 1926 the Communist party through its
demagogic propaganda and exaggerated promises was able to
attract many of our members. It thus managed to obtain control
of our New York organization and succeeded in plunging the
coat and suit industry into a general strike. After a futile eight-
week struggle the local Communist leaders had had enough. They

were ready to come to a settlement, but the Communist party, feeling that the Moscow line was about to change, ordered their agents inside the union to continue the strike—against their better judgment and against the interests of the workers.

The strike ended disastrously. This terrible fiasco unseated the Communists in our union. Since then, most of the leaders of that strike have broken with Communist totalitarianism and have returned to the union. These same leaders are now the most effective fighters against Communist influence and domination.

It took ten years for us to recover from the criminal and stupid Communist-led strike of 1926 which cost $3,500,000 and left in its wake a chaotic industry and a crippled union.

Other unions are going through the same experience we have had. Now and then the curtain is pulled aside and we see what is happening. Take the case of Joseph Curran of the CIO's National Maritime Union. He knows the story from the inside. He says that 500 Communist party members dominate his union of 80,000 members through tactics "no different than those practiced by the Nazis when they destroyed the trade union movement of Germany."

By means of its cells the Communist party, according to Mr. Curran, was able to take 107 out of 150 elective offices in this union, one of the most strategic in the nation's life. These 107 officials, says Mr. Curran, are "more interested in assuring that the National Maritime Union becomes a stooge union of the Communist party than they are in keeping it an instrument belonging to the rank and file seamen who built it."

Interference by the Communist party in union elections, finances and strike policies was but recently exposed by J. A. (Pat) Sullivan, president of the Canadian Seamen's Union, an affiliate of the Canadian Trades and Labor Congress.

For years prior to his frank confession of Communist affiliation Mr. Sullivan repeatedly denied that tie. He did so, he says, in order to win two elective positions—secretary-treasurer of the Canadian Trades and Labor Congress and head of the Canadian seamen's organization, strategic posts from which he could serve the Communist party.

The Communists are desperately working day and night to get

control of progressive unions. With these as a base they can then launch their attacks on more conservative union citadels. Once in control of a few key progressive unions, they have a toehold in the inner circles and policy-making body of the whole labor movement. This is no small achievement. It means representation on committees and bodies of all sorts, visiting the President, for example, having an entree to important Government departments and gaining access to what might otherwise be secret information and, naturally, passing it on to the party commissars.

One Communist-dominated union "suddenly" conceived the idea of organizing workers in the Panama Canal Zone. Overnight the organizer flew to that strategic area. In a comparatively short time the union boasted 13,000 members there. Was this display of activity solely an interest in trade unionism?

I will not deny that Communists, at times, fight to improve the lot of the wage-earners but only when such a policy coincides with the interests of the Soviet rulers. If it is to their advantage to forgo demands on their employers, to neglect grievances, to engage in the maximum of "class collaboration," they will do so.

Take their attitude toward President Roosevelt. When the New Deal was sponsoring important social legislation, Earl Browder saw in it "the clearest example of the tendencies toward fascism." Roosevelt's labor policies, according to Mr. Browder, constituted "the American brother to Mussolini's corporate state with state-controlled labor unions closely tied up and under the direction of the employers."

Subsequently, when the party line changed, no praise of Roosevelt was too great for Mr. Browder. However, during the Hitler-Stalin pact this ersatz fuehrer thundered in Madison Square Garden, "The Rooseveltism of the New Deal has capitulated to reactionaries."

Yet the moment Russia was forced into the war by Hitler everything changed again. The Communists buried their class struggle theory temporarily and they stopped strikes abruptly because they were no longer interested in embarrassing our defense preparations or sabotaging aid to Britain. In fact, they glorified F. D. R. in terms second only to those held in reserve for Stalin. In this and in their temporarily servile submission to American employers they had but one motive: to serve Russian interests, not those of the American people.

The unions under Communist domination reflected this sudden change faithfully because they are completely wired for Communist sound. Read their organs and you will learn that as soon as Russia entered the war they abandoned their campaign against lend-lease and frowned on any interruption of production. In this period one of the largest of these Communist-dominated unions even espoused an elaborate "incentive" production plan of the type denounced by labor for many years as "speed-up." It is hardly necessary to emphasize the reason.

For purely Communist purposes, the needs of Russian foreign policy, the Communists have brought discredit to the time-honored weapon of trade union picketing. They threw a picket line around a hotel to interfere with a dinner officially tendered to Winston Churchill by the City of New York. In another instance Philip Murray had to intervene to prevent the Communist-dominated New York City CIO-Industrial Council from proclaiming a two-hour city-wide political strike. The strike was called ostensibly to support another CIO union—also in the Communist orbit.

Harry Bridges, who runs the West Coast Longshoremen's Unions, is familiar with all the curves in the Communist party line. When American cooperation with the Soviet Union was the order of the day during the war he boldly proclaimed the idea of extending the no-strike pledge beyond the war period. But he dropped this line when the war ended and the party line changed. Behind this changed expression is his belief, shared by other Communist party line followers, that the political strike is more important than the economic strike. Keep that in mind. It is important. The reason is obvious. The political strike is a revolutionary weapon. The economic strike is not.

What would happen if the Communists should gain control of the American trade union movement?

Let Tomsky, prominent Russian trade union leader, a suicide in one of the party purges, give the answer:

"If for a moment we could imagine that tomorrow all the

trade unions of Germany would march hand in hand with the German Communist party, we would have no doubt that a Soviet Government would be established there within five minutes after that combination of forces took place. . . . If we could imagine for a moment a combination of the trade unions with the Communist party of England, then a Soviet Government would rapidly spring up also in England."

Obviously, the extent to which Communists succeed in capturing posts and securing domination over unions vitally concerns the entire nation and not merely the particular labor body affected.

Present-day France affords a striking and tragic confirmation of this truth. The Communists in France now dominate the General Confederation of Labor. No doubt the Communist party in France owes much of its electoral strength to the stranglehold it has over the great trade unions in the metal trades, coal fields, transportation and other key labor organizations. Through its air-tight control of the trade unions, the Communist party has, whenever it so desired, exercised veto power over the French Government's economic policies. Because of this Communist control of the General Confederation of Labor, the numerically largest political party in France is one whose policies are controlled by a foreign power and not by its membership.

We must never forget that the Communists took to resistance in France not when their own country was attacked but only after Russia was invaded. What a menace this development is to the stability and security of France is clear to all.

In many important respects, the situation now prevailing in Italy is similar.

Were the Communists ever to exercise such domination over the American trade union movement and thereby secure such a decisive political position, our own country would find itself just as unstable and insecure—its national independence vitally sapped —at the mercy and whim of a ruthless foreign totalitarian dictatorship.

Liberals render a distinct disservice to the nation when they allow themselves to be used as fig leaves, front men or transmission belts by the Communists. Some liberals deliberately allow themselves to be thus used; others may do so unwittingly. But in both cases such liberals lend most vital prestige indispensable to Communist success.

Non-Communist trade union leaders who join with the Communists in united front movements render an equally distinct disservice to the people as a whole and to organized labor in particular.

The present trend in the country against communism has so far resulted only in an increasing number of union members getting on to the Communist game. Some leaders of trade unions have left their posts in disgust because of their belated realization as to what the Communists have been doing right under their noses. But though more and more rank and file workers in Communist-dominated unions are waking up to the fact that they have been used as dupes by the Communist party, the Communists have not yet been dislodged from the control of any unions which they have been holding in their grip. In recent months the Communist party has been put on the defensive and has lost some ground. But it continues to maintain its stranglehold on a number of unions.

How much strength do the Communists have in the unions? It is impossible to give an exact figure of their trade union membership.

Today the Communist party claims 70,000 members. Let us assume that 35,000 of these are in the unions. That would give the party a maximum numerical strength of .0027 per cent of the 13,000,000 trade union members. But despite their insignificant numbers, the Communists and their fellow-travelers and party-liners dominate twelve to fifteen out of forty national CIO unions. They have a strong bloc on the CIO executive board.

None of the 110 national unions of the AFL is dominated by Communists, but they do control locals of an undetermined number, though not many.

It is safe to say that no important labor union in the United States has more than 2 per cent Communist membership. Because of their devious methods of operation, however, the Communists and their followers wield an influence far out of proportion to their numbers. It is truly a case of the Communist tail in some cases wagging the trade union dog.

The real danger from the Communists in trade unions is that they control strategically placed workers in key industries such as communications, transportation, shipping and maritime and electrical manufacturng.

Here and there influential labor leaders have felt they could use the Communists to their advantage. Uniformly, this policy has been a failure, sometimes a disaster. The history of the CIO is abundant proof of my statement. Free, democratic trade unionism and communism do not mix. One cancels out the other. To be free, the unions must keep the Communists out of leadership which they would use to advance their party interests.

How can this be done? We start from the assumption, which is a fact, that up to now the totalitarian success in trade unions has been scored largely by default. The Communists have broken through open doors.

Today the constructive trade union leader who is fighting the infiltration of Communists into his organization is faced with other grave obstacles. Curiously enough, these hindrances come from those anti-union legislators, on the national and State levels, who presumably are opposed to communism but who at the same time are doing all they can to break down the trade unions and thereby help to strengthen the Communist position.

Every anti-union law passed by Congress becomes a trump card in the hands of the Communists. Weaken the trade unions and you open wide the dikes for Communist propaganda to rush through. Nearsighted "regulators" of trade unionism in our legislative halls are the best pals the Communists could wish for in this country.

It is sheer nonsense for anyone to believe the Communists have a monopoly of organizational skill. They can be beaten by the conscious combined will of the progressive and democratic forces within the unions. Over and over again our experience in the ILGWU has supported this contention.

A local of the ILGWU with a membership of 25,000 held an election recently. It has less than 500 avowed or known Communists. Yet, because of their energy, discipline, unscrupulousness in creating false issues and propagandistic activity, they polled 5,000 votes. Suppose only 9,000 members had gone to the polls. Less than 500 Communists would have taken control of a local with such a huge membership. Only because the progressive forces were alert, were well led and were able to bring 80 per cent of the members out to vote did they succeed in defeating the Communist-led forces, 3 to 1.

Therefore, to meet the situation, trade union progressives must:

(1) Put at least as much energy in organizing the majority as the Communists do in organizing the minority.

(2) Enlightened trade unionists do not have to ban Communist propaganda to stop party infiltration. Outlawing the Communist party from the political arena or Communists from trade union membership is not an effective way of combating them. We must rely on education and discussions of daily problems confronting labor, on the systematic enlightenment of our members about the grave issues facing us.

(3) We must do everything we can to bring home to the rank and file the importance of attending their local meetings and sharing in the responsibilities of union membership. They must lead in handling grievances in the shops and factories. They must serve on committees that administer the policies of the union, no matter how dull this work seems to be—remembering that if progressive unionists fail in these tasks the Communists will undertake them for their party purposes.

(4) Local unions should make it obligatory for members to attend meetings and participate in elections in order to insure that all decisions reflect the will of the majority. This would serve as the most effective barrier to Communist minority control of unions.

Local unions must work out practical administrative methods of stimulating all members to take part in every phase of union life, to take time and patience to interest members in such a program. Efforts must continue despite discouragement.

(5) As trade union leaders we must be tireless in our efforts to solve the daily problems of the wage-earners in improving their

working conditions and living standards and safeguarding their political rights and interests.

(6) Constructive unionists must refrain from competing with Communists or others in making extravagant "pie-in-the-sky" promises that cannot be fulfilled.

If we follow these rules we can easily overcome the Communist nuclei in the trade unions in every test of strength. These strepto-Communist cells, like those of other diseases, thrive in darkness and ignorance. They do not multiply in unions where leaders and members are alert, honest and competent.

What the International Ladies' Garment Workers' Union has been able to do since it routed the Communists twenty years ago every progressive American labor union can do today.

On Labor's Future

by George Meany

WHEN THE American Federation of Labor and Congress of Industrial Organizations (A.F.L.-C.I.O.) convene as a single organization in New York's Seventy-first Regiment Armory tomorrow morning, the merger of the nation's two major labor federations will have just begun. It will undoubtedly take some time for integration or cooperative working agreements to be completed among affiliated national and international unions, as well as for the merger of state and local branches, numbering almost a thousand. Under the circumstances, it would be optimistic to expect too much too soon from the merger. Therefore, it is my purpose here to look ahead and discuss the more significant future role of the new organization that will take shape this week—specifically with regard to the national economy, the relations between management and labor, the security of the free way of life and the basic political and legislative trends of our land.

For some years now the formation of a united labor movement has gained increasing support as a necessary and inevitable forward step. Among workers, confused by rival union claims, the plan for consolidation was greeted by overwhelming popular acclaim. Among trade-union leaders the move stemmed from a general realization that division was costly and that organized labor had to be prepared for future responsibilities far more exigent than the pressure of current problems, serious as they are.

For the world has suddenly arrived at the threshold of the atomic age. To labor this betokens a new industrial revolution of considerable magnitude. It has been said, facetiously, of course, that atomic power, yoked to the electronic brain, could reverse the evolutionary process and make a monkey out of man. Whether or not there is any substance to this far-fetched idea, it is clear that labor has to guard against the possibility of this new industrial age breaking down the conditions of life and work that wage earners have achieved in the past.

Let me say as emphatically as I can that labor will not resist industrial progress. We welcome it. But it is not characteristic of the trade-union movement to sit back and let the future overtake it. It must try to guide that future. It must come up with realistic solutions for the human problems that are bound to arise from the practical application of new scientific knowledge.

This is one of the long-range reasons for the merger. Labor is seeking, through unity, to create an instrumentality capable of defending the interests of American workers in the eventful years to come—an instrumentality that can succeed in assuring proper consideration of human needs along with the requirements of industry and finance. In our opinion there is no other agency—not even the Government itself—that can adequately fulfill this vital responsibility.

By its very nature, the labor movement will perform its primary service to the nation and its workers in the economic field. Many qualified experts—as well as quacks—have prescribed various kinds of treatment and medicine for the future well-being of the American economy. Yet the simple fact remains that to remain healthy the national economy must keep growing. It must provide millions of additional jobs each year as our population expands. It must do this even during a period when the introduction of automatic, labor-saving machinery tends, at least temporarily, to cut down the number of employment opportunities normally available.

There is only one practical answer to this apparent dilemma—

steadily increasing production. Yet, obviously, increased production can itself become a major problem unless it is promptly consumed. In the unsettled state of world affairs it is idle for us to count too heavily upon foreign markets. Thus it is necessary that the American people enjoy sufficient income and purchasing power to buy and consume the swelling output of the country's farms and factories. Here is the economic challenge of the future which the united labor movement can help to meet. Labor will possess more power at the bargaining table. It will seek to exercise that power to the end that a fair share of expanding profits is put back into mass circulation through higher wages and reduced costs to the consumer.

Simultaneously, labor is determined to bring about the organization of millions of unorganized workers and raise their income and living standards. Thus our efforts will help to attain a healthy balance between production and consumption by lifting mass purchasing power in a period when industry and agriculture will have urgent need for broader markets.

Parenthetically, it might be well to point out here that the labor movement does not envisage a time when each and every worker in this country will be a union member. There will always be a sizable proportion of workers in the unorganized category—workers employed in many thousands of small establishments who do not seek collective bargaining representation because they are in a position to bargain directly and individually with their employers.

Yet it would be a mistake to assume that such workers will suffer an extreme competitive disadvantage against union members, for history shows that labor's legislative gains, such as workmen's compensation and social security, are enjoyed equally by all workers, unorganized as well as organized, and that the wage levels of nonunion workers tend to climb after union rates are increased.

It goes without saying that unskilled or semi-skilled production workers will have fewer employment opportunities in the age of automation. A number of unions, in anticipation of this trend, have initiated training and retraining programs to acquaint their members with the latest mechanical and electronic processes. In

my opinion, union-sponsored educational and apprenticeship programs of this forward-looking nature will be greatly expanded in
the years to come.

Labor must also face the harsh fact that there may come an
extended retooling period in many industries which would result
in widespread unemployment. In order to prevent needless suffering, unions in the mass-production industries already have taken
steps to secure, through collective bargaining, supplementary unemployment compensation or a guaranteed annual wage. Such
insurance against the human distress caused by unemployment will
also help to cushion the economic shock of the transition and
avert a tailspin.

Undoubtedly, labor will revive its drive for the shorter work
week. It is part of America's economic tradition that workers
share in the gains that are derived from improved methods of
production. The establishment of a thirty-hour week undoubtedly
will serve to multiply job opportunities and keep unemployment
from getting out of hand.

It will also permit more time for recreation, education and the
general pursuit of happiness, which everyone would like to have.
What good can new industrial techniques accomplish if they do
not lighten the burdens of the people and make for a fuller and
richer life?

Thus far I have discussed, in terms of the future, trade-union
policies and objectives which already have begun to take root but
which promise broader development under the cultivation of the
united labor movement.

The place to break new ground, I am convinced, is in the field
of labor-management relations. The A.F.L.-C.I.O. will be ready,
willing and able to make an important contribution to the establishment and maintenance of industrial peace.

Before that goal can be achieved, both sides at the bargaining
table will have to recognize and acknowledge certain facts and
considerations that they have not as yet succeeded in bringing
clearly into focus. Basic among these are:

1) *The interests of labor and management are interdependent,
rather than inimical.* The earnings of both are keyed to the con-

tinuing prosperity of a particular business and the nation as a whole. Neither can produce without the other.

2) *Free labor and free enterprise can exist only under a free system of government.* Their real enemy then—their common enemy—is totalitarianism.

3) *The totalitarian threat of our day is communism.* Under communism there can be no free labor unions, no private capital, no private ownership or management of industry. The free labor movement of America, therefore, is fighting communism—and fighting it effectively—both at home and in the rest of the free world. This unalterable opposition of the American labor movement to communism provides basic security for American business.

It has been proved time and again that, short of war, the Communists can seize control of a country only by subversion of mass organizations of labor. Is it not then to the direct interest of American business to keep the free and anti-Communist trade-union movement strong? Is it not short-sighted of business organizations to foster and support national and state legislation intended to weaken the security of the free labor movement?

4) *Certain business leaders may consider "big government" or socialism more of an immediate threat to their interests than communism.* Are they allowing themselves to be deluded by their own propaganda to the effect that organized labor in this country is in favor of big government or the nationalization of industry?

Nothing could be further from the truth. The main function of American trade unions is collective bargaining. It is impossible to bargain collectively with the Government. Unions, as well as employers, would vastly prefer to have even Government regulation of labor-management relations reduced to a minimum consistent with the protection of the public welfare.

5) *The vast majority of labor-management disputes can be settled amicably.* They are today. The real problem is to devise a method of settling the exceptional cases before they erupt into damaging strikes and lockouts. This, in my opinion, can be done with a high degree of effectiveness, provided that a live-and-let-live agreement can be reached at a national level by the top labor and business organizations.

It is not my purpose at this time to suggest how and when such a non-aggression pact can be negotiated. Success or failure may depend upon the proper timing and the right psychological approach. Labor would like to see it happen because it promises to strengthen our nation when America needs its total strength.

The A.F.L.-C.I.O. does not underestimate the critical nature of the present international situation. We are not to be beguiled by the smiling-face technique of Soviet Russia. We do not believe that the Communists subscribed to the "spirit of Geneva" for any purpose other than to gain a propaganda advantage from highly publicized lip service to peace.

Soviet leaders are interested in power, not peace. They demonstrated at the recent foreign ministers' conference at Geneva that they will not yield power or domination as a concession to peace. As always, the Communists still have their sights on one goal—world domination—and they will not hesitate to employ any kind of war to gain that end.

Since its whole future is tied to the preservation of peace and freedom, the united labor movement intends, in the years ahead, to expand its already far-flung program to halt the spread of communism. This will be no easy task. Communist-controlled unions are firmly entrenched in France and Italy, in South America and in other vital areas of the free world.

We are confident that with our help these subversive organizations can be supplanted by free trade unions. A good deal of progress has been scored in that direction in recent years. The Force Ouvrière in France and the C.I.S.L. in Italy have steadily gained ground against the Communist labor fronts. An even greater challenge to the cause of free labor may arise in the under-developed areas of the world where the low standard of living provides fertile soil for Communist propaganda.

The A.F.L.-C.I.O. hopes to carry on its world-wide campaign against communism primarily through the International Confederation of Free Trade Unions, the agency which already has succeeded in isolating and immobilizing the Communist-dominated World Federation of Trade Unions.

In the final analysis, the best answer to communism is proof that democracy works for the greater benefit of the people. We still have a long way to go before that fact becomes self-evident to the rest of the world. Our pride in the American way of life must be tempered by a realization of the serious shortcomings that still cry out for correction.

Through neglect, timidity and political paralysis, we have failed to provide decent schools for American children, to get rid of slums, to build protection against floods, to construct necessary modern highways and, above all, to assure the enjoyment of civil rights and equal protection under the law to all Americans.

In addition to these obvious flaws, there still exist manifest injustices in the laws governing labor-management relations and the farm economy.

The A.F.L.-C.I.O. plans to intensify its political-education activities to help bring about an effective solution of these problems. We are all taught in school that this is "one nation under God, indivisible, with liberty and justice for all." That it doesn't always work out that way is the result of political misdirection. Neither political party has had the strength or the courage consistently to attack economic and social problems on the basis that America is actually one nation, indivisible.

The purpose of labor's political-education program will be to awaken both parties and the American people to the need for this national approach to national problems. There is little likelihood in the foreseeable future that the A.F.L.-C.I.O. will seriously consider the formation of a Labor party. We are determined to work for our objectives within the framework of the existing American two-party system, on a nonpartisan basis. Our efforts will be concentrated, for the most part, on the election to Congress and the State Legislatures of candidates who support labor's progressive programs.

In other words, the united labor movement will not change political direction but will seek to evoke greater political consciousness and effectiveness among American workers.

While charting expanded activity in world and national affairs, the A.F.L.-C.I.O. has not overlooked its obligation to function in the years ahead as a responsible, self-disciplined organization. The constitution of the new organization establishes the machinery for keeping our own house clean of corrupt or subversive influences. That machinery will not be allowed to rust.

Labor's greatest asset is the respect and goodwill of the American people. We hope to earn and keep that goodwill. We hope to prove by our actions that free labor is a force for good in the life of our nation and the world.

Why They Cheer for Hoffa

by A. H. Raskin

DETROIT.

THE WAIL of a bagpipe cut through the shop steward's report that everything was O.K. at the barn of the Merchants Motor Freight. A chunky little man with the shoulders of a heavyweight boxer plowed past the six-footers in the overflow crowd at the rear of the union hall. Two truck drivers lifted him off his feet and bore him down the aisle. A thousand others leaped from their seats and cheered. Jimmy Hoffa was back with "the guys that made me."

Everyone wore a button with the slogan, "Hoffa—The Teamster's Teamster." Some wore two or three. This was the rank and file of Local 299 of the International Brotherhood of Teamsters —the local that started a tough, cheeky kid named James Riddle Hoffa on his climb from the loading platform of a grocery warehouse to the presidency of the country's biggest and strongest union.

And this was their answer to two years of effort by Senate rackets investigators to convince them that their union was being turned into a hoodlum empire by a faithless leader. Every instrument of mass communication—newspapers, magazines, television, radio and newsreels—had brought them the sordid record of union despoliation uncovered by the McClellan Committee.

They knew of the testimony that Hoffa had treated the union's money as his own, entered into subterranean relations with employers, suppressed the democratic rights of members by brute force and allied himself with the underworld. They knew of the Senators' charge that he had used his vast power in ways "tragic for the Teamsters' Union and dangerous for the country at large." They knew of the merged labor federation's decision that their failure to cast out Hoffa made them pariahs unfit to live inside labor's house. All this they knew—and they let Hoffa know it made no difference. He was still their boy.

When he rose to speak, they were on their feet again, whistling, shouting, stomping. He waved them down with a quick gesture. He spoke in a flat tone—confident, insistent, bare of oratorical adornment. There was none of the platform magic of a John L. Lewis or a Walter Reuther.

Yet the sensation that came across was of relentless, elemental strength. The 45-year-old Hoffa exuded it, from the glossy hair that bristled away from his scalp like a porcupine's quills, past the chill, hooded eyes, to the rocklike hands. He teetered a little on the balls of his feet in the manner of a fighter about to throw a punch. His navy blue suit strained across his thick chest and heavily muscled arms. Here was no Dave Beck softened by easy living. For all his Cadillacs, his $50,000-a-year salary, his limitless expense account and his free hand with the union's millions, Beck's successor still looks, talks and acts like a truck driver.

No note of apology marked Hoffa's report on his stewardship. Everything was black or white, with all the black on the side of his critics. He had taunts for Senator McClellan ("he's back in Arkansas now trying to straighten out Faubus, I guess"); the newspapers ("they propagandize the teamsters for only one reason—because of the size and strength and militancy of the Teamsters' Union"); college professors, and other longhairs with proposals for laws to clean up labor ("they only talk that way after they have had four long glasses of booze").

That still left Hoffa with a few jibes to fling at the two union chiefs he considers principally responsible for the Teamsters' expulsion from the A.F.L.-C.I.O.—George Meany ("he always hid in his office as a bookkeeper—he has yet to negotiate his first contract or meet his first scab on a picket line") and Walter Reuther ("here we talk a language the teamsters understand, not a language to change the United States into a socialistic country or to worry about what politician is elected").

He had a simple explanation for the charges that the union had become a homing ground for jailbirds: "All this hocus-pocus about racketeers and crooks is a smokescreen to carry you back to the days when they could drop you in the scrap heap like they do a worn-out truck." The teamsters applauded dutifully.

They kept applauding as he told them how much other unions owed them and how much they owed their union. He reminded them of the days when they worked seventy or eighty hours for $18 a week, without vacations, pensions, welfare, pay for breakdown time or seniority protection. "There are men here who used to pull Toledo for 75 cents or Chicago for $1.50; now the scale to Toledo is $17 and $34 or $36 to Chicago," he declared.

Always he was the teamster talking to teamsters: "You know me since I'm 17—the kid, you called me. They say I've got a police record. Sure, I've got a record and you know where I got it. It's no secret. There's not one thing there outside the labor movement. And I tell you Hoffa will have it again if they start kicking the truck driver around."

He warned them that the next five years would be "the five toughest years we ever saw in this union business," and this provided the jumping-off point for another slap at his detractors. "They even criticize me for calling this a business," he complained. "Well, what do you hire us for, if not to sell your labor at the highest buck we can get?"

There was much more, all designed to get across the point that "what we have had we can lose overnight, if we are foolish enough to become divided." And then it was time for the main business of the evening, a vote on whether Local 299 wanted to strip Hoffa and his executive board of their control over the union's finances and internal affairs.

"You are here for one purpose," Hoffa declaimed, "to show the solidarity and strength of this organization to those who think the teamster is a coward, that he can't find his way into his union hall or that he is the victim of a business agent who is a racketeer, a bum or a hoodlum. You and only you have established the rules of this organization, and only you—not the propaganda of the press and McClellan—will change the rules."

He waved a thick bundle of bills at the crowd. They represented all the local's obligations for the preceding month. He told the members they could insist on having each bill submitted to them for approval if they did not want to leave blanket authority in the officers' hands. "Send 'em to McClellan," was the bull-voiced suggestion of one rank-and-filer. The others shouted that they wanted the executive board to keep on using its judgment about how to spend the union's money.

The story was the same when Hoffa mentioned charges that the welfare and pension funds had been "stole blind" by investments he had made for his own profit or to help out his cronies. He lauded the funds' accomplishments, and he asked where his critics —"the great saviors of the workers"—had been when the union was battling to get the benefit programs set up. He contrasted the pension payments of $135 a month at age 60 with the lower standards in force in "many so-called progressive, clean unions."

When he got through and asked whether they wanted the union to change its way of doing business, there was a mass roar of "no, no, no." He was not satisfied with that. "Let's do this in an orderly way," he said, "so no one can charge I stole the vote." He called for a standing vote on whether the executive board should continue to have a blank check on the handling of union funds, the designation of convention delegates, the calling of strikes and all other matters of internal administration. Everybody stood up.

When the "nays" were called everybody sat down—except one brother, who had apparently had one beer too many on the way to the hall. When the crowd laughed, he slumped into his seat. That made it unanimous.

How significant was the whole performance? Should it be dismissed as the obeisance of cowed and servile men to a master armed with life-and-death power over their jobs? Did fear of physical violence against themselves or their families chain the members of Local 299 to the Hoffa truck? Was their vote an expression of insensate mass adoration akin to that extended to their fuehrers by the brain-washed populace of totalitarian lands?

None of these possible explanations seemed adequate for an observer who had spent three days before the meeting in individual contact with many of the drivers, talking to them privately in the terminals and on the loading docks.

Only two out of nearly 200 said they felt that the union was in a mess and that the membership was powerless to do anything about it. The others declared, with every indication of sincerity, that they felt Hoffa had done a stand-out job on wages, welfare, grievances and every other phase of union service. They brushed aside the accusations of gangsterism and racketeering as part of an attempt by outside forces to cut Hoffa down to size because he was doing too good a job in defense of the rank and file.

Their words added up to a hymn of contentment. Listen to Chad Virdin, an over-the-road driver, who shuttles the mail between Detroit and Jackson, Mich., on a night run: "So far as I'm concerned, the union is 100 per cent. Every year that old raise is there, and it has been ever since Hoffa took over." Or hear Robert E. Jones, a 345-pounder, who drives for the New York Central: "I think Jimmy Hoffa did more for the truck driver than anyone else who ever lived." Or these words from Clyde Miles, a loader on the dock at the Union Truck Company: "I'm only sorry there can't be more 299 locals and two Jimmy Hoffas. Where they get all that stuff in Washington, I don't know."

Some put their accent on the improvement in wages, from 65 cents an hour less than twenty years ago to $2.72 an hour now. Others enthuse about children delivered or operations performed at the expense of the welfare fund. Still others say that the thing they liked best was that Jimmy's office door was always open, that he was never too busy to listen to their gripes. Even now when he is in Washington, he will take a long-distance call collect if a member has an urgent problem.

He drives his staff harder than his members drive their trucks. A giant picture of Hoffa stares down, with the intensity of Big

Brother, from the wall of the room in which the business agents have their desks. The headquarters contains a steam bath and massage table for their use, but they get little chance to luxuriate under the masseur's fingers. Hoffa's partner, Owen Bert Brennan, whose standing with the McClellan Committee is no higher than Jimmy's own, laments that Hoffa never asks "how are you" or "how do you feel" when he telephones from the capital. His only query is, "What are you doing, and why the hell aren't you doing it right now?"

But even a casual visitor to the union offices is swiftly reminded that there is another side to the organization's affairs— the side that has caused the Senate investigators to bear down so heavily on underworld influence in the teamsters. The day that Hoffa was due back in town to attend the membership meeting, Philip Weiss, an industrialist with strong racket ties, strolled into the headquarters for a conference with Hoffa's aides.

Weiss was convicted two years ago of conspiring to steal $100,000 in auto parts, but his five-year jail sentence was set aside on a technicality. He is awaiting retrial in Detroit. When Hoffa was asked that night what Weiss was doing in the union, he shrugged indifferently. "He probably just dropped in to say hello; he does business with a lot of truck employers." And that was that.

The two union members who confided that they felt there was much that needed correcting in the local made it clear that they did not believe it would be healthy for them to try to do the correcting. "They have a way of eliminating you if you make trouble," said a car haulaway driver with twenty-two years in the organization. "What can one man do?" asked a platform loader. "Someone else is going to have to clean it up."

And what of the top-heavy majority who do not rebel because they see nothing to rebel against, whose fealty to Hoffa is so great that they are prepared to disregard or disbelieve all the venality disclosed at the Washington hearings? An observer comes away with no sense that these are callous, calculating men, sunk in cynicism or allergic to considerations of conventional morality. Many are church-goers, heads of families, war veterans. They seem to differ little from workers in auto plants or steel mills or other industries in the urges and satisfactions to which they respond.

If they lack polish, that is hardly a surprise. As Joseph Mc-Donald, a moon-faced, barrel-bellied movie driver, who has been a member of the local since it was born, puts it: "We didn't build our union in this tough industry in a town this size with feather pillows."

It is precisely because the rank and file of Local 299 has so much resemblance to most teamsters and most workers that the enthusiasm with which they embrace the Hoffa brand of leadership is in many ways more disquieting than Hoffa's own long record of moral delinquency. For it tends to lend substance to the creed by which Hoffa lives, namely, that anything goes so long as the union keeps delivering fatter pay envelopes, bigger pensions and better conditions to its members. He summed up his prescription for keeping workers' loyalty in one of his wire-tapped conversations with extortionist Johnny Dio. It was: "Treat 'em right, and you don't have to worry."

This is the philosophy of the slot machine, with the gamble eliminated. The wheel is set for a payoff on every spin and while the dollar signs keep coming up no one is disposed to check too carefully on what is happening in the back room. The teamsters hold no monopoly on this attitude; it pervades much of our economic, social and political life. We admire the man who can deliver—how he delivers is much less important.

This is a concept that holds dismal implications for those who look to increased democracy in unions as the answer to corruption. For it is distressingly apparent that Hoffa has emerged from all the attacks on him much more solidly entrenched than ever—not only in the allegiance of his home local but in every section of the 1,600,000-member brotherhood.

Votes of confidence have been piling up around him like confetti as he pilots his outcast teamsters uphill in wages and membership at a far faster clip than unions which proudly wear the Good Housekeeping seal of the A.F.L.-C.I.O. Against this backdrop of bread-and-butter gains, he has been mobilizing support for his fight to jettison his court-appointed monitors and win full control of the union at a new convention next March.

If the convention is held, the peppery little Detroiter seems sure to come out on top, and this time he will need none of the rigging tactics that cast so much shadow over his victory in Miami Beach a year ago. If Hoffa is stopped, it will be by the courts or other outside forces, not by any prohibitions from the rank and file.

No piling up of legislative safeguards for the exercise of democratic rights within the union seems likely to alter that fact in the near future. Unless Hoffa loses the energy and skill he has displayed as a delivery man for ever-expanding benefits for his members, there is every reason to believe he can count on their backing for an indefinite period.

That means that once again those who believe that unions should be something more than cash registers will have to rely on the long, slow road to reform. Public clamor and the multiplication of laws will not produce an overnight transformation, any more than they did when the State Crime Commission disclosed six years ago that underworld elements in the International Longshoremen's Association had hoisted the Jolly Roger over the Port of New York.

Only as we achieve loftier moral standards not only in labor but in business, politics and every other branch of our society can we hope for a real transformation. This is a road on which progress is sometimes agonizingly difficult, but it is an effort that must be made unless we are ready to concede that democracy itself is a failure.

Part 3

WORKERS IN AN AFFLUENT SOCIETY: 1946–1960

MOST OF the previous selections in this book have focused on working-class organizations, their relationship to the state, and their struggles with employers. Too often such reports fail to reveal the actual lives, activities, and aspirations of the individuals who compose the labor force. The following articles are concerned more with the lives and thoughts of American workingmen and women than with the labor organizations to which they may, or may not, have belonged.

The years after World War II are usually thought of as a time of prosperity and full employment, the beginning of what later became better known as the Age of Affluence. That the late 1940's and the 1950's were a better period for workers than the era of the Great Depression no one can deny. But that the postwar era brought either affluence or prosperity to most American workers is open to serious question, as the articles in this section demonstrate.

Steel workers in the Pittsburgh area, as described by David

Dempsey, scarcely conceived of themselves as members of an affluent society. As Dempsey's article makes abundantly clear, the men of steel worried constantly about security for the future and were haunted by images of a barebones, subsistence existence when they would leave the steel mill. A. H. Raskin's description of the style of life led by an allegedly typical New York City working-class family, the Garlands, hints at an existence of placid desperation. The Garland family, as portrayed in the article, apparently fights a losing battle against inflation, seldom can enjoy any pleasures outside the home, at best can barely afford the consumer appliances rolling off the assembly lines, and certainly is in no position to provide for material and financial security in the future. Yet the family shows no visible dissatisfaction with the nature of life in America; nor do its members conceive of any alternative to their existence. Why? Finally, Budd Schulberg's typical New York City longshoremen lead a life more desperate in many ways than those of coal miners, steel workers, or truck drivers. The research Schulberg conducted around the Port of New York resulted not only in the *New York Times* article included below, but also produced the award-winning motion picture *On the Waterfront,* which starred Marlon Brando as the unexpectedly aroused docker who fought exploitation and corruption on the docks and in the longshoremen's union. "Joe Docks" shows a group of men never certain of obtaining a day's work, regularly exploited by their union officials, and seldom out of the clutches of loan sharks.

As a change of pace, the article by Gertrude Samuels treats a long-neglected sector of the work force, yet one that was of growing significance: women. Miss Samuels explains clearly why more and more American women chose to work outside the home, and how the experience of World War II had altered the female consciousness of females. She also examines the satisfaction women received by becoming acknowledged, productive, and needed members of society.

Why Twenty Million Women Work

by Gertrude Samuels

THE PHENOMENON of World War II that appeared in a man's world and stayed to confound the critics—women in defense production—has in recent months quietly been manifesting itself again. At the peak of wartime employment, in July, 1944, there were 20.5 million women workers, or one-third of the labor force: truck drivers, welders, riveters, engineers, as well as in all the bench jobs. With the end of the war their numbers dropped to about 27 per cent of the working population. Today, in a record labor force of 63,700,000 persons, women number 19,467,000. The women's bureau of the Labor Department forecasts that if we continue on the present defense footing the percentage will soon go well beyond the wartime peak.

Many who are entering the labor market are going into traditional clerical, white-collar and domestic work. But in ever-increasing numbers others are following the trek to the manufacturing industries and defense factories—this time with a difference, however. There have been only a few short years between emergencies, and, unlike the doubtful, experimental years of 1940–41, their worth in all lines of work is now known. The welcome, especially for those with experience and skills, is large. Donning their badges, dungarees, sensible shoes and hair nets, grasping their tool and lunch boxes, they are gravitating to the industries they learned best in the last emergency.

Why do they do it? Why do they need, or want, to work at manual labor? Above all, since 50.9 per cent of all women workers today are married and another 16 per cent are widowed or divorced, many of them with young children, what effect is this outside work having on family life?

I came to Burbank—one of the greatest centers of aircraft production in the country—to work alongside the women and find the answers. For several days I became a structural assembly helper on a jet trainer assembly line in the Lockheed Aircraft Corporation. This is one of the many jobs that any beginner, moving from another field of work, might start at.

It was like moving to another country. Physically, the first impression is of a million strange noises, "foreign" terminology, and a confusing picture of men and women handling enormous, dangerous-looking tools and machines as though born to them. Emotionally, you feel drawn, despite the enveloping noise and movement, to a sort of magnificent calm which very busy people convey on jobs they apparently respect.

This huge plant sprawls over a square mile in the broiling heat and smog of the San Fernando Valley. Its planes have been flown by the great names—Doolittle, Lindbergh, Post, Earhart. Its F-80 jet Shooting Stars have seen action in Korea since June 1950. Its workers, numbering some 26,000 (at the war peak, it employed 90,000), come from the wide Los Angeles area or drive from sixty miles away—Ventura and Riverside—to work on the day, swing and graveyard shifts. Lockheed is presently hiring at the rate of 500 a week, with the emphasis for the present on the skilled and the experienced worker.

You "hire in" with a hundred others of both sexes. Soft music is being piped to the employment bureau as part of plant psychology "to calm applicants." The application blanks and the physical tests of fitness seem as exacting as military requirements.

Clerks take a complete dossier, including a loyalty pledge; you are photographed twice and fingerprinted twice. And when at day's end you have passed all the tests and received your round metal badge, identification card with thumbprint and clip of tool checks, you feel as though you have just crashed the blue book. You are good enough for defense work.

Indeed, this is the spirit that dominates the women workers here.

They are conscious of being defense workers. They feel a pride and self-respect in their work, and they know why they work. You hear very little about frustration here. They are working for the same reasons that men work—because they need the money, and also for specific goals: a house to pay for; children or relatives who need support: education for their youngsters; or for their marriage, when the husband's pay envelope cannot cover living costs.

The economic motivations are frankly in the foreground. But there are few who do not also remind you, significantly, that they "chose to be around planes." They feel they are "doing a job for others" as well as for their families. They eschew noble phrases but there is no mistaking that meaning.

From the outset you discover a conspicuous lack of envy of white-collar workers "who have to be on their feet all day, selling, or pounding a typewriter, being polite to everyone—that's hard work." And you also note the many who shoulder double jobs—rushing home to household work after the 3:30 whistle.

You find, too, that over the years the men have accepted them, on bench and assembly line, as equals and co-partners. This is especially true on the assembly line, where the younger women, still greatly outnumbered by men, scramble about plane sections like monkeys in familiar foliage. They are "all workers," giving the same production, working the same hours for the same pay. Wage scales range from $1.05 to $2.59 an hour.

It was into a section in the Fighter Assembly Division that I moved as Assembly Helper "A," $1.20 an hour. Bob Rhyme, who had started at Lockheed as a riveter on P-38's and now supervises "mid-fuselage, T-33 two-seater jet trainers," shows you around.

In this huge, high-roofed plant, clean and odorless, you marvel at the symmetry of dozens of plane sections—on one track are gleaming silver tails dwarfing the men and women below them; on another track a row of iridescent green fuselages; there the near-completed airframes, with plastic bubbles going over pilot seats; and all about and above the grinding, whining, whirring of air and electric motors and riveting guns.

Penny Sheppard, to whom I was assigned as helper, sits atop a fuselage, fitting on an engine access door, some twelve feet above ground. She seems beautifully serene up there, briskly drilling away with an air motor, so I go up to learn and to help. The job is to install the door—a drilling and fitting job—file down the sides to insure a snug fit to meet specifications, and mark and wrap the door for "shipment" to a final assembly line in another plant.

A person unaccustomed to climbing catwalks, straddling spaces twelve feet up and drilling with "guns" that seem to kick to the elbow, spine and thigh is liable to come down full of surprises when the whistle finally blows. For instance, you can locate every bone in your body—they all ache—while the gun has chewed redly into forefinger and thumb. You are certain that these women are blessed not only with courage and cleverness but immunity to the cacophony that beats about their heads.

But in the days that follow—on this 7-to-3:30 shift—it gives you a special thrill to find that you have a "mechanical aptitude," especially if you'd never been able to hang curtains straight in your life.

You catch on to the plant terminology, you distinguish between drills, you learn to handle the guns and tools with ease, to countersink holes to exact widths and do them speedily, testing for accuracy with rivets; to "spot face" the holes, burr them to clear away the roughness; to use a file the size of your arm, pound an engine door into place with a mallet along grease-pencil markings, ready it for a trim with the metal cutter.

The operations call for care, exactness and integrity and by this time you're trotting up and down the catwalk which has become just another stairway, fitting engine-access doors with confidence, running your flashlight over the sides to determine whether the clearance is exact, taking the door off to file some more.

You "break" for fifteen-minute smoker periods; bring in some sandwiches and coffee for the half-hour lunch which you eat with the others near the section tool-crib. A few minutes before the 3:30 whistle you help Penny check in the workers' tools, hand them back their tool check.

The story of Penny Sheppard is typical of the women who have voluntarily come into this man's world. She had taken her first factory job after high school graduation in a B-29 bomber plant in Cleveland, learning to drill, rivet, lay out work, read blueprints. It was 1942 and she had a patriotic pull to the work. Later she joined the Wac attached to the Air Force in Texas, working on the flight line. Today at 26 she is married and lives with her husband, Leon, a gunner in the last war, and their young son, Ricky, in the Roger Young Village of quonset huts not far from the plant for which they pay $29 a month rent. They are proud of their few possessions in their tiny, crude home—their big Kelvinator refrigerator, their new Chevvy, their son's neat nursery where her old Army foot-locker serves as his toy chest.

Their dreams are in the future: a home they are saving for; a career for Leon, who is now an apprentice printer; security for Ricky. While Penny works, Ricky is in an all-day nursery, a large expense for the young couple but they prefer this to "parking" the boy with strangers.

On a typical day, Penny gets up in the dark at 5:30; makes lunches for Leon and herself; gets the breakfast started; wakes Ricky up at 6:15. The Sheppards leave home at 6:30, Penny driving first to the nursery to deposit Ricky, then to Lockheed, clocking in at 6:55. She leaves the factory at 3:30, drives over for Ricky and gets home by 4:15; bathes the baby (in the kitchen sink for lack of a tub) and starts dinner. After dinner there are the dishes and baby to be played with until his 7:15 bedtime. Then, "I am free to do what I want."

This usually means baking once a week—a chocolate cake or cupcakes for Ricky; Friday is laundry night; another night for ironing; another for a drive-in movie or sewing (she makes her own blouses). She even finds a night to go to school, making ceramics. It can be a hard and weary pull, even for an enthusiastic 26-year-old.

Why—how—does she do it all? The blue eyes in the slender face are thoughtful and wise. "We're young. We're saving. We don't indulge in expensive hobbies or entertainment. We want things. We're putting enough aside for our home. I feel every young couple should have a home for their children.

"And I like working with my hands," she goes on, calmly. "When I started back in April after being away from it for seven years, everything seemed so strange to me. I recognized the various tools but it was all foreign in my hands. Then Bob Rhyme came along and showed me a T bulkhead and told me to make another like it—he started me off and left me on my own. I felt lost.

"I did the job after a struggle, but it took three times as long as I should. But no one stood over me and breathed down my neck, and I felt free to do it; he came back now and then to check, but didn't hang around. And then after about an hour of drilling and riveting, everything came back as if I'd never left the work.

"And I feel that my work is important," she says after a pause. "It sounds corny, because people just don't talk about being patriotic. But I really feel that anyone who is experienced and who isn't depriving their family in any way should be in this."

These are sentiments widely shared by other women—on the fighter line, on the bench jobs, in higher level positions in the engineering and draftsmen departments.

Florence Stickney—a pretty woman of 31 years who worked for Lockheed for two years during the last war and came back in April as a rigger—is married with three children. She averages $46 a week after deductions and she's "saving for a rainy day." This way, she tells you, "the children get more things by my working; it's easier to buy them their clothes and pay for school. We get more out of life."

Darlene Corder—a vivacious girl of 26, whose seaman husband is in a veterans' hospital—is a hydraulics and plumbing installer, making $62 a week with time and a half for overtime. (About 95 per cent of the plant is union organized, with women prominently represented.) She has a brother in Okinawa, another who is going into the Marines, and had a husband, father, brother and step-father in the last war. "So," she says quietly, "it's all very close to me."

Nearby is Pearl M. Washington, a handsome Negro girl who first came to Lockheed in 1942 and has been a rigger, plumber, frame worker, skin fitter. She took a man's job during the war, working on P-38 noses and doors "because I felt I wanted to help the boys across, and I have the same feeling now." She has bought her own home and car on her savings, and is finishing her college education as laboratory technician at night.

And Lee Stockford, the plant psychologist who also teaches at the University of Southern California, has this to add about women's morale:

"You find morale highest (by 51 per cent) among the married women—they stay with us longer, there is less turnover, they are better producers over the long-range hauls, and therefore they're considered the most stable labor group among women. On the whole they seem to feel that they are contributing something to home life, not detracting from it."

Perhaps the most significant tribute comes from the men they work among. The men tell you they were doubtful about the first women coming into the plant ten years ago. They thought mechanical work of this kind was out of the women's world. But "we were wrong."

Today the men feel that there are definite spots where women are doing the same high quality work as the men, are the equal of the men, passing the same inspection and work checks, "otherwise we couldn't give them the airplanes." On certain work—especially such bench jobs as marking harnesses, stamping and lugging wires, on the delicate, precision jobs—women are found to be "more valuable than men," who are unhappy and therefore less productive on routine work.

Many women in fact "are turning in good mechanical ideas, which eases both work and costs in the aircraft plant." Though women are not "natural mechanics," they are found to follow instructions more closely and often learn faster than men. And, adds one foreman ruefully, they're so fastidious about instructions that if you start them out wrong they'll make all the mistakes, too.

As for supervisors who may resent having women around, W. H. Grizzle, mild, rotund foreman of the electrical and precision assembly department, observed: "If they do, they don't stay here long. Best way to cure a supervisor with prejudices, I've discovered, is to shuttle in as many women as possible real quick. Then he has to make the best of it; usually he cures quick."

In dozens of plants, like Lockheed, the women are coming into production with a minimum of confusion. Their numbers are not yet spectacular, for most plants are still seeking experienced help; and many plants—not excepting Lockheed, according to observers —are still showing a heavy preference for male applicants over female for the advanced jobs. The greatest rise will come in the next twelve months as plants move into full production and men enter the services.

Soon a younger crop of girls going on their first jobs, and housewives who have never worked outside the home before, will join their numbers. Many will need training—and retraining— for in the years since the war even the skilled have not been able to keep up with the technological advances. Plants like this one are already setting up special training schools to cover basic requirements.

This time the women clearly expect to go ahead and no backtrack. They passed their tests with honors in the last war, and since the war they have challenged the limitations on so-called "women's jobs" that held back their upgradings and often hindered production. The Government is also urging supervisory training for those with the capabilities.

Further, the average woman worker today is married and older —her median age is 36—and she needs practical aids to lighten her burdens: nursery facilities, supplied by the plants where possible; rapid transportation; time for the family shopping. The double life she leads is of her own making—but since production is linked directly to morale, it would seem both realistic and profitable to guard her health, psychologically as well as physically, to understand her family as well as factory needs.

When I clocked out with the women on my last day it was with mixed emotions. I had come to enjoy the bustle of the place, the tools that had lost their fearsomeness, the plane sections that came together ingeniously before your eyes, the special sense of accomplishment that comes with the smallest job of hand labor. And it is hard to leave new friends. These were outgoing and goodhearted people and they were warm with purpose. I was going to miss them.

Steelworkers:
"Not Today's Wage,
Tomorrow's Security"

by David Dempsey

HOMESTEAD, PENNSYLVANIA.

THE MAIN entrance to the enormous Carnegie-Illinois steel works in Homestead is at Amity Street, and Henry J. Mikula is one of 14,000 workers for whom, in a city freighted with a legacy of strife and bloodshed, it symbolizes a new era in peaceful labor relations. Ever since the gate went up in 1942, when the plant was expanded for war production, Amity Street has pretty much lived up to its name. Except for a three-week strike in 1946, steel and labor have worked in harmony: the open hearths, slabbing mills, structural works and the big blast furnaces across the river in Pittsburgh have operated without interruption and at record capacity.

A few weeks ago labor called the second industry-wide strike in the history of steel. Narrowly averted at the last minute, the dispute is now in the hands of a three-man fact-finding board which will report its conclusions and recommendations to President Truman. If management or labor fails to go along, the gate at Amity Street will be closed.

Henry Mikula doesn't want to see this happen. To him—to most of the 940,000 steelworkers across the nation—a strike means a belt-tightening that would be costly and unpleasant. Yet the belt has been tightened before, Henry says; as a union man, he believes that labor has gained in the end. His attitude is especially significant in view of the fact that the present dispute is not primarily over wages—which are reasonably good for a non-craft industry—but the less immediate factors of better pensions, more sick benefits, and other aspects of social security.

To find out just how pressing this issue is, I spent several days with Henry Mikula and his shop buddies at the Homestead plant. For, as a worker who is in most aspects typical of the men who make up this largest of CIO unions, Henry is the keystone in the Amity Street arch. What kind of person is he, how does he feel about his job, why is he willing to strike if necessary for a cause that will chiefly benefit men thirty years his senior? These are simple questions, but in a complex situation such as this they do not admit of simple answers.

On the plantward side of the big Amity Street gate is emblazoned the slogan: "Steel Is Permanent." Henry sees this sign on his way home and he says it reminds him—at a time of day when he is all too conscious of the irony—that although steel is permanent, men are not. And this is the crux of Henry's dispute with the company. If he goes on strike, it will not be out of hunger or desperation, but for the new principle of welfare that has been added to labor's arsenal of demands, now that the basic wage-hours fight has been largely won.

To know Henry—to understand even the most ordinary facts about his life—you have to visualize Homestead, which might fittingly be called Steeltown, U. S. A. Although its sprawling mills, gushing clouds of smoke that settle over the city in a hazy smog, make up but a fraction of the plants that stretch for twenty-two miles along this industrial river valley, they dominate life in Homestead. Visible from almost every point in the city, which leans its way up the steep bluffs of the Monongahela River, they are the only major industries here, and nearly all of the wage-earners work in them.

Henry has been employed in the Carnegie-Illinois plant—a subsidiary of United States Steel—for twenty of his thirty-six years. Most of his fellow-workers also started at 16, although the minimum age is now 18. Most of them will work until they are 65, the compulsory retirement age. Most of them—like Henry—have fathers who worked in the mills and the great majority have children who are already helping to "cook" steel, or soon will be. Henry's stepfather, for example, is still a millhand; his oldest son, Jack, 14, will "probably" follow in the tradition. In Homestead, people talk, think, make, and "breathe" steel. Steel is the hard, pervasive fact of their existence, the image of their future, and the substance of their memories.

Memories here are long, and go back fifty-seven years to the great Homestead steel strike of 1892. To this city's steelworkers and their families, "the strike" is symbolically as important as is the Easter Week rebellion to an Irishman. Oldtimers vividly recall the pitched battle between "Pinkertons" and workers. A plaque on one of Homestead's main streets commemorates the seven union men who were killed. The incident is still good timber with which to fire up a mass meeting or a memorial service.

Henry was born here in Homestead, and thus grew up in the strongly labor-conscious tradition of its people. Not only his immediate family but his five brothers-in-law are employed in the mill. It would be strange if he were not biased in favor of the wage-earner. Yet, in a significant sense, Henry Mikula's bias is not born out of a feeling of exploitation or a sense of hopeless injustice. When his stepfather went on strike in 1919 it was in an effort to organize.

Today, after fifteen years of legally protected unionism and a company policy of harmonious labor relations, Henry is motivated by different reasons. It is security that has become the touchstone of Henry's world.

Nothing symbolizes so strikingly the gap between two generations of workers than this preoccupation with the intangible, or "fringe," benefits of the job. Until recent years most union demands centered on a fuller lunch pail. Today they are being extended to include the concept of a fuller life. To put it another way, in a phrase peculiar to steel, emphasis has been shifted from the hearth to the hearthside.

And as a result of this evolution in tactics, Henry now finds himself a sort of industrial guinea pig. No longer merely employe No. 45,118, a tractor operator in a slabbing mill, he is the subject of university research projects, Government surveys, newspaper interviews, fact-finding boards and a bewildering amount of solicitude on the part of both management and union.

And no longer is he an industrial Caliban, bumping his head against the lintel of an outdated system. Two wars, a New Deal and a Fair Deal have indoctrinated him with a new sense of importance in society. And thanks to a never-ending flow of union literature, he has grown amazingly articulate. Curious phrases like "unilateral action" have crept into his vocabulary. Statistics on the cost of living, company profits and wages are at hand to buttress his arguments.

Even the end product of Henry's labor has become more meaningful to him. During the war much of his time went into the production of armor plate and other necessary implements of battle. Right now the plant where Henry works is turning out steel for the United Nations headquarters in New York. The significance of this is not lost on him. He has bridged the barriers of his own small world to help build the physical core of a new one. All of this has given him, as an industrial worker, a new dimension largely unthinkable a generation ago.

Having learned to make new demands on the industrial system, Henry nevertheless no longer thinks of a strike as the only way of getting them. "We were relieved when the truce went in," he says. "Striking is no fun, especially when it's for something you won't get the main benefit from until you're an old man. We'd like a raise, of course, but this pension thing is more important. As long as the cost of living kept going up, pensions had to wait. Now seems like a good time to get started on them. We hope the whole thing can be settled without a showdown."

If Henry does go out, the placard that he will carry as a publicity weapon will be secondary to the heavy artillery which union brass have already moved into defiladed areas well to the rear of the company gates—the bulky reports on company earnings and workers' needs that have been prepared for them by private research organizations.

Although Henry and his buddies will be on the picket line, if necessary, they know that the real fighting will take place in Washington or New York, around the committee table, in the newspapers, and on the radio. That the statesmen of the nation, including the President, should make a special effort to solve their problems is something relatively new to the workers in this industry, where violence and bitterness were the order in years gone by. It is one more factor that has convinced Henry he counts for something in America.

Although Henry Mikula is a composite of all the steelworkers in this mill town—a symbol of the industrial wage-earner of 1949 —he is also an individual, with a wife and three boys, and this, too, bears on the present period of tension. In what way?

First of all, Henry earns a wage that no one would call excessive—$1.45 an hour, or about $255 a month. From this, about $8 is deducted for taxes, group insurance and union dues, leaving him a net of $247, or roughly $56 a week. Henry's pay is less than the industry average of $1.69 an hour, but it is substantially higher than the Government's enforced minimum of $1.23 for steel mills holding United States contracts, and it compares favorably with the national average for all industrial wage-earners of approximately $1.31.

By meticulous budgeting, making many of the children's clothes, keeping a garden, and "making out the grocery order with a pruning knife," the Mikulas have been able to get by and still have a little left for an occasional trip to the movies or a ball game. But there is nothing for savings and the war bonds which Henry bought regularly during the flush period when the mill worked overtime have long since been cashed in. Recently Henry bought a new furnace, and incurred a dental bill of $165. Both of these debts are being paid off in installments.

What might seem like a small miracle to the hard-pressed city worker—living on $56 a week—is explained in part by the fact that the Mikulas own their home, a four-room bungalow purchased eleven years ago, which is now entirely paid for. Taxes run $175 a year, fuel about $125. Maintenance is nil, since Henry does all his own repairs. Furnishings include a 13-year-old washing machine, and the house is surrounded by a good-sized yard in which the Mikulas have planted shrubs, hybrid roses and a blue spruce tree. Aside from the house, their only other major possession is a 1935 car, which Henry bought last year for $50.

As a home owner, Henry is no exception among workers here. Management long ago divested itself of company-owned houses and stores, and union officials estimate that half of the steel-mill employes with families own the homes they live in. Homestead is largely free of tenements, and the city's worst slums were razed during the war to make room for a new plant.

Replacing them is a low-cost housing development in which a family can rent a four-room apartment, complete with heat and utilities, for $35 a month. And despite the smoke, Homestead is surprisingly clean, bearing little resemblance to the mining towns close by. Nor does the district appear to be company dominated. In one borough the Burgess (Mayor) and ten out of sixteen public officials—all holding part-time offices—are steelworkers.

Two years ago Henry Mikula ran for the council in his own borough and was defeated by less than 200 votes. This year he's running again, and thinks he has a good chance of being elected. A Democrat (registration is about three to one Democratic in this area), he supports President Truman's Fair Deal. As a second generation American, he has no particular feeling of inferiority and casts no longing glances at the "new democracies," which do not seem to have improved the "old order" that his parents left when they emigrated to this country. Henry is a Roman Catholic and the head trustee of his local church. In the union he is assistant grievance chairman of his shop.

But the most important thing about Henry Mikula is the conviction that what is to him a fairly decent way of life can be made even better.

He has seen it happen with the older generation. Moreover, things have improved a lot in his own lifetime. When he went to work in the mill twenty years ago he made $2.28 a day operating the door on an open-hearth furnace. Since then the plant's increased productivity, the general rise in industrial wages and the union's astute bargaining tactics have brought him a long way. It is a measure of his progress—not his poverty—that he wants to go further.

Which brings him once more to the issue of security. In some respects, Henry gets what he calls "a pretty good deal." If he should be killed, or die from any cause whatsoever while in the company's employ, his family would receive $4,000 from a group insurance policy that costs him $1.93 a month. In the event of illness, he and his family are covered by a company medical plan that takes care of hospital costs and pays sick benefits of $15 a week up to thirteen weeks. Henry's share of the cost of this plan is $2.81 a month. In addition, he carries $1,000 worth of life insurance on himself, $1,000 on his wife, and $1,250 on each child. His premiums, including hospitalization and his group insurance, total $203.32 a year, or not quite one-fourteenth of his earnings. Henry works about three and a half weeks a year to pay for his "security."

The union is asking that a greater proportion of this insurance burden be shifted onto the company, and Henry makes no bones about the fact that such a plan would ease the economic squeeze for him.

Men earning the industry average of $68 a week, and the more highly paid $80-$90 a week employes, he says, can absorb these payments with less hardship. For the lower-bracket workers, both the high cost of "security" and its apparent inadequacy loom large. In this sense, Henry is a typical paradox among the industrial wage-earners: the man who needs security the most, yet who can least afford to provide for it.

Although it will be another twenty-nine years before he retires, the problem of "what to live on" is brought home by the fact that his father-in-law, who retired last year after forty-seven years in the plant, receives a combined pension-social security income of slightly less than $100 a month. And this is considerably above the average.

"We're asking for $150 a month, although I suppose we'll take less if we have to," Henry says. "What really burns us up, though, is that the company subtracts the amount of the Federal social security benefits from the pension they pay. Instead of getting social security plus the pension, the men only get the amount of the pension, with social security figured in as part of it."

This is not the case with some steel companies, but it is true in the plant where Henry works and remains a rankling grievance which the union has effectively exploited. And since an ever greater proportion of steel's labor force is approaching the retirement age, the men are becoming pension conscious.

A union study of 722 pensioners, who averaged thirty-four and a half years of service, forms the basis for indoctrinating the rank and file with the "facts" in the current dispute. According to this survey, the average monthly pension for the group studied is $6 which is paid by the company, and $31.83 under social security, or a total of $37.83.

A random check made by this writer of a much smaller—and perhaps not so representative—cross-section uncovered a high of $60.90 paid by the company, and a low of 62 cents, with the average amounting to $28.34. Social security benefits, which were in addition to company pensions, ranged from $40 a month down to $31.64, and averaged $36.05. About half of those interviewed had taken outside jobs in laundries, parks, etc., and earned another $3 to $6 a day. Thirty-eight out of fifty-six employes of the borough of near-by North Braddock, the union says, are retired steelworkers who must supplement their pensions.

Regardless of the sum now paid, Henry believes, it is not enough to dispel the fear of insecurity. And when union economists argue that the company can afford pensions of $125 a month, a pay rise and other fringe benefits at a rise in labor costs of 11 cents an hour per man, the plan seems feasible to him. Admittedly he is prejudiced in favor of the union's surveys. "But then, they haven't gone off half cocked on this thing," he says. "We're not asking for the impossible."

Management disagrees, and it is worth pointing out that the company regards Henry as a valued employe whose welfare is a matter of concern, since stability of employment—with consequent economy in labor costs—is a significant achievement in the steel industry.

"The fact that we have such a high proportion of men who stay here long enough to earn pensions," a company spokesman said, "is proof that our men are pretty well satisfied. Our company was the first to recognize the union and when Andrew Carnegie was still living it was the first to institute pensions. We anticipated a lot of social security years before the Government or most industries got around to it."

Henry agrees that his personal relations with management always were cordial. He had no trouble getting transferred from his old job at a blast furnace to his present job when he requested it two years ago. Safety conditions are good and the company has been fair in settling grievances, he says, but when it comes to boosting wages, pensions, and other security benefits—the total "package" comes to thirty cents an hour per man—management declares that existing prices will not support the rise.

"Our salesmen are fighting for every order they get," an industrial relations representative told me. "Steel is not a sellers' market. Our present cost structure won't stand a thirty-cents-an-hour hike without a substantial rise in price of the finished product and we don't think this is the time to raise prices."

It is along this front that the battle lines are drawn. "When a man gives forty or fifty years of his life to a job," Henry says, "he should be able to retire in comfort—a little comfort, anyway." Thirty years ago, in Homestead at least, this attitude would have been considered an impertinence by many. Today, to a generation of workers that has grown up in the midst of an increasing drive toward the "welfare state," Henry's point of view strikes him as anything but revolutionary.

He has, moreover, seen the company give way on three previous demands for higher wages—demands on which both union and management made concessions to avoid a strike—and he hopes for a similar solution this time.

But if it's fumbled, Amity Street will become enmity street; the big gate will be a barrier rather than a bridge, and Henry Mikula will be on the picket line. "It may be tough going," he says, "but if it will help these old guys get a better break, it'll be worth it. After all, I'm going to be in their shoes myself some day."

Life with
Tom and Helen Garland

by A. H. Raskin

TOM GARLAND thinks it's time someone blew the whistle on prices. What Tom thinks is important. Not because there is anything exceptional about Tom, but because there is nothing exceptional about him. Tom comes as close to being Mr. Average Worker as it is possible to find among New York's army of wage-earners. The State Labor Department picked Tom out as a man notable for his averageness—the holder of an average sort of job, in an average sort of company, with an average sort of pay envelope, and an average sort of family to feed and clothe. Nobody is exploiting Tom. He is not one of the ground-down wage slaves Moscow is always weeping over. The factory he works for prides itself on keeping its wages well ahead of its competitors, and it stays on cordial terms with the strong union to which Tom belongs.

Tom's pay as a stock selector at the Cutler-Hammer Electrical Company plant in the Bronx averages slightly less than $72 a week. That takes in his occasional overtime and the bonus the company distributes once a year. There was a time when Tom would have considered the $3,722 he earned last year a princely

From the *New York Times Magazine*, April 6, 1952, copyright © 1952 by The New York Times Company.

sum, but it doesn't seem to stretch very far these days. Tom is not used to lordly living. He has known a lot of poverty since he was born half a mile from the plant thirty-five years ago. His father, who had been a yard foreman for a coal company, lost his job during the depression and the family went on relief. Tom left school at 14 to take a job as a Western Union messenger.

He stayed at that for a year, making about $12 a week in delivery fees and tips, and then moved into a succession of off-and-on jobs as a grocery clerk, checkroom attendant, elevator operator and plumber's assistant. Nothing steady came along until he went to work for Cutler-Hammer in 1940 at 40 cents an hour. Uncle Sam pulled him out of that for four years of Army service, most of it in Panama and India. When he went back to making electrical switches in 1946, he found something besides his work to be interested in at the Bronx factory.

He fell in love with Helen Dippolito, a slim, brunette timekeeper, and they were married on St. Valentine's Day, 1948. Their first son, Thomas Joseph, is 3 years old; their second son, Gregory Robert, was born last October. Helen has to carry the baby up three flights of poorly lit stairs to the dingy six-room flat they share with her father and mother at 1244 Woodycrest Avenue in the Highbridge section of the Bronx. Helen's father used to be an iceman, but a spinal injury has kept him from working for the past fifteen years. Her mother makes umbrella straps and the Dippolitos pay the $43.55 monthly rent for the jointly occupied apartment. The Garlands pick up the bulk of the food bill by way of evening things.

They spend $8 a week for canned goods, coffee, sugar, cereals and other groceries. Butter is so high that Helen has switched to oleomargarine for her baking. The baking is an economy measure, too. Tom, a 200-pounder, has an insistent sweet tooth, and Helen has decided she can keep it satisfied herself for a good deal less money than the neighborhood baker charges. "Tom's favorite dessert is chocolate cream pie," Helen confides, "and a small one costs 85 cents at the bakery. I can make one twice as big for 50 or 60 cents."

Helen's hot oven doesn't shut the bakery shop out altogether. Tom still has to plank down $1 a week for bread and rolls. The butcher is a bigger problem. He puts a $6 dent in the family fortune. On weekends the Garlands splurge with round steak, roast fresh ham or chicken. Monday is leftover day. Tuesday they have pork chops, Wednesday chopped meat and Thursday spaghetti and meat balls. None of the family cares much for fish, so soup or eggs usually make up the main dish on Friday. Fruit and vegetables take another $6. The only reason it is not more, Tom explains, is that a brother-in-law runs the fruit store and gives them a break on prices. The milkman leaves five quarts of milk every two days. That nicks the budget for $4 a week and $2.50 more goes into strained foods, evaporated milk and dextri-maltose for the baby.

Ever since their marriage four years ago the Garlands have been trying to get enough ahead of their food bills to buy an electric mixing machine to help Helen with her baking. They are still trying. Tom keeps a coin can at the factory and tosses some change into it every day or so toward the mixer. The total has got up close to $20 several times now, but some domestic emergency always comes along to empty the can before there is money enough for the machine.

The Garlands do have a washing machine, in which Helen does all the family laundry—including the baby's diapers and Tom's work clothes. Tom invested his $157 bonus check in the washing machine two years ago and the family would be lost without it. The other main prop of the Garland household is a $309 television set. Tom bought it on the installment plan in 1950. He made the last payment a few weeks ago.

Television is pretty much the beginning and end of the Garland entertainment program. They live half an hour by subway from Times Square, but they see less of the Great White Way than the average farmer from Pumpkin Corners. It has been so long since they went to a movie that Helen says she wouldn't know how to buy a ticket any more. Drama, musical comedy, opera and night clubs are part of a world they know only through TV.

Tom bowls every Wednesday night with some of the fellows from the shop. What with dinner and one thing or another, his evening away from the cathode tube costs him $3.60. That is as much as he spends each week on lunches—usually a meat sandwich, a slab of pie and a pot of tea, consumed in the stock room.

When he has to work overtime, a dollar of his extra pay goes for supper at a diner near the plant. A co-worker drives him to and from home for the same $1 a week it would cost Tom to travel by subway.

Cigarettes are Tom's only vice. He smokes two packs a day. Forty-three cents burn away with the tobacco. There was a time when Tom drank a bit, but he has sworn off the stuff since his marriage. About the only time he touches whiskey now is New Year's Eve, when he shakes hands with all the men, kisses all the women and passes out blissfully at a big family party at home.

Uncle Sam dips into Tom's pay envelope for $4.33 a week in income taxes and another $1.08 comes out for social security. The state takes 30 cents more for disability insurance, leaving him with a net of $66.29 to take home out of his $72 basic average. Tom doesn't take all of it home, however. As one who knows crisis, he believes in putting something aside on a systematic basis.

He has the company take out $5 a week for defense savings bonds. In addition, he puts $2 a week into a Christmas Club account at a neighborhood savings bank. That buys Yule gifts for all the family—gifts with a heavy accent on practicality. Tom got some underwear, a tie and a handkerchief from Helen and the kids last year. Helen's portion was a skirt, a white satin blouse and a couple of pairs of stockings. Gregory was too young to care about anything except his bottle, but young Tom got a big bundle of toys.

Blue Cross hospital insurance for the family takes $6.12 a month of Tom's earnings. Another $2.50 a month goes for his dues as a member of the International Association of Machinists, A.F.L. Tom, who let his G.I. insurance lapse when he came out of the Army, has a $1,000 life insurance policy. So has Helen. They carry a $500 policy for young Tom and the same amount for Gregory. All told, the premiums come to $135.93 a year.

They have other fixed costs. Gas and electricity run to about $2.50 a week and the telephone costs half of that. It is harder to figure what they will have to pay the doctor and the dentist, to say nothing of the druggist. The other day Helen ran down to the drug store for a little salve and some odds and ends for Gregory. She returned with her purse $6.50 lighter.

The Garlands don't feel they have had more than their share

of bad luck when it comes to illness, but they have had to go into hock several times to keep up with their medical charges. Their worst siege was when young Tom was born with a slight foot deformity. They took the boy to a specialist once or twice a week until he was a year and a half old. That cost about $30 a month. It cost $25 more to buy his first pair of shoes. Friends told them they could get equally good treatment at a clinic, but they are glad they handled the problem the way they did. Their son bounds around like a gazelle these days.

If anyone wonders why business is so anemic in the garment trades, the Garlands are part of the answer. Helen didn't buy any clothes last year because she was pregnant, and she hasn't bought any yet. She has a mouton coat her mother gave her as a wedding present. That keeps her warm in the cold weather. She is waiting to see how much it will cost to get young Tom's tonsils out before she decides whether she will do anything about a new spring wardrobe. In the house Helen usually wears slacks to save her dresses and bedroom slippers to save her shoes.

Tom is not much of a dresser, either. At the factory he wears a sports shirt and a pair of trousers. The only difference at home is that the shirt and pants are cleaner. He feels he will be really well dressed when he can go to the closet and choose between a blue suit and a brown suit.

The last suit he bought was not for himself but for his father-in-law. He bought it as a Christmas gift, along with two shirts for his brother Joe, and he is paying for it in installments of $5 a week. A snow suit for Tommy set the Garlands back $18 this winter. A department-store time payment account costs them another $1.50 a week for miscellaneous items of clothing and household supplies. One major expenditure they are putting off is a bed for Tommy. He still sleeps in a crib and his parents feel it is past time for a change.

Tom and Helen are not feeling sorry for themselves. They have been through enough to see their problems in perspective. They knew plenty of people with greater troubles. At Tom's own factory a few weeks ago, a hundred workers were laid off because the company could not get enough metal and other materials to keep everybody on the job.

Tom not only has his job, he has more money on the way, at least theoretically. The company and the union agreed on a wage increase of 8 cents an hour nearly a year ago, but the raise is tied up in Government red tape. The Wage Stabilization Board has to pass on the contract before the extra money can be paid to Cutler-Hammer employes. When the increase is approved, it will be retroactive to July 1 of last year. That means a lump sum of about $100 for Tom, and $3.20 a week more in each pay check from then on.

However, in the last few weeks, the same shortage of materials that forced the layoff of 100 Cutler-Hammer employes has cut Tom's working hours. The result is that his weekly pay, before taxes and other deductions, has been running a shade under $63, or $9 less than his year-round average. That makes it practically impossible to balance the family budget, and Tom has no way of knowing how long it will be before his checks fatten up again.

But, tough as life may get, the Garlands are glad they are Americans. "We're a lot better off than we would be anywhere else in the world," Tom says. "We may not get everything we want, but at least we can choose what to do with our money. In other countries they don't even have a choice. No matter how bad things are, we're better off than they are."

Tom and Helen are happy about reports from Washington that the cost of living is coming down, but they would be happier if they saw the drop reflected in what they pay at the meat market and the grocery. Falling prices are still something they read about in the newspapers, and every optimistic report is counterbalanced by warnings of more inflation on the way.

Tom's idea is that the Government ought to put a stop sign somewhere along the road to higher living costs. "They should set a date six months from now," is the way Tom has it figured out, "and say on prices, that's it, and on wages, that's it. There's got to be a stopping point somewhere, or else we're all finished."

Helen has an even simpler idea. "I only wish the prices would come down," she says.

Joe Docks, Forgotten
Man of the Waterfront

by Budd Schulberg

WE ALL know the big names of the current investigation into crime
and corruption on New York's waterfront. The headlines are
hogged by Anastasia, Joe Ryan, Mike Clemente, "Big" Bill
McCormack, the polished executives of the great shipping lines
and influential stevedores. But there is a forgotten man on the
waterfront. His voice is lost among the gravel-throated alibis of
high-bracket hoodlums, the oily explanations of labor politicians
and the suavely martyred inflections of the shippers.

You whiz by him on the West Side Highway but you don't
see him. You hurry past him as you board ship for Europe or a
winter cruise through the Caribbean, and never notice his face.
But his muscles move your groceries and your steel; he carries
your baggage on his back. From his pocket comes the notorious
kickback you've been reading about. He's the one who has to
show up every morning for the "shapeup" you've been hearing
about. He is the human material with which racketeers, mas-
querading as union officials, pull flash strikes to shake down
shipping companies and force the employment of such key per-
sonnel as boss loader and hiring boss. He is the man who performs

From the *New York Times Magazine*, December 28, 1952, copyright ©
1952 by The New York Times Company.

the most dangerous work in America, according to the statistics on labor injury and death.

He's the longshoreman, the dock walloper, the little man who isn't there at investigations; the forgotten man in the great city of New York, the forgotten man of American labor. Miners, railroad men, even sailors were fighting fifty years ago against the kind of medievalism that passes for work conditions on the docks this very morning. In a day when social security and old age pensions are accepted as economic facts of life by both major parties, the longshoreman hasn't got job security from one day to the next.

If he's the forgotten man of the current investigation, here's the forgotten fact: it is this basic insecurity—breeding fear, dependence, shiftlessness, demoralization—that feeds the power of the mob. The weaker, more frightened and divided are the dock workers; the stronger and more brazen are the Anastasias, Bowers, Florios and Clementes who manipulate them.

Who are these longshoremen? What kind of lives do they lead? What do they think of these investigations? What are they after?

I went down to the waterfront two years ago for what I thought would be a few days' research for a film about the docks. Long after I had enough material for a dozen waterfront pictures I kept going back, drawn by these forgotten men performing a rugged, thankless job in a jungle of vice and violence where law and constitutional safeguards have never existed.

In the past few weeks I returned to watch the shapeup. I talked with dock wallopers in the bars from the Village to the mob hangouts along the midtown docks. I went to the homes of longshoremen who talked to me frankly (over cases of beer) about their lives, their fears and their hopes for a decent set-up on the piers. I talked to the defeated who shrug off every investigation as just one more political maneuver and who are resigned to grabbing a few crumbs from the gorillas who rule them. I talked to "insoigents"—as they call themselves—who think the time finally is at hand when honest unionism can remove the killers, grafters and seller-outers, and institute regular and honest employment on the docks.

About 35,000 men are paid longshoremen's wages in the course of a year. Of these, about half are regular longshoremen, men who depend on this work for their livelihood. The rest are what you might call casuals, now-and-theners who drift in to pick up an occasional extra check. Many of these are city employes, policemen and firemen who like to grab off the overtime money on nights and week-ends. Some 50 per cent, for instance, earn less than $1,000 a year. Another 10 per cent earn less than $2,000. About a third of all the longshoremen, fifteen thousand at most, earn from $2,000 to $4,000 a year. These are the regulars, the ones who have to hustle every day to keep meat and potatoes on the table for the wife and kids. An upper crust of favored workers averages more than $75 a week on a yearly basis. The base pay of $2.27 per hour sounds all right. It's the irregularity and mob intimidation that make longshoremen the most harassed workmen in America.

Nine out of ten are Catholic—if not Irish Catholic, then Italian or Austrian. This accounts for the influence of certain waterfront priests who have championed the dock workers, in a few dramatic cases going so far as to challenge known hoodlums face to face on the piers. You'll find the Irish on the West Side and in Brooklyn, some 6,000 of them, but they are now outnumbered by the Italians, which explains the growing influence of the Italian underworld that controls the Brooklyn waterfront, as well as the Jersey, Staten Island and East River docks. Irish longshoremen are devout. Before the 7:55 A.M. shape, you will see them going to Mass at St. Bernard's, St. Veronica's or St. Joseph's. Italians follow the Latin tradition of letting the wife handle the church responsibilities.

The Irish longshoremen, while kept in line by strong-arm boys and plagued by an inhuman hiring system, have a better deal than their fellow Italians, who in turn are a niche above the Negroes, who work in traveling gangs picking up the extra work when they can get it and are often relegated to the hold, the job nobody wants. The Irish are hardly ever asked to kick back any more. In other words, when the hiring boss picks his four or five gangs of twenty men each from the 200-250 men who shape themselves into an informal horseshoe around him, the Irish no longer return part of their day's pay to him in order to assure themselves of a job. But the Italians and Negroes systematically kick back as much as $5 per man per day. With seven or eight thousand men kicking back, this quickly becomes big business, some $30,000 or $40,000 a day in illegal fees being passed up from the hiring boss to his superiors as part of the $350,000,000 illegal take from the New York harbor each year.

"It's a stinkin' feelin' standin' there in the shape every mornin' while some thievin' hirin' boss looks you over like you were so much meat," one of the Irish dockers was telling me the other day. "But once in a while an Italian gang is brought into work with us and that really looks like something you've heard about in Europe, not America. They work in a short gang—sixteen instead of twenty—so the cowboys c'n pick up the extra checks for themselves. But they've got to do the work of twenty—or else. If they squawk, the boys work 'em over—or they don't get no more work. I've actually seen 'em beaten like cattle for a question.

"So the rules take a beatin'," my Irish friend went on. "In the first place, 90 per cent never read the contract. In the second place, it's just a piece of paper if the shop steward and the delegate are part of the mob. Jerry Anastasia, for instance, he's a delegate. A lotta help you get from a stiff like that. Half them I-talians are ship-jumpers, which leaves 'em at the mercy of the trigger boys. They ain't citizens and they can't even apply for unemployment insurance. The way I see it we got it lousy and they got it double lousy."

Today most of the Irish workers are picked up by gangs—in this case a legitimate work group, not the Mickey Bowers type. Each gang has its own leader and when the hiring boss points to him it means his whole crew works that day. But the Italians, Austrians and Negroes are still hired on an individual basis by gang carriers, exactly as Henry Mayhew described it in his book, "London Labour and the London Poor," a century ago:

> He who wishes to behold one of the most extraordinary and least-known scenes of his metropolis should wend his way to the docks at half past seven in the morning. . . . [When] the "calling foremen" have made their appearance, there begins the scuffling and scrambling forth of countless

hands high in the air, to catch the eye of him whose voice may give them work. . . . It is a sight to sadden the most callous to see thousands of men struggling for only one day's work, the scuffle made fiercer by the knowledge that hundreds out of the number must be left to idle the day out in want. . . . For weeks many have gone there, and gone through the same struggle, the same cries; and have gone away, after all, without the work they had screamed for.

Not a word need be changed in this description to apply it to hiring methods in New York Harbor a hundred years later. Now, as then, two or three times as many men as will be needed loiter near the dock entrance waiting for the hiring boss to blow his whistle when a ship is ready to be loaded or unloaded. Now, as then, he will pick them out according to his own whim and preference. But on too many docks in the great harbor of New York, the nod is given to the man who plays ball, kicks back, buys the ticket for the benefit he will not be expected to attend or signs up for haircuts in a barber shop where all the seats are filled by labor racketeers. Too often the numbered metal tag which a dock worker gets from the hiring boss, his admission card to a four- or eight-hour shift on the pier, is a badge of compliance, an acceptance of inferior status on the waterfront.

Thousands of longshoremen are wondering why a modern metropolis insists on maintaining a practice so barbarous that it was outlawed in England sixty years ago and is now abandoned in nearly all American coastal cities but not in the great Port of New York.

Work is slow right now and even the longshoreman who stands in with his hiring boss is lucky to pick up three split days a week. How does he make ends meet? "Ya live f' t'day—ya never put nuttin' away—if ya need money ya borry it," I was told. Borrowing comes easy on the docks and is deeply imbedded in the system. The men passed over in the shape must have eating money and they get it from the loan sharks who are part of the mob.

If you "borry" four dollars you pay back five and the interest keeps mounting each week. A rap of 30 per cent isn't unusual.

Nor is it unusual for a longshoreman getting the nod in a shape to turn over his work tab to the loan shark who collects the debtor's check directly from the pay office. So our longshoreman winds up a day's work by borrowing again.

"I was born in hock and I'll die in hock," a longshoreman told me in a Chelsea saloon. In some locals a longshoreman who wants to be hired has to go the route—come up with a bill for spurious "relief" drives and play the numbers and the horses with books belonging to the syndicate. In Brooklyn Albert Anastasia had everything for six blocks in from the river. Longshoremen have to buy their wine from the groceries and their meat.

Unquestionably their incomes are supplemented by regular filching of meat and liquor from the supplies flowing through the piers. Even the insurgents who are doing their best to buck the graft and large-scale pilferage are no different in this respect. Their ethics may be questionable but they stem from a deeply ingrained cynicism that is easy to understand. For years they have watched the fantastic loading racket make off with whole shipments of valuables. The pilferage of ten tons of steel reported to the Crime Commission by a shipping executive may have been front-page headlines to the general public but it was hardly news to the dock workers. "If 5 per cent of everything moving in and out is systematically siphoned off by the mob, why shouldn't I take a few steaks home for the wife and kids," a longshoreman figures.

"Takin' what you need for your own table is never considered pilferage," it was explained to me rather solemnly. Shortly before Thanksgiving a longshoreman who could double for Jackie Gleason noticed barrels of turkeys being unloaded from a truck. He was not working that day but he simply got in line and waited for a barrel to be lowered onto his back. Everybody in his tenement got a free turkey.

Another longshoreman, known for his moxie in standing up to the goons of a pistol local ("one of them locals where you vote every four years with a gun in your back"), told me he was starved out on the docks for sixty straight days. "I stand there lookin' the crummy hirin' boss right in the eye but he never sees me." In a whole year he made less than $1,500 and he had kids to feed. "We couldn't've made out if I hadn't scrounged the groceries on the dock," he said.

What are their politics? Traditionally Democratic, as befits good New York Irish and Italians, but you might say their universal party is cynicism. Because so many mobsters were aligned with the Democratic city machine, some longshoremen took to wearing Ike buttons on the docks as a sign of defiance and undoubtedly the President-elect was well supported. Like the majority of voters nationally, they hope our political change will break the ties between racketeers and the office holders who have been protecting them.

But longshoremen have a feeling of being political orphans inevitably betrayed by the people for whom they vote. They'll tell you their cause has been ignored by the politicians, the police and even the press. Still, they aren't fooled by communism. Despite periodic outcries against subversive influences on the docks—unfortunately used as a cover-up for various forms of racketeering—communism is as unpopular among longshoremen as among stock brokers, farmers or railroad workers. The insurgents who led the harbor-wide wildcat strike a year ago have a hatred for Joe Stalin and his slave labor system that burns just as fiercely as their feeling for Mickey Bowers, Mike Clemente and the whole waterfront system that keeps union racketeering in power.

Men in the Chelsea area are still bitter at the editorials calling their strike Communist-inspired. The local involved, 791, is made up of staunch Irish Catholics, many of them under the influence of the waterfront priest Father John Corridan, and are so rabidly anti-Communist that they have been refusing for years to load war materials headed for Russia or China. It is safer to call these men Communists in print than to deliver that opinion face to face.

"I belt guys for less 'n that," said an embattled member of 791, identified with opposition to Joe Ryan, to strong-arm methods, and to chronic insecurity on the docks. "Anastasia—that great patriot —he calls us Commies. Florio and Di Brizzi—to those bums we're Communists. Strange breed o'Commies who never miss Mass in the morning and who'll give up a day's pay before they'll work a

Russian ship. But I'll tell you one thing, if we don't clean this mess up ourselves, the Commies'll have a nice fat issue all ready to take over."

Father Corridan, of the Xavier Labor School on the Lower West Side, who has become a kind of one-man brain trust of the rank-and-file, sums up the Communist angle this way:

"In '45 the Communists did move in and try to take credit for the leaderless, rank-and-file strike. But right now their influence is nil, no matter what the I.L.A. brass says. The men down here —almost without exception—are loyal, God-fearing Americans. The way to fight Communism in the labor movement is to accentuate the positive—in other words find out what the men really need in order to live healthy, happy, dignified lives and then fight for it."

What longshoremen want has nothing to do with ideologies and millenniums. Their aims are so modest as to be taken for granted by some sixty million American wage earners. What they want most is an assurance that the job they're lucky enough to have today is the same one they'll have tomorrow—and next week— and next month. They don't want to keep wandering from pier to pier like a lot of miserable strays, begging for work.

An old man with forty years on the docks compared his status —or lack of it—with a railroad engineer's. "Look at him, he goes to work every morning knowing he's got a place in the world. The more time he's got behind him the more secure he feels. That's seniority. He knows if he does his job well his pay'll increase, his position improves and he'll finally retire with a good pension. He's got dignity, that's what he's got. Now take me. All my life on the dock. And I know my job. I know how to handle copper in the rain and how to get my fingers into a bag of flour. I c'n work fast. I like to take pride in my work. But what kind of pride can I feel when some punk comes out of the can and starts makin' five times as much as I am for doin' nothin' except pushin' us around?"

The old man insisted on buying me another drink. It may have been loan-shark money, but longshoremen are proud and open-handed and fine drinking companions when they feel they can trust you.

"After forty years I get up t'morra mornin' an' stan' over there on the dock like an orphan. I'll be lucky if I bring home twenty-five bucks this week. Is the hearings gonna change it? Well, lad, I'll tell ya one thing, it can't make it any worse. I just hope it goes all the way."

This hope is echoed all up and down the waterfront. Joe Docks, bottled up in his cramped cold-water flat or his waterfront bar, doesn't get much chance to tell us about his life. But he doesn't like it. Hard-drinking, two-fisted, high-strung, a rabid sports fan, an all-out friend, a dangerous enemy, he's also a loyal, religious, hard-working, responsible family man concerned with getting his kids through school and seeing them get a better break than their old man. He lives for the day when his job will be systematized through some plan of work rotation based on an adequate annual wage. He'd like some advance notice of where and when he's going to work. Today there is not even a central information service on shipping traffic, and the men pick up their information as to job chances in the same haphazard, chaotic way they did a hundred years ago.

Joe Docks thinks he deserves something better than the hopelessly outmoded hiring system that delivers him into the hands of hardened criminals. He's hoping, but not counting on the hearings, which are the most thorough ever held on the problem, to rescue him from underworld bondage and raise him to a level of dignity and security enjoyed by other American workers.

He's too solid and useful a citizen to be left to stew in his own bitterness and bewilderment in the waterfront bars. Anti-hoodlum, anti-corruption, anti-Communist, anti-uncertainty and anti-hunger, he is the real forgotten man of American labor.

The other morning a little fellow who sounded enough like Barry Fitzgerald to make the Ed Sullivan TV show was left standing on the dock by an ex-Sing Sing hiring boss for the fourth consecutive jobless day. "In Liverpool back in 1912 they knocked out this kinda hiring," he was saying. "I could tell them judges on the Crime Commission a thing or two about this stinkin' setup." Even now, early in the morning with another jobless day ahead and the Good Lord only knew what tomorrow, there was a twinkle in his eye. These are indestructible men (until a strong-arm man, a St. John or an Ackalitis, has the last word) and laughter comes easy to them for all their grief and frustration. "When those high mucky-mucks get all through and there's a zillion words of testimony all nicely bound, they'll know what we knew in the first place—down here it's really time for a change."

He gave his cap a jaunty poke, stuck his hands into his battered wind-breaker, pushed his chest out in a gesture of general defiance and crossed Forty-fourth Street to McGinty's Bar and Grill.

As you read this over Sunday breakfast or in the paper-littered parlor, Joe Docks may be in church, or playing with his kids, or lying in bed reading about the basketball games. He'll be back on the docks tomorrow morning around half past seven. If he's passed over he'll be over at McGinty's or some other place, looking for the loan shark, drinking a little beer, worrying about the wife and kids, playing a number, wondering if the Crime Commission can really get those gorillas off his neck, and waiting for the general public to respond to a golden challenge: "If you do it to the least of mine, you do it to me. . . ."

Part 4

WORKERS AND UNIONS SINCE 1960

SHORTLY AFTER the election of John F. Kennedy to the presidency in 1960, and more particularly after the publication of Michael Harrington's *The Other America* in 1962, public attention switched from the attractions of affluence to the affliction of poverty. Closely linked to the more general issue of malignant poverty in a wealthy society were the problems of technological change and racism. The following articles concern the related issues of unemployment, automation, racism, and their impact on the labor movement.

As the decade of the 1950's came to a close, Americans realized that something was wrong with their economy. Since the end of the Korean War in 1953, unemployment had become a permanent feature of working-class life in America, and by 1960 it was reaching totally unacceptable levels. In 1961 a team of *New York Times* reporters led by A. H. Raskin conducted a survey of unemployment in the United States. The Raskin article included below describes the extent of unemployment, the kinds of workers it most frequently affected, and the general working-class response to the lack of jobs.

Many economists conceived of unemployment as a problem that

could be overcome by a proper mixture of monetary and fiscal policies, that is, through the right combination of government credit management, taxes, and expenditures. Still other economists believed that the unemployment of the 1960's was a new problem, not amenable to solution by traditional fiscal and monetary measures. According to these analysts, a large proportion of unemployment flowed directly from the growth of automation in industry, namely the replacement of men by machines. In the article below, Gardner Ackley and John I. Snyder, Jr., discuss and debate the implications of automation. Ackley views the new technology largely as a long-term stimulant to the economy and a net producer of jobs and higher incomes; Snyder, however, sees automation as a direct threat to the jobs of millions of workers and as a force that must be carefully managed, not unthinkingly applauded.

Among those hit hardest by poverty, unemployment, and automation, nonwhite Americans bulked particularly large; indeed, their membership in the ranks of the poverty-stricken and the unemployed was out of all proportion to their representation in the total population. A new militancy began to grip large sectors of the nonwhite population, as reflected among Negroes in the Black Power movement and among Americans of Latin derivation in *La Raza*. The demands of these long-exploited Americans presented the labor movement with a threat as well as an opportunity. The news story that describes the clash between George Meany, president of the AFL-CIO, and Herbert Hill, labor adviser to the NAACP, suggests how and why many black Americans looked upon the labor movement as simply another racist institution reflecting the larger white society. As should be apparent from the story, Meany and Hill engaged in a dialogue of the deaf as representatives of constituencies who used the same vocabulary but drew different meanings from it. Dick Meister's portrayal of César Chavez and the Mexican-American farm workers he organized and led in California demonstrates why the labor movement was eventually able to arrange amicable relations with the United Farm Workers Organizing Committee. Unlike the blacks, Chavez and his Chicano followers in no way threatened the established distribution of power within the labor movement; in fact, they offered labor leaders the promise of increased membership and income and hence greater power. Meister's article further describes the tactics used by Chavez to organize previously unorganizable migratory workers and the relationship between racial and working-class consciousness.

While different problems arose for the American working class and struggles between and among workers took new forms, the old battle between unions and employers remained constant. But it, too, assumed a new shape. Traditionally, for example, employers in the nonferrous metals mining industry had been among the most anti-labor operators in the nation. Copper companies for decades had used every anti-union device available to American employers. The Phelps Dodge Company during World War I had employed Pinkertons, gunmen, and federal troops to drive labor unions out of its mines in the Bisbee, Arizona, district. This labor-busting had culminated on July 12, 1917, in the deportation at gun point of more than twelve hundred local workers and their sympathizers. It is thus hard to believe that A. H. Raskin's description of the 1967–1968 copper strike involves the Phelps Dodge Company and the Morenci, Arizona, community. In Morenci 1968-style, Raskin finds no workers being deported at gun point, no labor spies instigating trouble, and no troops maintaining order. Instead, the striking copper miners sit quietly in air-conditioned company-built and -rented homes, watching color television sets purchased on credit at the company store, eating food and wearing clothes provided by the company—also on credit—for the duration of the strike. Thus far had labor-management conflict evolved from the brutal days of World War I and the. turbulent decade preceding World War II.

Unemployment

by A. H. Raskin

UNEMPLOYMENT WEARS many faces, all of them dour. In a surplus foods warehouse in Charleston, W. Va., a jobless truck driver tugs at a sack of dried beans and sighs: "Well, at least I won't have to pay any gas bill this month. The company shut it off."

In Detroit a laid-off Chevrolet worker winds up a futile job-hunting tour that has led him from the Metropolitan Airport through the Michigan Bell Telephone Company and United States Rubber to the Chrysler tank arsenal.

"I still think there is a future for me and my boy here," he says. "At least in Detroit I know what to expect. If I go some place else, even if I had the money to do it, I wouldn't know anybody. I wouldn't have any background for getting a job."

In the town hall at Sanford, Me., a 57-year-old textile spinner, stranded when the community's only big mill moved to the South, paints a corridor in return for grocery credit slips.

"After 40 we're outcasts," he grumbles.

In Pittsburgh a furloughed steelworker, waiting to apply for extended unemployment insurance benefits under the emergency program just approved by Congress, says:

"Being out of work leaves a person with mental and spiritual frustration. It's painful, like living in a vacuum."

From the *New York Times,* April 8, 1961, copyright © 1961 by The New York Times Company.

These are the long-term jobless, the hard core of the 5,500,000 Americans for whom America has no work. Their plight is worse than that of newcomers to the unemployment rolls because many have been idle so long they have come to accept the idea that they are the unwanted, the useless, the rejects of a society built on the dignity of work.

The full story of disheartenment does not emerge from statistics showing 800,000 men and women out of jobs for more than six months and another 1,000,000 idle fifteen weeks or longer.

These figures make no allowance for those who have withdrawn into an unsought retirement because they have learned that their age makes it pointless to continue wasting shoe leather looking for jobs no one will give them.

Nor do the figures provide an index of those whose eagerness to avoid public charity prompts them to take catch-as-catch-can work at skills and pay far below their accustomed grade. These low-end jobs give them a precarious clutch on classification as employed workers and thus hold down the roster of chronic joblessness.

The unemployed tell their own saga of defeat against a backdrop of rusting mine tipples and sepulchral factories in places like West Virginia, where even the prospect of Federal aid to distressed areas has stirred little hope for an early revitalization of industry.

Ralph Sledd, who worked in the mines for twenty-nine years as a conveyor loader, lost his mining job in 1950 as a result of a shutdown. A muscular, soft-voiced man of 51, he haunts the Charleston warehouse district in search of platform jobs at truck terminals.

He used to earn $18.50 a day underground, now he makes $5 or $6 whenever he is lucky enough to pick up a day's work toting produce crates. His wife is dead and his four children have grown up and moved away. He lives in a tumbledown rooming house in the city's "black belt," but he refuses to take advantage of his right to draw surplus commodities to supplement his tenuous earnings.

"I leave that for the people who need them," he says. Then, without bitterness, he asks and answers a question:

"How does a man get along? Well, a man will live as long as the good Lord lets him. I believe the coal industry will eventually come back—but I won't live to see it."

Clarence Blankenship, who served as an Army medical corpsman in World War II, is a 40-year-old orphan of the mines. When his job as a coal cutting-machine operator gave out in 1952, he switched to work in a lumberyard at less than half the pay.

"We wasn't doing too bad," he recalls with a gap-toothed grin. But his wife, Anna, working as a hospital aide, tried to lift a heavy patient and ruptured a spinal disc in 1956. Ever since trouble has been Mr. Blankenship's portion.

His wife needed an operation to relieve blood clots and his savings were wiped out. Last year the lumberyard burned and his job went up in smoke. The family moved from Bluefield to Charleston so relatives could help care for the five children.

A few weeks ago Mr. Blankenship was one of 4,500 long-term unemployed picked from among 31,000 family heads who clamored for $1-an-hour jobs under a state emergency work relief program. That modest piece of good luck was balanced by his wife's need for a second operation, which left him with a $700 hospital bill and a continuing charge of $15 a week for medicine.

"I just can't make it on $40 a week," he says. "I just went and told the hospital people I can't pay. I never missed a payment before in my life, but now—I bought $1,600 worth of furniture before Anna got hurt, paid it down to $180. Now the store says its going to come and take it away. Ain't that a laugh?"

He doesn't sound very amused, and his tone is no lighter when he adds:

"They'll be work; they's got to be. You'll see a lot more robbing and stealing if they ain't."

The man who made the wry joke about not having to pay his gas bill was Kenneth Lester, still two years short of his fortieth birthday, who went from driving an Army tank in Europe to driving a truck in Charleston after V-E Day.

He lost his job when the small trucking company that had hired him was absorbed by a larger hauler five years ago. Since then he's been looking for steady work in almost any field but "there's always too many men in front of you."

He made a scratch living for himself and his family by doing chores in restaurants and service stations. Now he is employed on the make-work program at $1 an hour distributing Federal excess foodstuffs to his fellow unemployed.

His biggest anxiety at the moment is that his two infant daughters, one 2 years old and the other 2 months, cannot shake off their colds. He sees doctor bills ahead to chew into his slender take-home pay. A 5-year-old son has been parceled out to relatives to help make the money stretch farther.

Worries of this kind are plentiful in New England communities, like Sanford, where the migration of textile manufacturers has left pockets of permanent poverty. The paint on a sign at Sanford's municipal airport, inviting companies to move into a projected industrial park there, has been kept fresh for five years in token of the Maine community's boast that it is "the town that refused to die."

But aside from a struggling aircraft enterprise in a hangar, the 900-acre industrial park remains a bleak expanse of crab grass and dark undergrowth. The resignation etched on the faces of many of the 1,000 Sanfordites who receive surplus food and a dole is a human reflection of the town's deep economic distress.

The number taking Federal food would be much larger were it not for the Yankee reserve that keeps many from parading their want.

"If all those eligible for surplus commodities would apply, there would easily be another thousand," said Selectman Henry J. Desmarais, who operates a mobile canteen at a shoe factory. "But they are just too proud to walk out of the Town Hall carrying a bundle that represents to them charity."

Sanford's economy began sagging many years ago but its most crushing blow did not come until the big Goodall-Sanford Mills joined the Southern flight of textile makers in 1955. The stagnation left by its departure was manifest in visits made to some of the town's relief recipients by Miss Rachel Bergeron, a welfare nurse, whose bright young face contrasted with the creased countenances of those she came to help.

Outside a weather-battered tenement on the edge of the mill district, a mangy dog had jumped into an overflowing garbage pail and was gorging himself on refuse. In a first-floor kitchen, woolen socks were drying on the open door of a gas stove.

Here eight children peeked out of doorways or wandered around vacantly. The father, a former maintenance man at the mill, now receiving a welfare allowance of $26 a week, did not grumble.

"We do the best we can, and they won't get me out of Maine until they plant me six feet under," he vowed. His wife nodded mute assent.

Only one family had welcome tidings for the nurse. She had stopped at a rickety frame house, its back porch littered with the ruins of a partly dismantled washing machine and some crusty bits of metal that might once have been lawn furniture.

A young woman, no older than Miss Bergeron, answered her knock. From behind her eddied the heavy smells of a kitchen that had known many years of greasy cooking. Farther back were the squeals of six children of stepladder ages and the mewling of two kittens being mauled.

"I'm so glad you dropped by," the mother said. "He's been called back and we'll have a pay check again next week."

The little plane plant at the airport had some new orders, and her husband was going back as a riveter. He had been a woodsman, who moved into town because wood-cutting is spotty, seasonal work with pay on a day-to-day basis. Work in the machine shop, he has found, is spotty, too, and the pay of $1.40 an hour affords little basis for gracious living.

For engineers and industrialists, who for several decades have been making pilgrimages to Pittsburgh and Detroit as the fountainheads of mass production, the realization comes hard that both now officially rank as centers of chronic unemployment in the same class as the ghost towns of West Virginia and New England.

Pittsburgh's new Golden Triangle is a dazzling example of civic refurbishment. It is matched by Detroit's shiny new City Center and Exposition Hall. Both industrial metropolises still have sprawling factories and hundreds of thousands of busily engaged workers.

But the decentralization of the steel and auto industries, the onrush of automation and the unwillingness of many companies to spend tens of millions of dollars on modernizing outworn facilities have created huge pools of jobless men in Pittsburgh and Detroit.

So persistent has the glut of manpower proved in good times as well as bad that many of the idle fear their productive careers are over. This is especially true of those, still fifteen or twenty years away from the normal retirement age of 65, who are convinced they are no longer young enough to find work anywhere else.

John Fortner, a Detroit auto worker, is one victim of the ebbing of employment opportunities away from the motor capital, but he is buoyed up by the belief that he has not yet crossed the "unemployability age barrier."

Mr. Fortner, who is only 38, worked for a manufacturer of auto seat cushions for fourteen years. When the 1957–58 recession began, his employer moved away and two years of job-hunting brought him no work.

"I just ran out of everything," he recalled. "I did get unemployment compensation for twenty-six weeks, then for thirteen extra weeks. But when that ran out, I went to welfare. I got $62 every two weeks and put in thirty-two hours a week helping a janitor at a school."

In the fall of 1959 a revival in auto production enabled him to latch on to a job at Chevrolet's gear and axle plant. But his low seniority made him one of the early men to go when Chevrolet scaled down again in January. He is back on the unemployment insurance rolls and there are so many men with priority over him on the recall list that he is skeptical about his chances for returning to Chevrolet.

He is the man who has been tramping from one place to another in a fruitless search for other work, but who still feels his best chance lies in staying in Detroit. When he is not making his job rounds or checking in at the state unemployment office, he finds relief from the monotony of sitting at home by playing dominoes and listening to records at a friend's music shop.

J. C. Johnson, who has a family of six, has not been able to get an auto job since he was laid off at the Dodge forge shop in 1957. He got so used to taking domestic and service employment in his long siege of idleness that he has decided to make a business of it.

"I've been jobbing," he explained. "I got to taking service jobs at golf clubs and hotels. I worked at food preparation and at special parties. Jobbing here and there has helped me get by. And my daughter is working as a domestic. She's helping out a lot."

In Pittsburgh, Edward Dean, a 47-year-old electrician, has been learning something about age discrimination since he was laid off by Jones & Laughlin Steel Corporation last November.

Mr. Dean, who has twenty-four years of seniority at the company, is confident he will be called back in another month or so, but he is so disheartened by the frequency of shutdowns and lay-offs in the steel industry that he has been trying hard to find a new job.

"All the places I've been, they're pretty warm about hiring me till I mention my age," he reports. "Then they cool off. There seems to be a stigma about being over 40. They drop you like a hot potato."

The combination of steel strikes and production cutbacks has held Mr. Dean's average time on the J. & L. payroll to about eight months a year since 1951. He is concerned about the possibility that automation will make work even scarcer in the future, but he emphasizes that "you can't stop progress." His answer is a royalty system, under which workers will get compensation and retraining if their jobs are wiped out.

Another who is sure automation cannot be stopped is Edward Utzig, whose job as a patrolman on the Pennsylvania Railroad was abolished in December. Now in his mid-forties and the father of seven children, Mr. Utzig has worked for the Pennsy for twenty years.

"Thank God for the $51 a week we get in unemployment compensation," he declares. "Without that we couldn't survive."

His chief hope for work is a temporary job as a guard at the county jail. New technology had no direct effect on the closing out of his old post, but he feels it is worsening the job chances of many thousands of rail workers.

"Automation is wonderful for the employer, but it is rough on the worker," is his conclusion.

He has no solution, except that "something has got to be done." Asked who should do it, he replies—and a sudden note of reverence comes into his voice:

"With so many million out of work, I can't understand how Mr. Kennedy can handle the job alone. He needs the help of God."

George G. Frederici, another former patrolman on the Pennsylvania, feels doubly aggrieved about the scrapping of his job after twenty years with the railroad. "It's an injustice," he says. "My dad worked as a maintenance-of-way man on the Pennsy for forty-three years." Now his big worry is whether he can keep up the payments on his neat brick house and meet his daughter's tuition bills at an Indiana teachers' college.

For John McClasson, a 46-year-old millwright's helper at the Edgar Thomson Works of United States Steel, all thought of being restored to his job has vanished. The mill, established more than seventy years ago, is turning into a marginal operation with a skeleton payroll.

"The profits that made United States Steel were built here," says Mr. McClasson. "Now the company is letting the mill become obsolete and putting its production into new plants elsewhere. The workers are left to pay the price of the company's drive for profits."

Automation:
Threat and Promise

THREAT
by John I. Snyder, Jr.

"WHEN LOOMS weave by themselves, man's slavery will end," wrote Aristotle more than 2,000 years ago. Today, "man's slavery" is ending. His machines are becoming more and more automatic and rely on him less and less—and as they do, they are indeed eliminating much of the drudgery and menial tasks which man alone, up to now, performed in our factories and offices. This is automation's bright side—a view of progress and of hope.

But automation also has a dark side. Even as automated machines free men from drudgery, even as they cut the manufacturer's production costs and increase his output, even as they gain universal acceptance, they simultaneously displace men from jobs. If they did not, these machines would make no economic sense. And unless other jobs can somehow be found or created for the men displaced, they will swell the ranks of our unemployed—the

From the *New York Times Magazine*, March 22, 1964, copyright © 1964 by The New York Times Company growing army of unemployed that constitutes our major domestic problem at a time of great prosperity.

To my mind, there is no question that automation is already a major cause of unemployment in this country, or that automated machines will essentially take many more jobs from men than they have already.

Item: At one plant, one man today operates one machine which performs more than 500 separate manufacturing functions that formerly took some 70 men to perform.

Item: In a similar plant, 48 men using automated equipment today turn out a finished product in 20 minutes. Before automation, it took 400 men 40 minutes to do the same job.

Item: In an electronics plant where 200 men used to assemble 1,000 units a day, only two men now turn out just as many with the help of automatic machines.

Item: A three-man crew in a "robot" steel mill turns out 217 miles of rod per day at more than twice the old rate and at one-tenth the old labor cost.

Item: A major Government agency, using computers, has cut its clerical work force from 13,000 to 3,000 workers.

And so it goes—and so, indeed, it should go, for many different reasons. We have developed, and are still developing at even greater speed, a large number of incredibly sophisticated machines. We have perfected automatic sensing devices that simulate seeing, hearing and feeling. We have created computers that work out more than a million calculations in something like two minutes. Without them, the paperwork in our offices would overcome us, our missiles couldn't get off the ground, our basic capital- and consumer-goods industries wouldn't be able to compete and thus remain solvent and alive.

To a manufacturer of automation equipment, all this is welcome. It means, in essence, that as competition increases, the demand for automated machines will also increase—and like businessmen everywhere, I want to sell my product. But I believe it will be difficult to do just that if our unemployment problem continues to mushroom and adversely affects the economy. In my opinion, it should be clear to one and all that automation has displaced, is now displacing and will continue to displace men from certain jobs in growing numbers, and that these men are finding it increasingly difficult to find new jobs.

Obviously, however, this belief is not shared by one and all. There seems to exist a group of economists who genuinely believe either that men are not being displaced by machines at all or that such men find other jobs elsewhere and are not joining the army of unemployed. This, then, is the nub of the matter. Who is right? Are automated machines and devices displacing men in significant numbers or not? Are they adding to our growing rolls of unemployed, and if so, to what degree?

Secretary of Labor W. Willard Wirtz says that the figures are hard to arrive at. The American Foundation on Automation and Employment says that automation is a major factor, causing the elimination of 40,000 jobs a week, or more than two million a year. This is the estimate I submitted last fall to a Senate subcommittee investigating the country's unemployment situation. At that point, the issue was joined, for only a day or two before I testified, the productivity expert of the Bureau of Labor Statistics, Leon Greenberg, had told the subcommittee that automation was displacing 4,000 a week, one-tenth of my estimate.

The Automation Foundation's estimate of workers displaced by automation is based on a Department of Labor formula. The total employment figure for any given year is multiplied by the annual rate of increase of output per man-hour, the latter representing a sort of measure of automation's efficiency. In 1962, roughly 67 million workers were employed, and output per man-hour increased at a rate of better than 4 per cent. On this basis, the multiplication of 67 million by 4 per cent indicates that 2,680,000 workers a year, or 51,000 a week, had lost their jobs to machines that year. To allow for a reasonable margin of error, however, we maintained that automation had been a major factor in a loss of jobs, not at the rate of 51,000 a week, as the formula would indicate, but at a lower rate of 40,000 a week—which is still frightening enough.

We are not alone in this claim. Last June, Secretary Wirtz said that "we have to create jobs to replace every job which a machine takes away [and] it's running right now between 25,000 and 30,000 a week."

The late President, who regarded unemployment as "the major domestic challenge of the sixties," said we must maintain "full employment at a time when automation, of course, is replacing men." President Kennedy also said that "our Labor Department estimates that approximately 1.8 million persons holding jobs are replaced every year by machines." More recently, A.F.L.-C.I.O. president George Meany told his convention in New York that he had information that men are losing jobs to machines at the rate of 80,000 *per week!*

Prof. Charles Killingsworth of the University of Michigan says that accelerated technological change has produced a "structural imbalance" in our labor force, reducing the need for unskilled, semi-skilled, and blue-collar workers generally, while at the same time increasing the need for highly trained workers who are presently in very short supply.

Professor Killingsworth maintains further that our "real" unemployment rate is currently around 8 per cent, not 6 per cent as we have been told. According to his "iceberg theory," only a part of the unemployed can be seen or counted; a great many more are "hidden"—the unskilled and uneducated who have given up job hunting altogether. He estimates that there are about a million "hidden" unemployed, including those who have run out of unemployment benefits and have stopped reporting in, and those who have tired of looking for jobs completely.

Leaving aside the question of whose statistics are best, or the most correct, it seems clear that we do have on our hands an unemployment problem of considerable dimensions, and that automation is contributing to it.

The nation, however, remains unaroused. Too many of us seem eager to believe that the unemployment problem does not exist at all, or that if it does, automation is not contributing to it. And even when both points are conceded, we still like to think that people who lose their jobs to machines can be rapidly retrained and placed immediately in other jobs paying more money; that workers displaced by machines in one section of our country will find jobs with comparative ease in other areas, and that there is no relationship between automation and the Negro revolution.

All these, I believe, are serious misconceptions, and their continuance can have damaging effects not only on the national economy but on our position in the international marketplace.

How can we solve the problems automation is causing in this country today? How do we generate the three to four million new jobs we must have each year if we intend to lick the unemployment problem? These are the questions to which all Americans, whether in the ranks of labor, management or government, must address themselves in the coming months. We must begin a thorough search for answers that will work.

What about the solutions offered so far? Is the tax cut the answer? If it creates enough additional purchasing power to stimulate more production and thus additional employment, it can be a partial solution—but only partial. I believe a tax cut was necessary for the well-being of our economy, but we must remember that it won't help the unemployed worker who doesn't have any wages to tax! At best, it will help preserve the jobs of those now employed.

Some labor leaders feel that collective bargaining will provide a solution. But, by the very terms of automation, how can they negotiate the elimination of themselves or their members at the bargaining table? Leaving aside all other considerations, collective bargaining, at least as we have known it in the past, can't help us solve the human problems created by automation.

On the other hand, I *do* believe that the collective bargaining process will prove invaluable if it is employed with the kind of wisdom and vision that produced both the Kaiser steel agreement and the industry-wide steel agreement. These were negotiated without a timetable and without a deadline—which suggests that collective bargaining in the future ought to be a round-the-year process.

How about the shorter work week? I believe it has merit in the absence of other solutions—if only because of the long-term benefits it may produce. A shorter work week means more leisure time. More leisure time may lead to more constructive ways of using it. And a more constructive use of leisure time will mean new leisure-time industries—and thus more jobs.

As a country, we need to act now. Unemployment is our greatest domestic problem, and we must become totally preoccupied with it if we intend to solve it. As a result of automation, we have entered an era demanding totally new ideas and a totally new approach—perhaps far removed from any we have known before. Everyone should get a fair hearing, no matter how outlandish his ideas may seem, for our very salvation, in my opinion, depends on innovation and cooperation.

The complete solution to our unemployment problem, I believe, depends on planning for two objectives: the creation of new industries and the creation of new markets.

The service industries, for example, have been growing at a phenomenal rate in recent years. We should study this growth carefully and figure out how to accelerate the present pace so as to make new jobs. Similarly, the leisure-time industries and businesses already mentioned are constantly expanding and this, too, is an area that should be studied with a view to creating more jobs.

As a further example, we have yet to perfect our ability to relate the industrial techniques and skills developed in the defense and aerospace industries to the field of consumer products and services. I think that a study of these enormous industries would, without revealing any vital secrets, provide us with opportunities for establishing large new consumer industries. We cannot afford to let exaggerated considerations of national security stand in the way of releasing harmless secrets that can be turned into a new source of jobs.

A Presidential commission to examine what could be safely released to industry would be a sound approach.

All these new industries have now, or would soon have, strong domestic markets, but we must create new ones as well. I don't think we have related our place in the international market to the fact that developing nations have an imperative need for industrial products and machines. We should take another look at these potential markets in the light of our unemployment situation. We need them as much as they need us.

The suggestions I have offered might not all work out, but they are examples of the kind of thinking I am convinced we need to solve the unemployment problem as we know it today—as well as some of the other mammoth problems all around the globe. If we are to grapple with them effectively, find new answers and make them work for us, we shall need a far greater degree of cooperation between labor, management and government than mankind has ever known before. The Automation Foundation— representing the International Association of Machinists and my company, U.S. Industries, Inc.—is, perhaps, one of the first practical steps in this direction.

Regardless of which particular steps are finally agreed upon, the suggestions are put forward because the crisis is a *real* one. The handwriting is on the wall, and as Thorstein Veblen once said: "Invention is the mother of necessity."

PROMISE
by Gardner Ackley

UNEMPLOYMENT in America is, and has been for six years, excessive and distressing. Some people say it is the product of a new force in our economy—automation—and that this kind of unemployment is impossible to eradicate without new and drastic remedies. Against this, I will argue that the effects of automation on employment are nothing new; that any employment problems created by automation can be solved if we adopt the right policies, and that as we solve these problems, automation will prove a blessing, not a threat.

Engineers define automation as "the transference of control functions from human beings to computers and servo-mechanisms." To the economist, its meaning is much simpler—it reduces the number of workers needed to produce a given quantity of goods and services. In that sense, there can be no doubt that automation destroys jobs, but there is nothing particularly new about that. Technological change has been destroying jobs since the beginning of civilization—faster and faster since the Industrial Revolution—and yet the *total* number of jobs has, with occasional interruptions, risen continually.

For example, this year it will take about 2 million fewer

workers than were needed last year to produce the same total output (just as last year, the previous year's output could have been produced with about 2 million fewer workers). Yet, last year, total employment rose by about a million jobs, and we expect a rise of perhaps 1.4 million jobs this year. This means that about 3 million *new* jobs were created last year, and nearly 3.5 million new jobs will be created this year.

It is clearly one-sided, therefore, to concentrate on the job-*destroying* effects of automation without considering the job-*creating* ability of our economy as a whole.

Popular concern with "technological unemployment" has always varied over the years. We heard a tremendous amount about it during the nineteen-thirties, when unemployment was epidemic. But during World War II and the first postwar decade, when jobs were readily available despite radical changes in productive methods, it was seldom mentioned. Since 1957, however, unemployment has averaged 6 per cent of the labor force, and in no month has it fallen below 5 per cent. Once again some people have decided that technological change—called automation this time—is the primary cause of unemployment. In that regard, Europe's experience is instructive. There, the postwar technological revolution has been far more dramatic than here (because European industry started so far behind ours and has largely caught up). But full employment has been maintained and very little has been heard about the technological displacement of labor.

From the history of our economy, it is clear that technological change has always created more new jobs than it has destroyed. Our technologically progressive economy has continually offered more and better jobs and incomes, more and better goods and services for most of us to enjoy, and more leisure time in which to enjoy them. We are employing half again as many workers as we did in 1929. We are producing almost three times as much. And average earnings of employes and the self-employed have more than doubled—from $2,522 in 1929 to $5,224 today, in terms of present buying power.

But the fact that past technological gains have proved entirely consistent with rising total employment and increasing individual welfare does not make us satisfied with our present excessive unemployment. To get the unemployment rate down to 4 per cent by the end of 1965, we would need to create about 9 million new jobs during 1964 and 1965—about 4 million to offset productivity gains and 5 million to take care of the unemployed and those who will enter the labor force. Finding that many new jobs is our most challenging piece of domestic business. How can we do it?

Demand is the crucial factor. When it expands as fast as "potential output" (the output we *could* produce with *full* employment of both men and machines), then automation means more goods sold rather than fewer jobs—and we congratulate ourselves on the wonders of technological progress.

There are several ways in which technological change itself directly stimulates the demand for goods and services, and hence creates as well as destroys jobs. In the first place, greater productivity means higher incomes for the workingman and the owner of a business, and with their higher incomes they buy more goods and services. In each of the years 1949 to 1963, American families spent between 92 and 94 per cent of their after-tax incomes on goods and services. Over this period, both the purchasing power of the average family and the actual quantity of goods and services bought by the average family rose by one-third. And since the number of families increased by one-fifth, total consumer spending, at constant prices, rose about 60 per cent.

Second, technological change stimulates consumer buying. It not only reduces the cost of existing products, but also creates new products. Without TV sets, air conditioners, dishwashers, "miracle fabrics" and many other innovations, it is possible that the percentage of incomes spent in consumer markets might well have slipped over the years.

Then again, new technologies provide a powerful incentive to business spending on new plants, machinery and equipment. Expenditure on automation alone—to replace older but still usable equipment—has in itself recently constituted a significant part of the total demand for goods and services.

Yet it is clear that, since 1957, over-all demand has not been growing as fast as our potential output. Those who fear automation say this shows that our productive powers are now outstripping our wants, that the public is satiated, that our private and public needs have been met so adequately that from now on it will be hard for demand to keep pace with productive capacity.

But there seems little evidence to support this view. The fact that American families have been spending a constant proportion of their after-tax incomes on goods and services at a time when average family incomes have been continually expanding hardly suggests satiation. Very few families indeed seem to have much of a problem deciding how to spend another $1,000 a year. Even in our affluent society, the average family income is still only about $6,000 annually—and one family in five gets less than $3,000. In my view, no conceivable rate of technical progress, and of associated gains in personal incomes, could lead to consumer satiation in our lifetime. Give consumers the incomes they could earn with full employment and they will find plenty of ways to spend them.

As I see it, our problem of insufficient demand has arisen from a tax "brake" that has kept consumer and business purchasing power from moving up at the same rate as our potential output. The present tax system is a legacy from the days when postwar backlogs of consumer and business demand, together with the requirements of the Korean conflict, kept our men and machines fully employed.

If, today, the economy were operating at only a 4 per cent level of unemployment, the Federal Government's tax receipts would exceed its expenditures by some $8 billion. The Federal budget has thus been exerting a strong restraining influence on private demand—which could only be justified if private and public demand together were sufficient to maintain full employment—a condition not seen since 1957.

The slack markets and high unemployment of today are thus neither new nor mysterious—and a major part of the cure is now at hand. The $11.5 billion tax-reduction program will turn the Federal budget from a restraining into an expansionary influence. Releasing the tax brake will permit the economy to respond fully to the opportunities provided by automation by creating a high and growing demand for goods and services and thus an adequate growth in the number of jobs.

These new jobs will not always appear in the same industries in which jobs are destroyed. Sometimes they do. In the nineteen-twenties, for instance, cost-reducing innovations in the automobile industry stimulated national demand for cars, gasoline products and highway construction and greatly expanded the number of jobs in these areas. In other cases, however, productivity gains can cause a loss of jobs in an industry, because demand for its products does not keep in step. Striking productivity gains in farming and mining, for example, have not been matched by a rising consumption of wheat and coal.

A progressive, growing economy thus often requires a shift of workers from declining to growing industries, and the uneven impact of automation may increase the need for this migration. Moreover, automation, like all other technological changes, demands different kinds and degrees of skills, increasing the risk of mismatching between the qualifications sought by employers and those offered by workers.

The design, construction and installation of automated equipment require highly trained specialists. And the use of such equipment reduces our relative need for unskilled and semiskilled workers. But changes in job requirements are generally paralleled by the evolution of appropriate skills among the labor force.

Each year, the working population contains more and more highly trained—often college-trained—workers. Just since 1941, the average number of school years completed by adult male workers has risen by 50 per cent. New recruits to the labor force are considerably better educated than those leaving it. By 1970, 30 per cent of it will consist of persons who entered the job market after 1960—and their training will be readily adaptable to the demands of new technology.

But while the skill requirements of automation can be, and are being, met, there is no room for complacency. There are far too many high-school dropouts. There are far too many high-school graduates whose intellectual capacity would permit them to complete college, but who do not for lack of money or lack of motivation. And our graduate and professional schools—even though growing more rapidly than any other part of our educational system—must grow still faster.

Moreover, it is not only academic education that is important. We also need better vocational training, and, particularly, better vocational *retraining* programs; improved labor-market information; and better guidance and placement services.

The human cost of rapid technological change has always been high, but we can reduce it by helping workers to adjust effectively to change. With the affluence technological change has brought us, we can also afford to do more than we have in the past to alleviate the plight of those too old, too limited in education or otherwise unable to share in it.

To meet the challenge of automation, then, we need, first, policies to maintain a strong and growing demand for goods and services, and thus a sufficient over-all demand for labor; and, second, policies to help workers adjust to change. The first will be primarily monetary and fiscal measures; the second, "labor-market" or "structural" policies.

This complementary approach can not only meet the challenge of automation, but convert it from a threat to jobs to a source of strength and well-being for us all. Properly harnessed, automation can also make a major contribution to solving our balance-of-payments problem in world trade. Lower costs of production, and the rapid introduction of new and better products, will improve our competitive position and help end the drain on our gold supply.

Automation is not our enemy. On the contrary, like all past technological change, it can confer the blessings of higher incomes and better living, and more leisure to enjoy them, if we but pursue the proper policies.

George Meany
and Herbert Hill Clash

by Stanley Levey

GEORGE MEANY accused the labor secretary of the National Association for the Advancement of Colored People yesterday of false-
hoods, smears and a political attack on labor.

The words of the president of the American Federation of
Labor and Congress of Industrial Organizations—blunt, bitter
and scornful—were directed against Herbert Hill. He is the author
and prosecutor of the association's antidiscrimination drive in the
labor movement.

Mr. Meany pointedly chose the convention of the Negro American Labor Council for his forum. He did so in the knowledge that
many members and leaders of the organization approved Mr.
Hill's objectives, if not his tactics.

The speech brought into sharp focus the differences that divide
the labor movement and the Negro community. Each has accused
the other of responsibility for the gap between them.

Factors in the Dispute

These feelings—simmering beneath the surface for some time—
boiled over in August when a special House subcommittee, with

From the *New York Times,* November 10, 1962, copyright © 1962 by
The New York Times Company.

Mr. Hill as an expert consultant, began an inquiry into alleged discrimination by the International Ladies' Garment Workers' Union against Negroes and Puerto Ricans.

A second cause of the irritation was the decision last month by the N.A.A.C.P. to press for decertification by the National Labor Relations Board of unions guilty of discrimination. One of the targets in that drive was a local of the United Steelworkers Union in Atlanta.

Mr. Meany referred to both incidents in his speech last night to the Negro labor council at the Americana Hotel. Of the garment union case he said:

"When anyone tries to say that the trade unions are the chief barrier to the economic opportunities of Negroes in this country, I resent it and I reject it, for it is simply not true.

"Yet the labor secretary of the N.A.A.C.P. was the chief prosecution 'expert' last August in a political attack on the I.L.G.W.U., a union whose record shines like a beacon in the history of human progress."

Of the steel union case Mr. Meany declared that it was "fantastic" to accuse the union of trying to perpetuate the distinction between Negro and white workers. Over the years, he said, the union has been fighting to break down barriers.

"Let me tell you something else," he went on. "At the time the steelworkers organized this plant several years ago there was a conference between the president of the steelworkers, David J. McDonald, and the executive secretary of the N.A.A.C.P., Roy Wilkins. They discussed the practices in the plant as they then existed and agreed on the program the union would follow in an effort to correct them.

"More than that, a special committee was set up to meet every three months to evaluate what had been done and to discuss any problems that may have arisen. The members of that committee were Frank Shane, the civil rights director of the steelworkers, and Herbie Hill.

"I am told by the steelworkers that Herbie Hill has never sought nor attended a meeting with Frank Shane from the time the committee was set up until the day the decertification action was brought against the union."

Reached by telephone, Mr. Hill said that he had never described all unions as barriers to economic opportunities for Negroes, but that he had identified the "old line craft unions" as the obstructionists. On the steel case, he said:

"The record will show that the charge of no meetings is simply not true. There have been several meetings, including one in Washington when Arthur Goldberg was counsel for the steelworkers. I was accompanied by Robert Carter, general counsel for the N.A.A.C.P."

Mr. Meany rejected a proposal made by A. Philip Randolph, head of the Negro council, and other Negro trade unionists, that unions found guilty of discrimination be expelled from the merged labor federation.

"I think," he said, "that we will get further—and that we are getting further—by keeping the unions within the federation and helping their officers to fight the evil."

In a two-hour keynote speech at the opening session of the convention at the Sheraton Atlantic Hotel, Mr. Randolph sought to maintain a balance between the activist elements in his organization and the point of view of the A.F.L.-C.I.O.

He deplored the conflict between the garment union and the N.A.A.C.P., which has backed Mr. Hill. As a solution he proposed that Mr. Wilkins and David Dubinsky, head of the I.L.G.W.U., try to work out their differences. If they could not, he said, they should turn their disagreement over to arbitration by a panel of prominent citizens.

The convention will continue today with Walter P. Reuther, head of the United Automobile Workers, as the chief speaker.

A Kind of Economic Holy War

by A. H. Raskin

MORENCI, ARIZONA.

YOU STEP off the jet airliner at Phoenix, speed in an air-conditioned car over the superhighways that were once Apache trails and suddenly you are in a feudal empire in which the automated marvels of ultramodern technology keep alive—or encapsulated —a seignorial economic relationship that might have been lifted whole out of the Middle Ages. This is the empire of Arizona's great open-pit copper mines, and the company towns around them, which normally are the source of more than half of all American copper.

Here for the last seven months has been the central battleground of what many experts consider the most fundamental test of strength between Big Labor and Big Business since the mass-production industries were unionized in New Deal days. The nationwide copper strike, which passed its 200th day at the end of January, has pitted the full resources of the American Federation of Labor and Congress of Industrial Organizations against those of the Big Four copper companies, acting as standard-

From the *New York Times Magazine,* February 18, 1968, copyright © 1968 by The New York Times Company

bearers for most of the rest of the country's corporate giants. Both sides consider the contest a kind of economic holy war.

Yet, it is hard for a visitor to shake off the sense that this battle is being fought on the far side of the moon, so alien does 20th-century America seem in this strange land of copper. True, the reminders are plain enough. Mammoth electric shovels and rotary drills sit toylike on the shelves of the silent mine; a train of 80-ton dump cars rusts on its snowy floor; electronic controls await the return of absent mine and mill employes. And in the parlors of the strikers, curtains are drawn against the blazing sun to avoid interference with the blazing hues on the color TV set.

But, even in its torpor, the mine is omnipresent as creator and destroyer. The community exists only to serve it and feed on its bounty. And that bounty is far harder to come by in copper than it is in coal, which lies densely packed and ready to burn when it is torn from its inky tomb. Copper's sterner story is told in the limitless waste dumps that rim every mine. In most places 6,000 pounds of earth must be moved to get an ultimate yield of 15 pounds of copper. At Twin Buttes, near Tucson, Anaconda has hauled out 153-million tons of over-burden—half of a Panama Canal—and is just reaching its first touch of ore. Another 50-million tons will have to come out before the mine starts operating.

The result of all this dross is that man-made mountains of waste grow until they rival the red granite hills from which the copper is dug. The mesquite and cactus disappear under huge piles of rock, dirt and sludge, and "tailings" from the concentration plants form a chalky mush that engulfs two or three square miles near each large mine. Seen from above, the tailings look like a bilious gray-white sea. Viewed from the highway or the window of a miner's home, their crusty side wall has the aspect of a windowless Pentagon fronting for a full mile and rising a hundred feet above the desert.

To the men of the mining camps, as to their employers, all these mounds symbolize jobs, not waste. More than half the workers are of Mexican descent. Many have followed their fathers into the Arizona pits and some represent the third generation of their families to work there.

To them the mine is birthplace, sustainer and sometimes grave-yard. And not infrequently it gulps down the house in which they were born, as it did for Joe Gonzalez, the 39-year-old financial secretary of Steelworkers Local 915 at Kennecott's Ray mine. The whole town of Sonora, his birthplace, was eaten up by expansion of the mine.

This state—with a quarter of its land still set aside for Indian reservations and only 15 per cent privately owned, with no more people in all of its 114,000 square miles than the island of Manhattan has in 22—has become the improbable zone of decision for the colossi of capital and labor in a battle to shape the pattern of industrial relations in the automation era.

Arizona produces nearly three times as much copper as Utah, which stands second, far ahead of Montana, New Mexico and Nevada, the other chief American sources of the red metal. Lead and zinc mines, refineries and fabricating plants owned by the struck companies are scattered through all parts of the country—two shut wire mills are just north of the Bronx in Yonkers and Hastings-on-Hudson. But the chief upset to local economies in lost wages, lost taxes and disruption of tributary industries has been in the five Western mining states.

The national economy has taken a beating, too. The long shutdown has pushed up the already swollen defense budget by forcing the use of high-priced foreign copper on military orders, throwing the balance of payments several hundred million dollars deeper into the red.

It has threatened a permanent export of mine jobs to South America and Africa, and impelled some of copper's customers to switch—perhaps forever—to aluminum and other substitute materials.

In Washington hearings three weeks ago before a special White House peace panel, union and industry leaders traded moral imperatives about the evils of overcentralized economic power—each side, of course, identifying the other with too much bigness and depicting itself as the resolute defender of individual liberty. Everybody was so intransigent that the panel gave up in despair. All this sloganeering echoes distantly in the mountain fastnesses of the mine camps, where 15,000 Arizona strikers watch the battle of titans with only one real interest: When will it be over? There is little grumbling, little acute hardship, just the grinding emptiness of day after day with nothing much to do except hope that this will be the day it ends.

Never has a labor dispute provided more intriguing insights into the complexity of the American economy and the extent to which many ancient shibboleths of labor-management warfare need consignment to the slag heap of history. Nor could any necromancer conjure up a more fanciful laboratory in which to assay the contradictions of current industrial practice than exists in the Southwest's storied blend of desert and highlands. This is where the "Wobblies"—the old Industrial Workers of the World—struck a half-century ago in a walkout that helped speed them toward extinction but set in motion the "one big union" philosophy underlying the current A.F.L.-C.I.O. drive.

The pooled power of 26 unions, headed by the million-member United Steelworkers of America, is being used in an attempt to compel the copper Big Four—Kennecott, Anaconda, Phelps Dodge and American Smelting and Refining—to sign company-wide contracts, a process that would give the unions vastly increased leverage for standardizing wages and benefits. The companies are fighting to keep things the way they always have been—scores of separate agreements covering mines, smelters, refineries and fabricating plants scattered all over the country. The unions accuse management of wanting to keep the labor front fragmented as a whip to beat wages down. The company retort is that labor seeks to make them guinea pigs in a plot to get dictatorial control over the whole economy through massed union strength.

The essence of the battle: Can the unions substitute "unite and conquer" for the old company practice of "divide and conquer"? Who wins will have a decisive effect on the power balance in many other key industries—and on how often Uncle Sam must intervene in future bargaining deadlocks so massive they chill the economy.

But all these cosmic issues and the bitterness they have engendered in the Eastern capitals of economic and political authority seem ludicrously unreal when you come into a town like Morenci,

120 miles north of Mexico, where everything begins and ends with Phelps Dodge. Its huge open pit, the largest in Arizona, dominates the landscape and the lives of 6,000 men, women and children.

The Morenci mine is a cannibalistic master that literally swallows up the town it spawned in its greed for red metal. More than a billion tons of earth and rock have been hauled out of the pit since 1937. Dynamite blasts and electric shovels have scooped it out in the shape of a classic amphitheater, a mile and a half across and a quarter-mile deep. The calling of the strike last July 15 forced a delay in plans for making the big circle bigger still. That has meant a stay of execution for the old section of the town, built around the turn of the century when Morenci was a center for underground mining. Now the doomed structures sit a few dozen feet from the lip of the crater, marked for destruction soon after the back-to-work signal is given. Homes, stores, offices and the still plush, if somewhat seedy, Hotel Morenci ("When it was built, there was no finer hotel between San Francisco and Kansas City," says Dewey Tidwell, its assistant manager) will all vanish into the pit. Some day, in the intricate process of copper extraction, their pulverized remains will be washing down a pipe as slurry bound for a waste dump.

The displaced workers and their families are being rehoused by the company in a handsome new town on the safe side of the mine—where there are no copper veins to tap. The solicitude that goes into the resettlement discredits analogy between today's corporate welfare state and the paternalism of George Pullman, whose "model town" in Illinois spawned the bloody railroad strike of 1894, or other early practitioners of "enlightened" union-busting through employer-nurtured Shangri-La's. Perhaps the highest tribute to the effectiveness of the Phelps Dodge approach —and the most striking evidence of the muddled state of labor-management relations—is the virtual unanimity with which staunch unionists in Morenci salute the company as a "good employer" at the same time that they vow to stay out forever if that is their union's order.

Last year, before the strike turned the whole operation into a ghost town, there were 1,000 people on the waiting list for jobs

at the Morenci mine or its auxiliaries—the concentrator, where
ore is ground to a consistency finer than face powder, and the
smelter, where most of the impurities are melted out. The bulk of
the job-hunters were relatives of the 1,900 workers already on
the payroll, like Alex Florez, whose father has worked at Morenci
as a boilermaker for 24 years. Young Florez applied to Phelps
Dodge right after being graduated from the local high school—
for which the company pays 98 per cent of the property taxes—
but he had to work at a market for a year before he was called
up as a brickmason's helper. Raúl Villareal, a spoutsman at the
smelter, had better luck. He got his job fresh out of high school;
his father has been in the pit 20 years.

The workers pay less for a house than New Yorkers pay for
each room in a subsidized middle-income housing project. Rents
on the company houses range from $14 a month in the old section
to $30 for a three-bedroom ranch-type dwelling in the new. If
there is a house in Morenci without a color television set, I didn't
come across it. Practically all the sets come from the shiny new
company store, as big and elaborately stocked as any suburban
shopping center in Long Island or Westchester County. Almost as
omnipresent as color TV in the Morenci homes were tinted
photographs of President Kennedy and of sons in the armed
forces. The town includes a 42-bed hospital and medical center
maintained by the company, a 10-lane bowling alley, a swimming
pool and most of the other attributes of suburbia.

The chief complaint of the hard-rock miners before the strike
was that they had no time to enjoy any of these appurtenances of
gracious living. For three years, the standard work schedule in all
branches was 26 consecutive days without a single day off. Then
would come two days to recuperate, followed by another 26-day
stint, and so on for three years. The sixth and seventh day of each
week would be at time and a half, and many of the men liked the
overtime so much that they worked for months at a time without
any days off at all.

One effect of the never-stop schedule was to put the Phelps
Dodge workers at the top of the Arizona industrial list in annual
earnings. For the state as a whole, copper workers averaged
$8,061 in 1966, according to the Arizona Employment Security

Commission. That was more than any other nonfarm group earned, and the Phelps Dodge workers were well ahead of the copper average. The company, fearing the copper boom might end, preferred paying overtime to moving in workers it would later have to fire.

However, the 26-day grind made a good many miners welcome the strike as a much-needed sabbatical. L. R. Brokaw, a mechanic at the power plant, was one. He was delighted at the chance to install an underground sprinkler system for his lawn. Then he started tinkering with the three Brokaw automobiles—his own, his wife's and one belonging to a son who has just gone into the Army. "Now I'd like to see it settled," he says, "but on a fair basis, not any old way."

Others have been spending their time going out on the Coronado Trail after elk, antelope, quail, wild turkey or even mountain lion. But the intrepid hunters have had it, too. They're ready to look at copper again, and not just in cartridge cases.

One thing that makes it certain they will not start back until the union gives the signal, however, is the extent to which Phelps Dodge itself has removed any danger that the strikers will be starved into submission. Through the credit policy it pursues in its stores and houses—not only at Morenci but at its other big Arizona installations at Ajo, Bisbee and Douglas—the company is doing more to subsidize the strike than the sponsoring unions. That policy helps illustrate how much things have changed since "Big Bill" Haywood of the old Western Federation of Miners addressed the 1905 founding convention of the I.W.W. as "the Continental Congress of the working class" and summoned it to violent overthrow of the whole wage system.

It also indicates why in the seventh month of this epic strike the pickets wave cheerfully at John O'Neil, the Morenci general manager, every time he drives past. And why Orville Larson, co-chairman of the top union negotiating committee at Phelps Dodge, says the company is "smarter in labor relations than any of the others; it's just a captive of the industry or we'd have had a contract there long ago."

The company allows each striker an average of $35 a week—$40 one week and $30 the next—in interest-free charge coupons for purchases of food, clothing or anything else. Rents also go uncollected until pay checks start coming in again. Shortly before Christmas the company distributed $500,000 in vacation checks to workers who had not had their three-week vacations before the strike. That lessened the gloom, but half of the turkeys the company store had expected to sell in the Thanksgiving-Christmas season are still in the deep freeze.

The friendly spirit even extends to the picket shacks, at which shifting crews of two or three unionists maintain a languid patrol around the clock. The company supplied the building material for the shacks, the electric lights and the stoves for protection against the chill night air. The strike committee furnishes coffee, cookies, soda pop and a television set. Drinking alcohol is forbidden. Union benefits for picket duty—usually one four-hour turn every two or three weeks—run from $10 to $25 a week. The unions also pay their members' utility bills and supply gas for their cars.

(The United Steelworkers, which has been spending an estimated $500,000 a week on the strike, is holding a special convention next month in Atlantic City to assess all its working members in steel, aluminum, can and other industries $5 a month for five months to build up the strike fund. That means a war chest of roughly $25-million to carry on this battle and any that may arise later this year in other sectors of its jurisdiction.)

If the combination of credit and benefits insulates the union rank and file in towns like Morenci against much of the immediate financial squeeze that might increase its eagerness to settle, it is only fair to note that most of the industry also has a thick layer of insulation in the form of expanded profits from overseas copper holdings. The earnings of all the companies are down drastically from the record levels of 1966 but they are still in the black. Kennecott has extensive production in Chile and Canada, and Asarco in Peru, Australia and Mexico. Ironically, Phelps Dodge, with the most generous policy in underwriting its strikers' living expenses, has the smallest offset in foreign operations—a one-sixth share in one Peruvian company.

The long sleep in the American mines has, of course, created a boom market—along with inflated prices—for all the foreign copper producers. (Chile and Zambia rank behind this country as the free world's biggest, with Canada and the Congo next in line.) Even before the strike, the United States, its demands swollen by the requirements of the Vietnam war, had to import some copper; now it is flooding in.

No one has calculated with precision what share of this shower of riches winds up on the plus side of the struck companies' balance sheets. But, when taken together with the financial life rafts available to the strikers, it is enough to render suspect the hallowed notion that the function of a strike is to tighten the financial pinch on both sides until one or the other gives up or both decide it is time to listen to reason. In this strike both warriors have more built-in protections than does the national economy.

When you go into the homes of the strikers or talk to them in the picket huts, fatalism is the most assertive note. The one thing clear to the rank and file—those who support the tie-up just as much as those who wish it had never happened—is that the final decision on both the management and union sides will be made by the big brass far away from the mine head. The officers of the local unions dutifully deny that there will be any top-down determination for labor (a denial made obligatory by the one-note insistence of all company statements, advertisements and telephone recordings that the whole strike is a "power grab" in which the union members are voiceless pawns).

But the members appear little disturbed by the charge. They are satisfied, by and large, that the negotiating program reflects the ideas the locals put forward, that the vote to quit work was an overwhelming and uncoerced one in all areas and that the only way to conduct meaningful contract talks is to trust the men the unions send to the bargaining table.

"The people in Pittsburgh have to tell us what to do," says Luciano Romero, picket captain for Steelworkers Local 5738 at Kennecott's Hayden smelter. "We are ready to go back any time we get a decent contract."

And through it all is the awareness that, whatever the merit of the immediate issues, the workers' only strength lies in their togetherness as expressed through their union. Practically all the strikers went through a six-month shutdown in 1959. It was a conventional battle over the buck, blotted out of public view by national concern over the 116-day strike of a half-million steel-workers in that same year. It took most of the hard-rock miners two or three years to pay off the debts they piled up then. "It was hard, but it was worthwhile," is the verdict of Juan Ortiz, a trucker at the Phelps Dodge smelter in Morenci. "To get anything I feel you must go through a lot of hardships." His thin, sad-faced wife adds a footnote: "I can't say who's right this time. It's been going on a long time, too long, and there's two sides to every story. But the poor must stick together or they would have nothing."

Needless to say, there are dissenters. Take Dennis I. Stutzman, for 44 years a boilershop welder for Phelps Dodge in Bisbee and now two years away from retirement. His son is just back from service as a Mormon missionary in the Tonga islands and is entering college this month. Stutzman had hoped to be able to help pay the youth's college expenses and also put aside enough money to buy a little farm in Nevada where his wife's folks have a place. "The longer this goes on, the farther away that gets," he mourns.

In San Pedro, near Kennecott's Hayden smelter, Elias Gonzalez was caustic about the strike that was keeping him off the job he has held for 27 years. "We don't have nothing to do here," he complains. "It's all happening in Pittsburgh; the main people are over there keeping us out of work." His widowed sister, whose husband also had worked at the smelter, was even angrier. "They're sitting in their golden chairs; they don't care about us poor people."

Many of the skilled workers have gone to other states in search of jobs to fill their time and pocketbooks until the Arizona mines and mills reopen. One such was Daniel F. Crow, a welder in the machine shop at Morenci, who took a post as tool clerk in a Sperry Rand plant in Louisiana. It lasted for two months—until the plant was shut by a strike.

His son, Olan, an electrician's helper at the Ray mine, got a job in a California plant making specialized bolts for space capsules. But he had to come back at the beginning of January to be on hand for the birth of his first child in the Kennecott hospital in Kearny. A former Marine, with service in Vietnam, young Crow considers the mine strike "ridiculous." The only reason he intends to stay on is that he is next in line for apprentice status in the electrical department, so he is keeping his family in a trailer park at Kearny till the mine goes back into production.

One paradox is that the unions themselves have been uncommonly generous in permitting their members to work for the struck companies on operations divorced from the direct mining and concentrating of copper. The green light extends beyond such customary authorizations as the assignment of men to keep power plants and pumping stations in operation or to prevent fires from going out in reverberatory furnaces and thus wrecking costly smelter equipment. At the Ray mine Kennecott is being allowed to go ahead on construction of a $42-million plant for treating 10,000 tons of copper silicate ore each day. And at Twin Buttes an intricate network of conveyor belts and earthmovers is fast turning what John B. Knaebel, Anaconda's vice president, calls the biggest gravel pit in the world into an engineering marvel comparable to Egypt's Aswan High Dam. It is designed to produce a minimum of 30,000 tons of ore a day.

Union officials explain their willingness to let these massive projects roll forward on the ground that no copper is being produced by them—and thus money is flowing out of the company coffers with none flowing back in. Knaebel discounts this explanation, even though the 950 men working for Anaconda at Twin Buttes earn roughly $25,000 a day. He insists that outlay doesn't weaken his company's ability to hold out because of the profits it draws from its Chilean operations. He thinks the union's real objective is to avoid a revolt by men chopped off the payroll.

But the evidence is scant that the strike will ever crack because the men walk away from their leaders. Even in cities like Butte, Mont., where there are no company stores and many strikers have had to go on public relief, hardship has merely stiffened resolve. Miners have a tradition of standing against the world when they feel their union under attack. That is as true in the copper mines as it was in coal when John L. Lewis defied the White House, Congress and all the forces of public opinion with his wartime strikes a quarter-century ago. A few abortive back-to-work attempts have been made in the copper strike, but they have flubbed out quickly. The one that seemed most likely to pick up steam was started by the Rev. Robert Hyman, a Roman Catholic priest in Douglas, right on the Mexican border, where Phelps Dodge has a big smelter. But the priest did some homework of his own and decided that the unions had better arguments on their side than the companies. That turned him into a champion of companywide bargaining, instead of a foe.

The pastoral conversion has not started any comparable trend toward reassessment of position in management, nor is any in prospect. Government troubleshooters, who have been trying for weeks to find some sign of give in the approach of either side, tend to view the strike with much the same sense of desperation that diplomats do the prospects for peace in Vietnam.

The two conflicts have at least one thing in common. Both represent situations in which a dubious initial excursion has now been escalated to such dimensions that monumental stakes have been created by the very fact of escalation. What might have been just another strike, with no issues broader than the companies and workers directly affected, has been magnified into a siege which George Meany has told the A.F.L.-C.I.O. "we cannot afford to lose." And the resolution is no less strong in the National Association of Manufacturers and the United States Chamber of Commerce.

As with most global showdowns, the road to this one was paved with ironies. Example: Multi-unit contracts are no novelty in the Big Four—a whole checkerboard of combinations leaping state lines has existed for years in the industry. So it takes a lot of cant on both sides to polarize their present battle into a test of grassroots vs. nationwide bargaining. Even stranger, the showdown would not have developed at all if last year had not seen the fruition in the union camp of a merger for which the copper companies had long been hoping in the belief that it would help promote labor peace. This involved the absorption into the United Steelworkers of the 40,000-member international Union of Mine, Mill and Smelter Workers, which had been expelled from the old C.I.O. in 1950 on charges of Communist domination but which had successfully resisted a decade and a half of raids on its membership by the steel union.

The merger became official last July 1, but the end of inter-union rivalry did not bring the reduction of militancy which the employers had expected to accompany the wedding bells. On the contrary, the fact that the exiled Mine, Mill and Smelter Workers had been brought back into good standing in the House of Labor made it possible for the A.F.L.-C.I.O. to fasten on the copper industry as a prime target in its campaign for "coalition bargaining." This is a process under which a dozen or more unions with footholds in various units of a major industry join forces to increase their muscle in strikes and settlements.

The expiration of the first of the copper contracts in mid-July gave the federation the opportunity for applying the technique in copper, and the squeeze has spread as more and more contracts ran out. Higher wages and higher pensions have taken second place in the union priority scale to the establishment of company-wide bargaining agreements covering all unions with members in copper.

Labor considers this coordination a necessary answer to the flood tide of corporate mergers, especially the conglomerate mergers that tie together a hodge-podge of giant companies in unrelated industries. Kennecott is currently in the final stages of just such a merger, one that will bring the big Peabody Coal Company under its umbrella before the end of this month unless the antitrust authorities say no.

In the last two years inconclusive preliminary skirmishes in labor's coalition drive have been fought against such giant corporations as General Electric, Westinghouse and Union Carbide, but there has not yet been any final demonstration of either its effectiveness or its legality. Which is why the stakes are so high in the federation's declared intention to go for broke this time.

For all the doomsday atmosphere on both sides, however, there is nothing startlingly new about the idea of companywide bargaining. Indeed, it has been practiced for years by companies that dwarf the copper producers and that seem in no imminent peril of ending up in bankruptcy court. General Motors, Ford, Chrysler, Alcoa, American Can and many others negotiate a single basic contract for their production and maintenance employes. United States Steel, Bethlehem, Republic and eight other big steel-makers have an even more embracing unit: they bargain on an industry-wide basis.

So do the whole soft coal industry and what is left of hard coal, the iron ore mines, the railroads, the truck operators and the merchant marine. What differentiates all these negotiations from those being sought in copper, however, is that both the bargaining units and the bargaining agents have formal certification from the National Labor Relations Board. They do not represent an informal pooling of certifications won for different groups at different places in different branches of each company by 26 distinct unions.

It would be fatuous, though, to pretend that such legalisms are really what the fight is all about. The copper companies have studied the fruits of companywide bargaining in other places and they consider it bad for everybody but the union leaders. The industry's view is that local or regional agreements are particularly important for workers as well as management in companies like theirs that mine not only copper but also lead and zinc and that encompass such diverse enterprises as brass mills, scrap conversion plants, refineries and factories making everything from wire to plumbing fixtures.

More compelling still, in the industry's scale of values, is its certainty that companywide bargaining would quickly lead to the institutionalization of a uniform industry-wide strike date for all operations. And the conviction that this, in turn, would insure Government as a perpetual intervenor in the bargaining process— always on the union side. Management's fears on this score were reinforced last month when the Johnson Administration bypassed the no-strike injunction provisions of the Taft-Hartley Act and set up its short-lived fact-finding panel, a move the A.F.L.-C.I.O. had long urged.

Labor sees the vehemence of the industry's resistance to companywide negotiations as proof positive that the companies count on continued fragmentation to hold down pay scales and working conditions by playing one union off against another. "These public-be-damned, employe-be-damned corporations must be dragged belatedly kicking and screaming into the 20th century," proclaimed the A.F.L.-C.I.O. in a resolution unanimously adopted at its Florida convention in December.

Kermit Hoyt, an electric shovel operator, who is vice president of Steelworkers Local 5252 at the Ray mine, put it less luridly but a good deal more practically in the plywood union office in Kearny: "We got our first contract from Kennecott in 1955 and it covered just our members in the Ray mine," he recalled. "I know what it is to bargain against a giant when you are all alone. It is like an ant crawling up an elephant's leg."

That comes close to saying what the fight is about for most of the 15,000 Arizona strikers and the 45,000 who are striking with them in 22 other states. But each weary day of immobility makes it plain that, in the end, not much is likely to be decided.

The size of the money package no longer is in much doubt— an increase of about 95 cents an hour over the next three and a half years. The strikers themselves, for all the privations many of them have gone through at companies other than Phelps Dodge, are curiously detached about how much more goes into their pay checks. In one town after another, they grumble that prices go up faster than wages, no matter how big the package. They would like to see a cost-of-living escalator in the contract to keep their purchasing power steady. But most are much more interested in bigger pensions and in early retirement.

On the tougher question of companywide bargaining, worried Government officials in Washington search for a face-saver that will enable the men of power in labor and industry to retire from the battlefield with their dignity and press releases relatively unfractured.

While the peacemakers grope, the strikers molder in their society out of the Middle Ages and say with J. M. Patterson, a maintenance machinist at the Morenci powerhouse: "What's been lost, we'll never get it back, but it will help future generations." For most of them, that hope makes it all worthwhile. But it is at least as likely that what will finally evolve is a papering over of the issue that will settle everything by settling nothing—and both sides will limp away to fight another day.

La Huelga Becomes La Causa

by Dick Meister

SAN FRANCISCO.

"NEXT S.O.B. gets in my way, I run over." Truck drivers are notorious for idle threats, but this one, on the waterfront here, sounded as if he really meant it. Burly and unshaven, he jumped from his truck, slammed the cab door, and furiously thrust his hands deep into the pockets of his sheepskin jacket. He pounded his foot. "Move, dammit! Move!'

Fifteen weary men and women stared back. The 15 of them, swarthy farm workers and long-haired young activists, began singing "We Shall Overcome," then switched to Spanish: *"Nosotros venceremos . . . Nosotros venceremos . . ."* They waved crimson and black picket signs at the driver; they leaned, defiant if not calm, against the front bumper of his truck. But they would not move, not even if he did mean it. "Not after eight days, we won't move," declared one of the demonstrators.

For eight days last month, he and his fellow pickets had held back the truck, and more than a dozen others like it, all filled with table grapes which had been trucked 200 to 300 miles north from the magnificently fertile Central Valley of California for

San Francisco longshoremen to load onto ships bound for Manila, Saigon and other distant ports. The demonstrators would move, they vowed, only if the grape growers whose product was in the trucks in front of their picket line granted them what the long-shoremen who waited behind the picket line had won 34 years ago—union contracts, contracts that would give vineyard workers the economic protection guaranteed the country's urban workers.

They did not get any contracts from the grape growers. Instead, they got a court order that threatened them with jail unless they moved. It finally broke their waterfront blockade and sent tons of juicy California grapes off to the boys in Vietnam. "O.K., O.K.," said the infuriated but no less determined picket captain, a terribly intense young woman named Kathy Murguia. "If we can't stop grapes here, we'll stop them someplace else." And off went her band to a supermarket, to picket and to shout: "Don't buy grapes . . . don't buy grapes . . ."

The plea should sound familiar, for it is being sounded all over the country today. If it is not at a supermarket in San Francisco or a chilly pier on the city's waterfront, then it is outside a crowded supermarket in New York City, Boston or Detroit, at a school cafeteria, church, government office, Congressional hearing room or political rally.

The locales are a long way from the hot, dusty vineyards around Delano, Calif., the nondescript valley town of 12,000 inhabitants where grape pickers, most of them Mexican-Americans, called The Strike—*La Huelga*—in September, 1965. But Kathy Murguia and thousands of others—students, clergymen, politicians—have made the cry an essential part of the same struggle: the most successful effort yet in 50 years and more of futile efforts to organize farm workers and win them collective bargaining rights.

The development has been remarkable and swift. What started just a little more than three years ago as a barely noticed local strike quickly became a compelling social movement that has drawn together such diverse elements as the old left and the new, young activists and old-line union men, civil-rights organizations, religious groups and big industrial unions. This fall, it evolved into a national boycott as well—and a major political issue argued by

Presidential candidates. As remarkable as the movement is the man who has led it all—a uniquely gifted, truly charismatic figure named Cesar Chavez.

Ask a striker or boycott supporter why it happened and you're likely to draw an incredulous stare—and an angry question in return ("You ever try raising four kids on $1.50 an hour?"). Grape growers and their allies have different responses, often couched in language, not surprisingly, like that used by urban employers during the equally turbulent organizing drives by industrial unions in the nineteen-thirties. The growers, fearful of losing an almost unique upper hand in labor relations, will tell you it's primarily a move by "union bosses, radicals" and all manner of "outside agitators" to force their employes into something they neither want nor need. The harsh fact, nevertheless, is that vineyard workers share the plight of farm workers generally—working and living conditions that, in the words of the United States Senate Subcommittee on Migratory Labor, "must be recognized for what they are—a national disgrace." Most farm workers live, at best, in sterile, prisonlike compounds and, at worst, in crumbling shanties in rural slums, and have little voice in community affairs. Nor do they have much say on the job, where they may work 10 or 12 hours a day, six and seven days a week, often lacking such simple amenities as toilets and clean drinking water.

California's vineyard workers always have been better off than most farm workers. Their generally prevailing base wage of $1.50 an hour is higher than most, for instance, and, on some days, individuals can make two or even three times as much through piece rates that provide bonuses—generally 15 cents to 25 cents —for every box of grapes picked. Growers repeatedly point to these wages and the fact that vineyard workers are less migratory than most, and note that they have injury insurance and are covered by state housing, safety and sanitation regulations and, in some cases, by minimum-wage laws.

Yet the vineyard workers also average far less on a yearly basis than the $3,000 poverty-level figure (somewhere between $2,000 and $2,300, according to union figures), are lucky to find more than six months of work in any year, and are rare indeed if they can afford to keep their children from joining them in the vineyards. Overtime pay, paid holidays, vacations, sick leaves, pensions and unemployment-insurance benefits generally are denied them, and those few laws that are supposed to provide them some rudimentary protections are but laxly enforced. Practically nothing is guaranteed them; they can be fired at any time, for any reason.

In brief, says a strike leader: "The work is back-breaking, it is temporary, and it still leaves us almost at the bottom, standing ahead only of even more destitute farm workers in other states."

Now at least some of the vineyard workers want union bargaining rights—the weapon that has been dangled before them for so long as the only way to give them a voice in their own destinies. But here, too, the law has ignored them. Under the National Labor Relations Act, most industrial employers must bargain collectively with their workers if a majority of the workers prove they want to bargain, and then must sign a contract with the workers' union. But farm employers have managed, thanks in part to a powerful lobby, to remain exempt from the law since it was enacted in 1935.

That, in essence, is why the pickets are in front of the supermarkets. If the law will not make grape growers bargain, the pickets and their supporters hope they can, by shutting off sales of the growers' produce.

The pickets were not at the markets at the beginning, three years ago. They were lining back-country roads, outside the vineyards that sprawl over the 400 square miles where most of the country's grapes are grown, hidden from urban concern in the heartland of California's $4-billion-a-year farm industry. Although Mexican-Americans dominate the work force in the vineyards, as they do throughout California agriculture, it was another minority group that called the strike—a band of Filipinos under the banner of the A.F.L.-C.I.O.'s previously ineffective Agricultural Workers Organizing Committee. Within eight days, they were joined by the Mexican-Americans' independent National Farm Workers Association, and it immediately became certain that this was not to be a standard organizing attempt. Chavez, the brilliant, virtually self-educated leader of the Mexican-American group, would try it differently.

A glance makes clear this is a union leader seen but rarely in California's valleys: a stocky, sad-eyed, disarmingly soft-spoken man, shining black hair trailing over the edge of a face brushed with traces of Indian ancestry; a man who talks of militance in calm, measured tones, a soft trace of Mexico in the quiet voice; an incredibly patient man who hides great strategic talent behind shy smiles and an attitude of utter candor; a devout Roman Catholic.

Growers call Chavez "a dumb Mex . . . revolutionary . . . political opportunist . . . Trotskyite." But to his followers he is a messiah who inspires utter devotion. "Here was Cesar," recalls an eloquent but typical enthusiast, "burning with a patient fire, poor like us, dark like us, talking quietly, moving people to talk about their problems, attacking the little problems first, and suggesting, always suggesting—never more than that—solutions that seemed attainable. We didn't know it until we met him, but he was the leader we had been waiting for."

Chavez, starting out as a migratory worker from Yuma, Ariz., in the late nineteen-thirties, has been through what they have been through—in the vineyards, cotton fields and fruit orchards of Arizona and California—for most of his 41 years. He has seen the Anglo organizers come and go, the A.F.L. and C.I.O. men who have promised so much for so long, and he has learned from their failures.

Ten years with Saul Alinsky's Community Services Organization, first as an organizer in California's valley towns, then as national director at its Los Angeles headquarters, taught Chavez other valuable lessons about organizing his fellow Mexican-Americans. He does not march among them preaching the virtues of Samuel Gompers and trying to organize them as if they were so many Anglo plumbers. He tries to build from within—to let his people organize themselves, in their own way. "Grass roots with a vengeance," Chavez calls it.

To be successful, his union could not be "a neat business operation with no heart" that promised merely the negotiation of better wages, hours and working conditions in return for the payment of dues. Farm workers had seen too much of that kind of unionism. Their union would have to teach them the unified, self-directed action the outsiders never had taught. As Chavez says, they'd have to learn to do everything for themselves, "from the most mundane office work to the most sophisticated bargaining"—and their union would have to offer "programs which guarantee a new life."

It was slow going. Chavez, after resigning from the Community Services Organization in anger over what he saw as its lack of concern for the farm worker, settled in Delano in the early sixties with his wife, Helen, and their eight children. For three years preceding the strike, and while working in the vineyards himself, he patiently gathered a core of vineyard workers and their families into his association—more properly a combination community organization and civil-rights group, rather than a union. They formed their own credit union, where they could borrow the money they always seemed to need, and banded together to buy tires for their battered autos and to get other necessities at discount prices they could afford.

"I thought it would be four years, maybe five, before we'd be ready for a strike," says Chavez, "and I was really scared we might go too soon and get crushed." But the A.F.L.-C.I.O. group jumped the gun. It had won a 15-cents-an-hour increase in the then prevailing base wage of $1.25 from nearby growers during the early phase of the 1965 harvest season and, when its members moved into the Delano area vineyards, they demanded the same. Had they gotten it, that would have been that. But growers, fearful, they said, of weakening the incentive of pickers to go all-out for piece-rates bonuses, were adamant; they would not even discuss the demand.

The strike was on and, once on the picket lines, the strikers demanded far more than just higher base pay. They would settle for nothing less than the whole range of union rights: their pay, and everything else, would have to be negotiated by their own representatives and guaranteed in writing. Chavez held back for a few days, but his members were too eager. They were willing, if not as ready as they thought, to try the ultimate test—even if it meant, as it did, losing a $286,000 Federal antipovery grant their association had just won.

Chavez knew they could not do it alone. There were at least 5,000 vineyard workers in the strike area and probably no more than 300 local families in his association, perhaps 200 in the A.F.L.-C.I.O. group. Besides, growers, undeterred by law and able to recruit from a steady stream of migrants, would replace strikers as quickly as they left their jobs. It was essential that financing, manpower and pressures also come from elsewhere, through what Chavez calls "a strong, broad coalition of forces willing to throw their full weight into the battle." So, with perfect timing—this is the day of the civil-rights movement and the War on Poverty, after all—he immediately sought and won active outside support, from unions, minority and antipoverty organizations, students, political leaders, clergymen, and liberals and radicals generally.

The farm workers' economic battle quickly became a cause— a civil-rights movement with religious overtones as well as a strike. Outsiders flocked to the vineyards with money, food, clothing, tactical advice and picket signs; they made the strike headline news, and they split once-sleepy Delano, and eventually the entire state, into warring camps. "I'm here," announced an early arrival in clerical garb, "because this is a movement by the poor people themselves to improve their position, and where the poor people are, Christ should be, and is." Other supporters may have been less poetic, but all said much the same thing in their own way: This was part of their own battle against society's power structure.

Naturally, the power structure in Delano and elsewhere did not much care for "these outsiders," as a Delano housewife declared, "coming to our town and meddling in our affairs." Her attitude was shared by the growers, of course, and by the men who run the commercial, religious and governmental affairs of the little town whose economy they dominate. "There's no civil-rights problem here," said one, taking what has become a classic position, "and no wage problem either . . . and those pickers don't want a union; it's just an idea of Chavez and all those bleeding hearts. I think maybe the Communists got something to do with it, too."

The "bleeding hearts" persisted, nonetheless. Led by the Northern California Council of Churches, a Protestant group which adopted the strike as the main activity of its Migrant Ministry, they set up well-stocked commissaries in the strike area, ground out tons of propaganda, and personally pleaded with nonstrikers and others to join what had mushroomed from *"La Huelga"* into *"La Causa."* They solicited contributions all over the state; spoke at university rallies, church affairs, political gatherings and union meetings; petitioned legislators, and inspired lesser versions of their movement among farm workers and their allies in several other states. They demonstrated at the metropolitan headquarters of the larger growers and at markets that sold their grapes and grape products. They braved the threats of growers and armed guards who descended on their picket lines outside the vineyards; hundreds of them, clergymen included, eagerly went to jail to test stringent picketing regulations hastily drawn up by unsympathetic local officials.

Just six months after the strike began, they gathered, in March, 1966, nearly 10,000 strong, before the steps of the State Capitol in Sacramento, to demand "a new social order for the farm worker." There they met 80 strikers who had marched in a dramatic 25-day pilgrimage north from Delano, planting the seeds of their movement all along the 300-mile route. That was perhaps the most dramatic of the outsiders' activities, but it was not the last; they have continued the other activities, and much else, to this day, without a noticeable slackening of pace.

It often has been self-serving, inefficient and disorganized work the outsiders have performed; the wild distortions, and sometimes outright lies, of the single-minded, naive, uninformed and inexperienced partisans among them can be maddening. So can their impromptu style, especially to the well-programed men of organized labor who try to bring some method to it all. ("I love these people," remarked a top San Francisco union official. "But, God, they're like a bunch of hippies sometimes. They come bouncing down to a warehouse—all of a sudden like—and tell us, 'Quit unloading those scab grapes!' Hell, why don't they tell us these things in advance? We could arrange something.") But, if not always well done, the outsiders' activities have been absolutely essential; they have kept the effort from dying as so many farm organizing efforts before have died, from lack of public attention and support.

During this second phase, big labor's first serious notice came from Walter Reuther, who marched through the streets of Delano and outside the vineyards in a demonstration that made growers reconsider their wishful premise that this would be a standard, quickly abandoned farm strike. His United Auto Workers union, Reuther told cheering farm workers, would contribute at least $5,000 a month "for as long as it takes to win this strike." That was just before Christmas Day in 1965. Seven months later, the A.F.L.-C.I.O.—doggedly reluctant to put more than token financing into what had been a losing cause for so long, and hesitant over the unorthodox ways of the Mexican-Americans—nevertheless chartered Chavez's group as the United Farm Workers Organizing Committee, merged its own organizing committee into it, and made its efforts a major concern. William Kircher, the A.F.L.-C.I.O.'s strapping, bulldoglike director of organization, was dispatched to Delano on an almost full-time basis, backed by a monthly budget of $10,000 at the minimum (not counting the $3.50 a month in dues the union is getting sporadically from what it claims now to be 17,000 members throughout the country, and outside contributions of more than $250,000 a year).

Yet the growers have retained the upper hand; they have their own powerful allies within the state's business, financial and political hierarchies. However unprecedented, the concrete gains of the farm workers have been relatively slight: 11 contracts or union-recognition agreements from the 100 or so growers involved, covering only a few thousands of California's 300,000 farm workers; and, because of strike pressures, an increase of about 25 cents an hour in the base pay of most vineyard workers.

The pay of those under contract has gone up considerably more, to a base guarantee of as much as $2.55 an hour, returning what the union says is an average of more than $3 an hour including piece-rate bonuses. The contracts also provide some of the first employer-paid holidays, vacations, pensions and health-care services in the history of farm labor and, among other things, require growers to provide nonprofit housing, field toilets, drinking water and tools.

Most of the growers who have signed contracts raise wine grapes, and strikers hardly have touched the more numerous growers of table grapes—most especially not the largest grower of all: Joseph Giumarra, whose family-owned corporation oversees 5,000 acres of vineyards spread over two California counties. As many as 3,000 workers pick 52 million to 65 million pounds of grapes every year for Giumarra, bringing the corporation a gross return of anywhere from $5.5-million to $7.5-million. "If Giumarra the giant signs," reasons a hopeful union organizer, "the others will fall too." It is true, at any rate, that Giumarra is, if not the leader, then certainly a grower whose views and tactics are precisely those of most growers.

Joe Giumarra, a raw-boned, slight, gray-haired man of 69, is typical of California grape growers in other ways as well. He is an immigrant, a proud, independent man who still works a full day in his vineyards and who, like many table-grape growers, came to Delano from Southern Europe in the early nineteen-twenties, saved frugally, bought cheap parcels of land here and there, and then hit it big when subsidized Federal water began pouring into the area.

Strikers like to picture Joe Giumarra and his fellow growers as devils. They are not, but they do seem quaintly out of touch with what has been going on beyond the vineyards since they moved into the valley beside the Mexican-Americans three decades ago. They often seem sincerely perplexed that anyone would suggest farm workers need—or want—anything but what the *patron* grants them. *They* didn't need a union; they merely needed a chance to work hard.

Joe Giumarra doesn't talk much to interviewers. He leaves that to his nephew, John Giumarra, Jr., a young man typical of growers only in his views. John, a clean-cut 27-year-old Stanford Law School graduate who looks like a clean-cut Stanford Law School undergraduate, is a pleasant, eager and articulate advocate. The words roll out rapidly; John Giumarra knows what he wants to say, and he knows the grape business as well as any man in the country:

"Joe, my three other uncles and my father came over from Sicily—it was right after the first war. It was bad, believe me. The Italian Government needed money—foreign credit and that sort of thing. Confiscated everything. Even my grandmother's wedding ring—really! They started a little fruit stand in L.A. Sold what they grew up here—all through the Depression. Then . . . Well, there's 11 Giumarra families around here now, all of them on this farm. Over 50 people, and they all work here, every day. Except the kids, of course. They're in school."

Certainly, they have a multimillion-dollar corporation, he says, but they're on a slim margin, just like all the growers. "You're lucky to break even—and some years you can't even do that. Sure, you make it some years, but not by all that much." Take the $3 or so growers are being paid these days for the standard 26-pound lug of grapes. "The box alone costs 50 cents to 55 cents; then there's another, say, 70 cents for the picker. Then you've got property taxes, equipment, all sorts of growing costs. And the weather can kill you. It's like going to Las Vegas and rolling the dice—a very risky business. It's not easy like people think. . . ."

Even so, he says, the Giumarra Corporation "is willing to sit down with any responsible union." Chavez's organization, however, doesn't make the grade. It's "a rebel outfit that doesn't represent anybody." John Giumarra isn't sure the vineyard workers need a union, anyway. "You have to go slow-motion to get less than $2.10 an hour. And it doesn't matter where they live, they get free transportation. If they don't live around here, we give them a place to stay, too. Absolutely free." Nor is he sure the Giumarra Corporation can afford a union. "It's competition. Those other states don't pay farm workers like us . . . a union could drive the pay way out of line—the price too. Believe me, the consumer better look out." (He scoffs at Labor Department studies showing that labor costs amount to only 2 cents to 5 cents of every dollar spent by growers, and that even doubling current wages would add no more than a few cents a pound to the price.)

John Giumarra insists that his family's corporation actually has not been struck, anyway. He concedes that a strike was called, but, he says: "Our workers weren't willing to go on strike in favor of Chavez—that's why he called the boycott. If they did go on strike, they could have us at the bargaining table within a week. Our crop is perishable; it has to be harvested."

He voiced that argument as he stood outside the Delano High

School auditorium recently with other grower spokesmen who were boycotting a House subcommittee that was holding another of what have come to be seemingly endless hearings on the vineyard dispute. Inside the auditorium, Chavez, cheered on by 600 strikers who filled the seats behind him, attacked the logic of Giumarra's argument—one most growers utter at the drop of the words "strike" or "boycott."

Most of the pickers working in Giumarra's vineyard and in those of other struck growers, Chavez contended, are Mexican nationals brought here in massive numbers to replace his striking members during the harvest, as part of a work force of 350,000 nationals now working at various jobs in California. The nationals —and there are indeed an undetermined but comparatively large number in the vineyards—carry permits, commonly called "green cards," that allow them to live and work in this country without becoming citizens. They are supposed to live here permanently and are not supposed to replace strikers, but legally determining their residence status and what constitutes "strikebreaking" is a tricky matter. Chavez has demanded that the immigration laws be enforced strictly and that most of the "green-carders" be sent home to Mexico. The Labor Department and a group of liberal Democratic Congressmen have made similar demands of the Justice Department, but Giumarra and the other growers have held them off with assertions that their workers actually did not strike, or at least that those who did strike have abandoned the picket lines. Some assert as well that the "green-carders" actually began working for them before a strike was called.

In any case, there are Mexican nationals in the vineyards who, Chavez told the subcommittee, "can afford to work for much less than workers who maintain residence in our country . . . because the standard of living where they live is much lower." (And who, whether working legally or not, have little affinity with a locally based American union.) Jim Drake, a chunky, 30-year-old Protestant minister who serves as Chavez's administrative assistant, put it in harsher terms: "The growers are using the poorest of the poor of another country to defeat the poorest of the poor in this country. That's about as low as you can get."

Outside the auditorium, John Giumarra, Jr. showed his first

real sign of anger: "It's nothing but a damn lie!" Around the building, near the rear doors of the auditorium, a dozen or so grape pickers huddled in the shade. The men had the same dark, sinewy look as the men inside, and they, too, wore faded jeans and denim shirts; the women, chubby for the most part, wore, like those inside, floppy straw sombreros, loose, baggy slacks, and faded red kerchiefs knotted around their necks. But no, said one, who decided *someone* should talk to the reporters: "No, sir! We're working. We don't want anything to do with that damn Cesar. Nobody does—nobody that's a real worker, anyway. Look at me —I make $2.50 an hour. Who needs a union?"

They weren't afraid; they were going to march in and tell the subcommittee "the truth." Four of them did, echoing, in halting English, the words Giumarra was voicing rapid-fire outside the auditorium. (One woman, though, added a new element to the dialogue. She had heard, she told the subcommittee, that the union didn't favor children working in the fields. "How," she asked plaintively, "do they expect me to keep my 14-year-old out of trouble?")

How had the dissenters got to the auditorium? "Well," said a woman, "the boss came up to us in the field and asked us, 'You want to go to the high school and tell them the truth?' He brought us here in his own trucks, too. *Si, si*—right over there. . . ."

It may be the easy availability of strikebreakers; it may be a reluctance of marginal workers to risk what little they now have by walking off the job for an uncertain future: it may be that farm workers really do not want a union. But, whatever the reasons, orthodox strike activities, even in the unorthodox manner of Cesar Chavez, cannot do the job.

Thus the boycott. Chavez's union had used the tactic to win its first major contracts, in 1966 at the Schenley and DiGiorgio Corporations. Both came after national boycotts against the easily identified liquors of Schenley and canned goods of DiGiorgio (then including S&W Fine Foods, which the company subsequently sold). As Schenley vice president James Woolsey says, it wasn't the strike that brought his corporation to the bargaining table but "a threat of serious damage to our business on a nationwide scale . . . the adverse publicity generated against us."

The present boycott began last fall, with Giumarra's grapes as the sole target, at a time when farm-union organizers were at an apparent dead end. It did not improve their situation significantly, however. Then Chavez, following a superb instinct for the dramatic, and sincerely concerned that his members might turn to violence in their frustration, began a fast. It was to reaffirm, he said, a commitment to the Gandhian principles of nonviolence that had guided him from the beginning.

There had been no serious violence in the vineyard dispute, despite a spate of minor attacks and extreme provocations for which union and grower forces blamed each other, but there was a danger that Chavez, emerging as a Martin Luther King of the newly aroused Mexican-American, would be supplanted by men from the Southwest who preached a "brown power" version of the black militants' call to arms. The frustration hit its peak when the strike was extended to the nearby Coachella Valley this spring and Chavez became convinced that "someone would hurt someone." The pickets were removed from the Coachella area; Chavez announced that "no union movement is worth the life of one farm worker and his child or one grower and his child," and retired to a private retreat, to fast, pray, and read the Bible and the writings of Gandhi.

After 25 days, he broke the fast in March, before 4,000 supporters at an ecumenical mass in Delano's city park. Senator Robert F. Kennedy was at Chavez's side as he slumped in a chair set up on a flatbed truck and nibbled feebly at a tiny bit of bread handed him by a priest. Senator Kennedy took a portion from the same home-baked loaf, then hailed Chavez as "one of the heroic figures of our time" and congratulated those who were "locked with Cesar in the struggle for justice for the farm worker and the struggle for justice for Spanish-speaking Americans."

Chavez feels that by his fast he managed to turn his followers from the path which militants everywhere else seem to be skirting: "It made our nonviolent position clear; everyone can understand it now, both ourselves and our adversaries." The ordeal eventually sent Chavez to a hospital where he lay immobilized for three weeks. Even now, he still must spend most of his time in bed, although he has resumed full direction of the union.

Chavez's fast focused national attention on Delano again, and the unbending growers of table grapes began feeling pressure. Swiftly, the Giumarra-only boycott was expanded to include the grapes of all the growers. In one way, the growers brought it on themselves, by allowing Giumarra to use their labels on some of the containers the corporation shipped to market, in an attempt to hide them from strikers. But they would have been involved anyway; the union was faced with nearly insurmountable problems in trying to single out one grower among many who shipped grapes to the same stores. "It was the only way we could do it— take on the whole industry," says Chavez. "The grape itself had to become a label."

The boycott soon became the main activity of strikers and their allies. By now, the vineyard picket lines have been all but abandoned. Some strikers actually have returned to work, to ease the strain on their union's treasury, and about 200 of them and their families have been sent off, on union salaries of $5 a week, to more than 30 cities in this country and Canada to wage probably the most extensive boycott in American labor history.

Backed by their allies' muscle and financing, strikers are demanding that markets, school cafeterias, city agencies and other buyers and sellers of food quit handling grapes or face picketing, demonstrations and the opposition of the strikers' influential supporters. The supporters have made their own forays into many other communities, as far abroad as Western Europe, and many stores have gone along with the demands (so many thousands, says Chavez, that "we can't begin to count them"; growers "can't count them" either, but feel Chavez is guilty of gross exaggeration —"as usual," most of them add).

Some large universities also have joined the boycott and even a few school districts. The union-oriented mayors of a half-dozen major industrial cities, including New York, have ordered municipal purchases cut off. Also, the nation's chief religious organizations, Catholic, Protestant and Jewish, have asked their millions of members to bypass grapes.

In New York, where California growers normally sell about 20 per cent of their table-grape crop, sales dropped by 90 per cent at one point this summer. Shippers were forced to put grapes in cold storage or ship them to other areas—where the resulting surplus drove prices down (some grower sources estimate the summer boycott activities cost growers $2-million to $2.5-million).

Grape sales have picked up recently, however, and Alan Mills of the growers' Grape and Tree Fruit League claims that, by now, the bulk of the 1968 crop has been harvested, sold to wholesalers and shipped out of the vineyard area. He acknowledges there were some problems, but insists "they were problems that were overcome." Chavez is no more precise in his estimate of the boycott's concrete effects, although he insists that "prices are shot to hell" and that sales are down 50 per cent in major Eastern marketing areas.

It is obvious that growers are being hurt, although it is impossible to measure the specific harm. Prices are down compared with 1967 and, although the over-all volume of grape shipments actually is above last year, so is the tonnage of grapes being stored for future sale. How much of this is the result of a heavier crop this year and how much the result of the boycott can only be speculated on at this point; sales between now and February should tell the story.

One thing is clear: growers, who once talked as if Chavez's union didn't exist, are worried about what the California Farm Bureau Federation is calling "one of the greatest threats ever to face our state's agriculture." They are spending thousands of dollars on a nationwide advertising and public-relations campaign that urges us to "feel better in all respects" by "buying and enjoying fresh California grapes," and are bringing their own considerable pressures to bear on food-store owners and public and church officials, in part through newspaper editorialists, chambers of commerce and other business groups.

Growers also have filed damage suits for millions of dollars against some of the industrial unions that have helped in the boycott, charging them with violating the law against secondary boycotts. (Ironically, the law does not cover farm workers because of their exclusion from the National Labor Relations Act.) "Their hearts are with us," noted a disgruntled picket as she watched a group of previously cooperative teamsters unloading grapes in front of a picket line in San Francisco the other day, "but their bread and butter is elsewhere. They don't want to be sued." The legal action has indeed made the unions cautious—especially in New York City, where they have backed off from picketing and other pressures that made the boycott so successful there this summer.

Chavez's union nevertheless has scored a significant victory. The boycott finally has made its cause a major national issue; it has forced politicians to take sides. During this year's election campaign, Vice President Humphrey, Senator Eugene McCarthy and other liberal Democrats, following the early lead of Senator Kennedy, repeatedly voiced their support of the boycott and its aim of winning bargaining rights for farm workers. Republicans, led by Richard Nixon and Gov. Ronald Reagan of California, generally opposed the grape pickers' efforts (with the major exception of Senator Jacob Javits in New York).

McCarthy was the first to raise the issue when, during the primaries, he declared that the grape boycott should be supported by "all those who are concerned with human dignity and determined to lift poverty from our land." Humphrey followed with a similar statement. "As more people know that the boycott is almost your only effective organizing device," he told Chavez's union, "more and more will support it." (Ed Muskie must not have been listening; long after his running mate had delivered that statement, he told a group of astounded California reporters that he hadn't even heard of the boycott.) Mr. Nixon was silent until after the national party conventions. Then he spoke out against the boycott, and at a California campaign rally gleefully plopped grapes into his mouth.

This is a crucial development, for political action is essential to Chavez's strikers. Like the industrial workers of the nineteen-thirties, they need the protection of the National Labor Relations Act to allow them to win what they are struggling for on the picket line by simply casting a ballot in a union election or signing a union authorization card, and they need a law to protect them from "green card" strikebreakers.

A growing number of Congressmen have been speaking out in favor of granting legal bargaining rights to farm workers, if only as a way to ease the pressures of the boycott and demonstrations.

But counterpressures from the White House—now that Mr. Nixon has been elected—probably will be enough to keep Congress from acting, at least in the near future.

Even Chavez's most enthusiastic Congressional supporters feel this way. Representative Phillip Burton of California concedes, for instance, "We don't have a prayer now—not in the next Congress anyway." Chavez agrees, and fears, in fact, that Mr. Nixon will launch legal counterattacks on the vineyard strikers and their boycott. "We're going to get the business," says Chavez. "There's no question about that."

Nevertheless, there is a definite political trend in the farm workers' direction, and one that seems unstoppable. The election undoubtedly will slow the pace. But, although the drive to grant farm workers the legal rights held by most other Americans who work for a living may be with us for a much longer time than its supporters had hoped, it apparently is here to stay. Politicians who once discussed the "farm problem" solely in terms of such cold and complex matters as parity and soil banks will have to talk as well of farm workers. Chavez and his grape pickers will not let them do otherwise; they have brought their struggle out from isolated vineyards and into the mainstream of American economic and political life; they have laid a solid foundation for farm unionization, and they are not about to quit.

"With or without a law we will continue to struggle," promises Cesar Chavez. Suddenly, the shy smile that has driven once supremely self-sure growers to distraction creases the dark face. "They said we couldn't do what we're doing, didn't they? Well, we're doing it, aren't we?" The tone remains soft, almost childlike, but the fleeting grin passes. "Sure, we know it will take time. But when we win in Delano, we'll win everywhere; we're fighting the strike of the century for our people.

"How can I say it without sounding presumptuous? Really, it's a nonviolent fight to the death. They destroy our union or we conquer them. We'll take them on everywhere, wherever there are grapes—anywhere. Any way we can do it, we'll do it. There's no turning back now."

Part 5

LABOR TODAY

WHERE AMERICAN workers and their unions stand today and what the future may hold for them are questions beyond the historian's purview. Still, the following selections offer a selective impression of the situation of the American worker and his unions as this book goes to press.

Speaking in August 1969, George Meany by and large takes satisfaction in the progress of the American labor movement and its workers since the Great Depression. Not unaware of labor's problems or the less than perfect nature of prosperity, Meany nevertheless seems gratified by what he describes as the middle-class, suburban orientation of American workers. The news dispatch from Flint, Michigan, on Labor Day, 1969, substantiates Meany's thoughts, as it portrays auto workers, generally unmindful of the turbulent 1937 sit-down strike that built their union, about to leave in their cars (many with attached house trailers or boats) for a weekend of camping and fishing. Auto workers, as well as plumbers, had apparently become contented members of a consumer society in which, despite the dissatisfactions associated with work itself, their wages enabled them to enjoy objects once reserved for the middle and upper classes. Finally, the report on the demonstration in New York City during which hard-hat construction workers attacked and beat citizens protesting the war in

Vietnam (while the police looked on passively) offers additional support to Meany's image of union members: workers who are basically satisfied with their society and more devoted to its defense than many other citizens.

Yet, for many American workers as 1969 passed into 1970, Meany's picture of a prosperous, suburban, middle-class working class grew blurred. Once again from 1969 through 1970 unemployment rose appreciably, and by December 1970 affected almost 6 per cent of the work force. During the same period wages failed to keep pace with prices, resulting in 1969 and 1970 in the most serious wave of major strikes since 1946. Some of the difficulties still endured by American workers are described in the news story of July 4, 1970, assessing unemployment around the nation.

An Interview
with George Meany

by Damon Stetson

GEORGE MEANY has expressed alarm at inflation's continuing toll
and has said that the only way to stop it is by controls—not only
on wages but on prices, profits and dividends as well.

The burly, outspoken A.F.L.-C.I.O. president, who was 75
years old on Aug. 16, made it clear that he was not advocating
controls but said unequivocally that the imposition of "legal controls" was the only method that could end the current inflationary
cycle.

In a rare and far-ranging interview in his Washington office,
which looks across Lafayette Park to the White House, Mr. Meany
reminisced about his long career in the labor movement and pronounced the movement in better condition than ever, while ac-
knowledging that it had become more conservative and middle
class than in its more militant years.

Mr. Meany did not comment specifically on the recent marches
and demonstrations in Pittsburgh and Chicago where Negro activists have been pressing for job opportunities in the construction
trades. But when asked about the problem of bringing in the poor

and the Negroes so that they, too, could "own a house and have a piece of the action," he did speak critically of black militants.

"We face it," he said, "by doing what we have always done and we continue our constructive work. As far as the black militants are concerned, some of them I don't think want improvement. I think they want the issue. I think they want to be militant. I think they want to demonstrate.

"I don't know what I can do for them, but as far as the black, nonwhite minority is concerned, there is no question that they still have a long way to go—but there is no question that they have come a long way. The statistics will show that.

"Of course, the militants say, we don't want to know what happened last year, we don't want to know how much improvement, we don't want to know how many black families are now in certain levels—and this is going up all the time. Any corporation in America that sells to the general public that have something to sell, they will tell you—they are paying attention to the black market because the black market is getting more and more ability to buy all the time. They are going up.

"But the black militants don't want to hear about that. They don't want to know what happened yesterday or the day before. They want sort of instant solutions for all these problems. And, of course, they are not going to get it."

Dressed in a light gray suit and blue shirt, Mr. Meany sat in a relaxed fashion, smoking his habitual cigar, as he talked last Thursday for 90 minutes with five labor reporters whom he had known for several years. In a rambling discussion that went all the way from his days as a union plumber in New York to his current concern about inflation, he made these major points:

¶Former President Johnson did more for the working man than any other President he has known, including Franklin D. Roosevelt.

¶It is too early to draw conclusions about President Nixon, although he has done things "to warm the cockles of [Senator] Strom Thurmond's heart" and other things that civil rights people think are "all right." The President's tax position and welfare approach have been pluses for labor.

¶Senator Edward M. Kennedy has been hurt "badly" by the

recent accident that killed a secretary and is "too young" for the Presidency anyway. Senator Edmund S. Muskie has "great possibilities" and Hubert H. Humphrey would welcome "another shot" at the Presidency.

¶Walter P. Reuther, president of the United Automobile Workers, did not have the justification that the late John L. Lewis had in splitting the labor movement. Mr. Reuther was more interested in heading the American Federation of Labor and Congress of Industrial Organizations than in putting over the program that he failed to promote while in the federation.

¶The Congress of Industrial Organizations formed by Mr. Lewis in the mid-thirties was a "shot in the arm" for the labor movement. But the A.F.L.-C.I.O. today is moving, is not decadent and does not need a shot in the arm.

¶Always a hawk on Vietnam, the labor leader said he had not changed his mind.

In his comments on the problem of inflation, Mr. Meany said that high profits and prices, land costs and skyrocketing interest rates, rather than wage increases, were mainly responsible for the rise in the cost of living. He expressed doubt that the monetary and fiscal policies the Administration was using would solve the problem.

Asked whether there was any voluntary way by which labor and industry could place some restraint on wage settlements, Mr. Meany said that the answer would have to come from leaders of big unions such as the United Steelworkers and the auto workers.

"I know they wouldn't buy wage controls unless it was a national emergency, unless the President said that our commitments overseas were such that we had to have this," he said. "Then they would buy wage controls and we repeatedly have said this, that we would take wage controls if the President thinks this is necessary, providing there are controls of all the other elements that go into the economy. This would include profits, income of all sorts."

Nothing stops the big corporations when they want to invest for expansion—even high interest rates and repeal of the 7 per cent tax credit, Mr. Meany said.

"They don't let anything get in their way," he said. "If they want to expand, and the figures for expansion of the big corporations in America—I just saw a report today—are still doing what they were doing a year ago. They are still going up. Now, the whole idea of this Arthur Burns [counsel to the President] and Dave Kennedy [Secretary of the Treasury] plan and this high interest rate was to cool it—bring it down and stop this. Well, it hasn't stopped it."

Mr. Meany repeatedly turned aside any suggestions that today's labor leaders were out of tune with the younger generation or not responsive to the rank and file. He chided labor critics who thought they knew better than labor what was good for labor.

He said that he did not bother trying to determine whether the rank and file was behind the leadership but rather acted on the basis of "what happens in the organization."

"I am not looking over my shoulder to see if the rank and file is following," he went on. "I am quite sure that if we are doing things the rank and file don't want, we will learn it in the very same way as we find out about the things that they do want. . . . All of these things come up through the labor movement."

Mr. Meany said the domestic challenges for labor were the same ones that were facing the American people, including the rising cost of living, civil rights, pollution and consumer problems.

Following are excerpts from an interview with George Meany, president of the American Federation of Labor and Congress of Industrial Organizations, which was held last Thursday in his office in Washington:

Q. Would you say that the labor movement is in better or worse condition this Labor Day than all the others that you can recall?

A. I think the movement is in better condition than it ever was. When I look back, it is hard really to realize the progress that is being made when you are so close to it, but if you take a leap back a few years and try to think of what was going on then—for instance, this business of welfare funds and pension and holidays with pay—this was a dream at one time. This is now accepted as commonplace. People say, well, we have so many paid holidays, vacations with pay and we have got pensions and hospitalization and welfare. You say, so what, everybody has got it. But I remember a time when this was unthought about.

Q. The laboring man has become middle class, has advantages that he didn't have before, more conservative than he was. Some people think that labor people now—leaders—are out of tune with the generation.

A. Actually I think the labor leaders are out of tune with the people who feel that they know better than labor does what is best for labor. We have always had that type of people. We have people who are constantly worrying about the lack of militancy on the part of labor. Labor, to some extent, has become middle class. When you have no property, you don't have anything, you have nothing to lose by these radical actions. But when you become a person who has a home and has property, to some extent you become conservative. And, I would say to that extent, labor has become conservative. I don't think there is any question of that. But, at the same time, the programs of the trade union movement—the things we lived for—there is nothing conservative about that. We still want to break through with new ideas.

Q. How do you assure that the rank and file—the man and woman in the home in the suburb—is behind the leadership as you look for new areas of . . .

A. I don't. I go by what happens in the organization. For instance, when you say the rank and file who owns a home—he might not have attended a union meeting for 10 years. So he is pretty hard to reach. But still you will find that from his union, from the local union level, these problems come into the movement and I am not looking over my shoulder to see if the rank and file is following. I am quite sure that if we are doing things the rank and file don't want, we will learn it in the very same way as we find out about the things that they do want.

Q. In other words, you are doing what you think is right and good for the labor movement.

A. Yes, and doing it on the basis of what we know about the labor movement. The heads of the trade union movement and the so-called liberals that were on the fringe of the movement, they didn't go off into a smoke-filled room, as you say, and come up with the idea that workmen's compensation is a good thing. That isn't the way it happened. Workmen's compensation came right out of the shop.

I don't think about what the rank and file wants because I know I will hear what they want. I don't go searching out and hold a referendum here and a referendum there because these things have a way of coming to the trade union structure.

Q. What is the answer, Mr. Meany, to bringing in today's militant groups—the poor and the black and others—so that they own a house and they have a piece of the action and perhaps are less militant and stop creating the same kind of disturbances that labor perhaps once had created?

A. What is the answer to bringing them in? I don't know what you mean.

Q. How do we face this particular problem?

A. We face it by doing what we have always done and we continue our constructive work. As far as the black militants are concerned, some of them I don't think want improvement. I think they want the issue. I think they want to be militant. I think they want to demonstrate. I don't know what I can do for them but as far as the black, non-white minority is concerned, there is no question that they still have a long way to go—but there is no question that they have come a long way.

They are going up. But the black militants don't want to hear about that. They don't want to know what happened yesterday or the day before, they want sort of instant solutions for all these problems. And, of course, they are not going to get it.

Q. There seems to be no doubt that a great many young people are either suspicious of the labor movement or downright openly hostile to it. How can the labor movement expect to have much of a future if that feeling is as wide as it seems to be?

A. I don't know and I don't spend any time worrying about it because I don't think there is any justification for it.

Q. You don't think there should be some special steps to awaken the interest of the young people in the labor movement?

A. No.

Q. Some labor statisticians of late have been proving that workers are on a treadmill, that they are not really getting any place. What do you think about the state of collective bargaining? Is it really working?

A. This doesn't represent a failure of collective bargaining at all. In fact, this shows that by the collective bargaining process, at least he is keeping pace with the treadmill. He is not gaining anything, maybe he is losing a little bit, but if he didn't have collective bargaining, where would he be?

Q. Secretary [of Labor George P.] Shultz has been making quite a case in recent public statements to the effect that unions should not make the basic assumption that inflation is a condition that is going to persist forever and that sooner or later there is going to be a downturn and if they continue to negotiate these high-cost contracts, they are going to be pricing the guy who they work for out of the market, and also their own labor out of the market. What do you think of that line of thinking?

A. I don't buy it. I think there is some logic to it. But let me say this: If Shultz was the head of a big steelworkers union and made those sort of observations to his members, he wouldn't be the head of that union next year. Now this is a very practical situation.

Q. What is the answer to inflation? How are we going to stop it? Controls on everything?

A. The only way you are going to stop it—and I am not advocating this, but you are asking me and I can only go by my experience and I don't pretend to be an expert but I do have some experience—the only way you are going to stop it is by controls.

Q. Legal controls?

A. Legal controls. And we will not accept legal controls unless they control all forms of income, prices, dividends, profits and everything else.

Q. Do you think it is coming to that, Mr. Meany?

A. I don't know. I hope not, but you ask how do I see the end. I don't see the end to this.

Q. That statement yesterday over at Commerce [Assistant Secretary William H. Chartener] wasn't very encouraging, was it, George?

A. I don't see the end of this. You see, if Dave Kennedy is right and the President is right and Arthur Burns is right, we should be seeing the end to this within a few months. If they are right. I hope, I don't know. You see, this high interest rate and the squeeze, this is supposed to cut down the demand for money and it is supposed to cool the economy.

Q. Would the labor leader who is being pressed for bigger raises by his members have been better off if the Nixon Administration kept a voluntary guide post on wages and prices as some argument to use against his own members?

A. I suppose so, but most of the people that go to the bargaining table try to think in terms of satisfying their members. I think this is only natural.

Q. Is there any voluntary way you can work it out between labor and industry to resume some restraint on wage settlement?

A. The fellows who have this responsibility directly—I don't have it directly—wouldn't buy wage controls unless it was a national emergency, unless the President said that our commitments overseas were such that we had to have this.

Q. Looking way ahead, philosophically, where is the labor movement going to end up?

A. The labor movement isn't going to end up. It is going to keep on whirling along.

Q. After all these years in the labor movement, are you able to look back and reflect and say if things had been different you would have preferred to do something else other than what you have done?

A. No, if I look back, I don't know of anything else I would prefer doing. I don't know of anything that could ever possibly have given me the excitement, if you want to put it that way, the interest or the satisfaction.

Q. What stands out as you look back on this career of yours in the labor movement?

A. Five years as head of New York State Federation of Labor [1935–1939] when they put more legislation on the statute books of that state in favor of labor than had ever been put on in any period before or since by any other state union.

Q. How were you able to do that?

A. I worked hard but I was damn lucky. I was very lucky. I came in there at the Depression. It is an amazing thing how the

attitude of a state legislature toward labor could be influenced by a
depression. I put 72 new laws on the statute books in one year,
1935, out of a program of 112 bills. But I had a governor who
was without parallel in my book in the field of public service:
Herbert Lehman.

Q. Which President do you think has done the most for the
working man while you have been watching things?

A. Johnson.

Q. Are you including Roosevelt with this?

A. Yes. You are talking about quantity and quality of the two.
Now, of course, Roosevelt couldn't possibly have done what Johnson has done because there were different times. Johnson couldn't
have done what he did if there hadn't been a Roosevelt before
him. It was a difference of 30 years.

Q. What about Nixon? Can you size that up yet?

A. Well, I have been trying and waiting and up to the present
time, I just can't size it up. He seems to come out with statements,
he has a little bit for everybody. He has got some for people on
each side. He has certainly done things to warm the cockles of
Strom Thurmond's heart and, at the same time, he has been doing
things that the civil rights people think are all right, too, in certain
areas.

Q. You say something for everybody. What has he given labor?

A. Well, I think that some of the things on his tax position
were favorable. I think as far as the common people, merely by
opening up this welfare thing with the statement from the highest
level, the White House, I think this was a great plus. That doesn't
mean I agree with the remedies he proposes, but the mere fact
that he said this business has got to be overhauled, it is out of
date, it is bad and so forth, I think this will be helpful.

Q. Are you with him on Vietnam now?

A. I haven't changed my mind on Vietnam. I think that we
made a commitment there. I think it is unfortunate the way we
got into it. I don't see how we can get out of it unless we can, in
some way, insure that this area is not going to fall over, one
country after another, to the Communists. I can't see anything
that changes my theory that, if they take Vietnam, they will keep
going. They will take Laos, Cambodia and they will be knocking

at the doors. I wasn't a critic of Johnson on this war and I certainly am not going to be a critic of what Nixon inherited. But I think Johnson inherited it. Now, frankly, I think Nixon would like to get out of this war.

I know Johnson would have done almost anything within his power to get out of this war except surrender and withdraw unilaterally. And I don't think Nixon will do that.

Q. Do you object to his present steps of kind of disengaging?

A. No. I do not. That part of the war I had better leave to the strategists. I am not a military strategist. I know something about international communism. I know that it has got to feed on this sort of thing.

Q. What do you think labor's program, looking ahead, has got to be in the next few years? What are some of the major challenges that are confronting the A.F.L.-C.I.O. labor generally?

A. Any number of things. I think this inflation thing is a real problem. I think we have got a long way to go before we can say that the job is done in the field of civil rights. And I think something that we talk about more and more is becoming more and more important and that is the question of how do we live in this country, what happens to our air and our water. This is a tremendous threat.

Q. On a broader basis, Mr. Meany, what kind of a situation does the formation of the A.L.A. [Alliance for Labor Action] present? Does it indicate perhaps some splitting of the labor movement?

A. That's the purpose of it. Whether it succeeds or not, I don't know. I don't see signs of any great success. This is history repeating itself. We had this back in 1934 and 1935 [when John L. Lewis formed the rival Congress of Industrial Organizations].

Q. Would you carry the comparison to the next logical step and say that [Walter] Reuther, like [John L.] Lewis, was interested only in splitting [labor by forming the A.L.A.]?

A. I think that he [Reuther] is interested only in being head of an organization. He would like it to be the whole thing, in other words as many as he can.

Q. Do you think Reuther could have done better if he stayed inside instead of going alone?

A. Oh yes. By far.

Q. Looking back, do you think the C.I.O. helped the labor movement by pepping things up?

A. Yes. The formation of the C.I.O.—and I don't think Lewis had this in mind, I don't think Lewis even thought about it—the formation of the C.I.O. was a shot in the arm to the labor movement.

Q. The next question of course is will the A.L.A. . . .

A. We don't need a shot in the arm. No, you see this is not a decadent organization. This is an organization that is moving, moving all the time into everything. We are in more activities now than I ever thought would be part of the routine work of the trade union movement.

Q. How damaging is it, Mr. Meany, to have a split at this time with the social issues?

A. I don't know. It certainly isn't strengthening the organization. After all, if the A.L.A. believes in the things it believes in, they believe in a lot of the things we believe in and there shouldn't be any difference of opinion. There shouldn't be any difference of opinion, for instance, on legislation.

Q. Can you look ahead, since you have seen the cyclical nature of these things in the past, to the rejoining of this element at some distant date to the federation?

A. I don't know. It took 20 years the last time. I don't want to look ahead that far.

Q. What essentially beat [Vice President] Humphrey [in the 1968 Presidential election]?

A. Oh, I think what beat Humphrey really was the lack of a party machine. He didn't have a party machine.

Q. You substituted for the party machine.

A. We substituted to whatever extent we could.

Q. What do you think about [Senator Edward M.] Kennedy?

A. I feel that this is a very unfortunate thing that happened up there. I don't know what the facts are and I am certainly not going to pass judgment on him, but looking at it from the point of view of the stark naked facts of political life, I think the thing has hurt him badly.

Q. For good?

A. Oh, I don't know. Who can say? As of now, I think it has hurt him very badly because I think what the average person feels is that no matter what happened, when it did happen, he sort of panicked. He practically says that himself.

Q. Aside from the merits of that, George, what do you think about his qualifications for the presidency?

A. I think he is too young. I think he needs a good deal more experience. I was certainly a great admirer of John Kennedy but I don't think being the brother of a President is, in itself, any qualification at any time. I think Teddy works harder as Senator. I think he has done a good job for the people of Massachusetts. But I feel that he needs a whole lot more experience before he could convince me that he has the qualifications of President of the United States.

Q. What about [Senator Edmund S.] Muskie?

A. I think Muskie made a lot of progress and drew a lot of attention as the Vice Presidential candidate. I don't know. I think Muskie has great possibilities. I think Hubert would certainly welcome another shot.

Q. Would you welcome his welcoming another shot?

A. I don't know. I wouldn't want to make the decision on that. I surely was very much for him. If he was the candidate in 1972, I suppose he would get a lot of support from our people. But I think it is a little too early.

Labor Day 1969: Affluence and Quiet

by William Borders

FLINT, MICHIGAN.

THE LABOR DAY weekend is passing quietly in Flint this year, with no speeches and no parades.

There used to be plenty of both, as workers from the General Motors plants that dominate this industrial city gloried in the successes that made Flint in the 1930's a nationwide symbol of the strength of organized labor.

"Those were the days right after we, the workers, conquered G.M., and we stood proud," recalled 76-year-old Lloyd E. Metiva, who helped stack up engine parts to block the doors of the Buick plant here during the crucial sitdown strike of 1937.

This quiet little city 60 miles northwest of Detroit is still very much a union town, with one out of every four residents a member of the United Automobile Workers of America.

But in Flint, as in many other American cities where unions have flourished, organized labor these days has gone into a second generation, and old attitudes have changed.

The American Federation of Labor and Congress of Industrial Organizations has found that 46 per cent of the nation's union members earn between $7,500 and $15,000 a year. Of the union members under 40, about 75 per cent now live in the suburbs.

Nearly half of the union members are 39 or younger—too young to remember the days before the sitdown strikes and, as Mr. Metiva puts it, "the youngsters don't care what we cared about."

As union leaders all over America are discovering, there is less loyalty to the old causes. George Meany, president of the labor federation, acknowledged the other day that labor "to some extent has become middle class."

Explaining why such tactics as the sitdown strike had become passé, he said:

"When you have no property, you don't have anything, you have nothing to lose by these radical actions. But when you become a person who has a home and has property, to some extent, you become conservative."

Instead of marching in parades or singing about solidarity, the workers of Flint preferred to spend this sunny weekend playing golf or vacationing at lake resorts in the cool pine forests, to the north.

The union has won prosperity for them, and many have moved from downtown Flint to pleasant tracts far from town.

Often they have taken their loyalties with them, leaving the union "stung by its own success," as one official here put it. The membership, which is now financially comfortable, tends to eschew many of the union's liberal goals and to consider the bloody sitdown strikes of 1937 as simply a moment in history.

Those strikes, in which National Guardsmen patrolled Flint with machine guns and 14 union men were shot, were a turning point in trade union history because they won for labor the organization of the automobile industry.

Describing company attempts to starve the workers out of one Fisher Body plant that they had seized here, a union newspaper wrote at the time:

"When outside strikers came with food for the evening meal, they found the door blocked. They began passing it through the windows. Guards attempted to prevent that. A teargas bomb went through the window.

"Then came the first shot! A striker fell. Police were firing into the crowd. Union sympathizers were retaliating with the only means of defense they had—stones, lumps of coal, steel hinges, milk bottles."

But that was 1937, and W. W. Wilson, who now earns $3.68 an hour spraying paint on Buicks, had not even been born yet.

"I can't really care that much about the sitdowns and all," 29-year-old Mr. Wilson said as he began the three-day weekend with a beer in Ethel's Bar, a squat brick building across the street from the huge Fisher plant, where he has worked since 1962.

"That's when I came up from North Carolina. I was making $1.25 there, unskilled. Now I still have got no skills, but I can live the life of an average class person."

Benefits Already Won

"I'll admit the reason we don't care so much about the union is that we've already got all those benefits, and, sure, they're benefits that this guy fought for," said Mr. Wilson, gesturing down the bar toward an older man who had just told him, with some heat, "You're getting twice what I got when I was a kid."

Mr. Wilson, and others who think as he does, would rather toss a baseball with his son in the back yard than lounge around the union hall, and the result is that the halls that dot this city are seldom the scene of dances or bull sessions any more, and most of them are open only during regular business hours.

"The union used to be like a church, and you'd do everything, even social things, together," said a concerned U.A.W. official in Flint. "But now, everyone's got their cars, and it's easy, for example, to drive to the ball game in Detroit on your own, so they think, why go together in a bus?"

Last Friday—outside the plants where the first generation of union men here bloodied the heads of strikebreakers in a struggle for job security—cars were parked with boats already tied to the top, so their owners could get a quick start on fishing trips at the end of the shift.

Others in the plant were picked up in campers or station wagons by well-dressed wives who had already packed up the children for what was, to these families, the last weekend of summer rather than a holiday to celebrate the dignity of labor.

The new rank-and-file conservatism of organized labor in Flint takes many forms, and some of them are causing deep distress among union leaders trained in automatic allegiance to certain progressive goals.

Although virtually no one here contends that they would ignore a strike call, the modern young members of the auto union often care more about suburban school taxes and the sanctity of their neighborhoods than they do about workmen's compensation or the union shop.

"I don't even know what the minimum wage is nowadays, but pulling down $3.54 an hour myself, I guess it's not too important to me," said Dennis Comstock, a curly-haired 29-year-old truck driver at Fisher.

He said that he had "never experienced a hard time, like the old guys did."

Says Unionists Forget

In a survey two years ago, the labor federation found that 75 per cent of the American union members under the age of 40 were living in the suburbs, often with a different point of view from the city dweller or from the trade union orthodoxy.

Civil rights, for example, is a goal that labor traditionalists talk a great deal about. But 12 per cent of Flint voted for George C. Wallace for President last year, and in some neighborhoods the percentage was 20 or 30.

The union leadership, in fact, had feared a much larger Wallace vote here, perhaps 25 per cent citywide, and it waged an intensive last-minute campaign against the former Alabama Governor.

The average union member here, said one man who knows many members well, is also "very anti all this student turmoil on the campuses." "He forgets that the sitdown was just exactly how he got where he is, that the union, too, was once revolutionary, not establishment, as it is now," he said.

Like the boy who accepts his father's color television set as a fact of life without worrying about the work that was done to get it, the young union members sometimes irritate their elders, like Mr. Metiva, who said:

"They should have been there when I was there, when we got raised from 25 cents to 40 cents.

"In those days, why, the foreman just looked at you crossways and you could be done for—laid off and not taken back. I just don't understand these younger ones."

But Mr. Metiva's son, Lloyd D. Metiva, also a Buick worker, is 39 years old, and he understands.

Rising Unemployment

by Francis X. Clines

HOD CARRYING in Pittsburgh has been heavy work for 18 years for William Brown, but the heaviest burden of all has come from the addition of his name and those of his seven children to the welfare roll.

"I am bitter," Mr. Brown declared this week as he told of the press of economic conditions that has seen him slip since January from the payroll to the unemployment compensation line and, now, to the welfare line.

"I don't think it's right that a man who wants to work should have to go on public assistance," the restless, frustrated 45-year-old man declared. His comments echoed those of growing numbers of laid-off workers resentful over conditions that are driving them to the dole.

Mr. Brown is a victim of the paradoxical ways of modern economy.

He is a figure in the rising unemployment that some economic specialists prescribe as beneficial in the long run but that welfare specialists are warning will be costly in the immediate future.

Throughout the nation, welfare officials are watching the rise in unemployment for possible effects in public assistance outlays. Slowly but clearly the welfare ramifications are appearing in some areas, particularly those where a severe jobless problem has out-lasted the duration of unemployment aid.

But in other areas, officials are hoping the public assistance budget will be spared such severe increases as those predicted for New York State, where specialists expect a 21 per cent rise in costs and a 7 per cent rise in needy individuals this year because of continuing inflation and unemployment.

In San Diego, the severity of the problem is measurable in the types of men who have had to take hat in hand. Skilled, well-paid engineers and technicians laid off in the aerospace and electronics industries are now receiving welfare.

"This has been the most horrible time of my life," said a father of five children who was dropped from his $1,100-a-month job as an engineer at Convair in San Diego last September.

There was a brief layoff in the engineer's career in the past and he expected much the same this time. But he has not found a job despite a search that has approached the frantic level at times, with the dispatch of 120 resumes to various cities. Unemployment insurance of $65 a week was exhausted, and so the man finally applied for welfare, which his family was granted at the rate of $239 a month.

The jobless engineer is a cautious man, born in Russia, who wants his name withheld to spare his family additional embarrassment. But he compares his present way of life to the years he spent in a German concentration camp. "I don't know what to do," he says. "I'm not the only one in this fix."

At 54 years of age, the man said last week he had decided to join a state training program for computer programing and seek a new start.

Welfare officials in San Diego estimate that such cases, combined with inflation, will push up the welfare budget there from $76-million for the fiscal year just ended to $98.6-million in the new year. A 30 per cent increase is forecast in aid for dependent children, the costliest relief category.

In Illinois, where the caseload last month was 619,000 persons compared with an average of 577,000 last year, officials told of how quickly the pinch had come on. "We never anticipated anything like this," Gershon Hurwitz, deputy state director of public aid, declared. He said that the effects of the national economic slowdown had been compounded by the long labor dispute in the trucking industry.

In economics, last year's Illinois welfare budget was $651-million while this year's is $858-million. In people, there is the case of Doroteo Cruz, the head of a family of six who is now jobless after 17 years of steady employment.

"Sometimes I have nothing in my pocket," says Mr. Cruz, who lost a $2.80-an-hour cabinetmaker's job last March after seven years but thought he had beaten the slowdown by getting a job as a $2.30-an-hour toolmaker. The truck strike closed this out, and he had to turn to welfare aid of $268 a month.

"I may go back to my country [Puerto Rico]," Mr. Cruz says. "There's so much trouble here, everything's going up. I have trouble getting by even when I'm working."

Unemployment insurance, which has less social stigma than welfare, is serving some areas more as a dam for an expected welfare flood than as a bridge to re-employment.

In Washington, the unemployment rate in the Seattle, Tacoma and Everett areas, where tens of thousands of aircraft workers have been laid off, is 10 per cent, over twice the national average. More than 69,000 workers are receiving unemployment aid there, $70 a week for up to 39 weeks, and a crisis is expected in September when this runs out.

In St. Louis, there were more unemployment aid recipients this spring than in more than a decade. But this is not expected to translate eventually into increased welfare aid because the truck strike has since ended and the state's welfare standards are considered too stringent. In fact, there are only 110 families in the state receiving aid to dependent children.

For those able to get welfare, there are problems of pride. "My ego really suffered," said a Portland, Ore., family man who lost his job as a clerk, used up the available unemployment aid, and held out from applying for welfare until the electric company man walked up to his house and shut off the power, including the stove.

A similarly situated man in Louisville, Ky., was laid off in a military economy drive from his $150-a-week job sacking gunpowder at an arsenal. He says he feels the problem as much in the social embarrassment of his two daughters' not having 50 cents for the local swimming pool, as in the absence of roast beef on Sundays.

The man did not want his name used because of the stigma of welfare. But he was philosophical in accepting the public assistance of $140 a month. "We've been in close places before," he said, "and the Good Lord always took care of us."

Hard-Hats Attack Demonstrators

by Homer Bigart

HELMETED CONSTRUCTION workers broke up a student anti-war demonstration in Wall Street yesterday, chasing youths through the canyons of the financial district in a wild noontime melee that left about 70 persons injured.

The workers then stormed City Hall, cowing policemen and forcing officials to raise the American flag to full staff from half staff, where it had been placed in mourning for the four students killed at Kent State University on Monday.

At nearby Pace College a group of construction workers who said they had been pelted with missiles by students from the roof, twice invaded a building, smashing windows with clubs and crowbars and beating up students.

Earlier the workers ripped a Red Cross banner from the gates of Trinity Church and tried to tear down the flag of the Episcopal Church.

"This is senseless," said the Rev. Dr. John Vernon Butler, rector of Trinity Parish. "I suppose they thought it was a Vietcong flag."

From the *New York Times,* May 9, 1970, copyright © 1970 by The New York Times Company.

Twice Father Butler ordered the gates closed against menacing construction workers.

Inside the church, doctors and nurses from the New York University Medical Center had set up a first-aid station, treating 40 to 60 youths who had been beaten by the workers.

The Mayor issued a statement saying that "a mob came perilously close to overwhelming the police guard at City Hall."

He added his "deep regrets" that the day of memory for the four students killed by Ohio National Guardsmen at Kent had been defiled by violence.

The police said that six persons had been arrested and that 19 persons, including four patrolmen, had been injured. However, Beekman-Downtown Hospital alone reported that 23 persons had been brought by ambulance from the Wall Street area suffering from cuts and bruises, none of them serious.

Fighting Erupts

It was about five minutes to noon when Wall Street suddenly erupted in a melee of fist-fighting that entrapped thousands of employes headed for lunch.

Starting at 7:30 A.M., hundreds of youths, mostly from New York University and others from Hunter College and city high schools, gathered at Broad and Wall Streets in a demonstration demanding the immediate withdrawal of American troops from Vietnam and Cambodia, the immediate release of all "political prisoners in America" and the cessation of military-oriented work by the universities.

All accounts agree that the demonstration was without violence until the construction workers reached the scene.

The construction workers, most of them wearing brown overalls and orange and yellow hard hats, descended on Wall Street from four directions. A thin line of policemen had blocked off the steps of the Federal Hall National Memorial at Nassau and Wall Streets, from about a thousand students who were sitting on the sidewalk and pavement listening to speakers denounce the war abroad and repression at home.

The morning was chilly, with a light rain. But toward noon the sky lightened and the day became warm and humid. The students were in good humor; they cheered a Broad Street lawyer, Charles F. Appel, 56 years old, who told the youths: "You brought down one President and you'll bring down another."

Then came the moment of confrontation. The construction workers, marching behind a cluster of American flags, swept the policemen aside and moved on the students. The youths scattered, seeking refuge in the lunch-hour crowds.

The workers sought them out, some selecting those youths with the most hair and swatting them with their helmets.

There did not seem to be more than 200 construction workers, but they were reinforced by hundreds of persons who had been drawn into the march by chants of "All the way, U.S.A." and "Love it or leave it."

On reaching the Federal Hall National Memorial, the workers at first pushed halfheartedly against the police line. "All we want to do is put our flag up on those steps," one worker said quietly to Inspector Harold Schryner. "If you try, there'll be blood to pay," the inspector replied.

But within two minutes the workers had surged over the memorial's steps, planting American flags on the statue of George Washington. Then they outflanked the police, driving demonstrators before them and hitting the youths with their helmets.

A Staged Assault?

From his 32d-floor office at 63 Wall Street, Edward Shufro of the brokerage firm of Shufro, Rose & Ehrman watched through binoculars two men in gray suits and gray hats who, he said, seemed to be directing the workers.

"These guys were directing the construction workers with hand motions," Mr. Shufro said.

At Exchange Place, Robert A. Bernhard, a partner at Lehman Brothers, tried to protect a youth from assault by a worker. The worker grabbed Mr. Bernhard and pushed him against a telephone pole.

A man who came to the aid of Mr. Bernhard was himself attacked by a worker and struck with a pair of pliers. Bleeding from a head wound the man was taken to Beekman-Downtown Hospital.

Near City Hall, a Wall Street lawyer, Michael Berknap, 29, a Democratic candidate for the State Senate, was beaten and kicked by a group of construction workers yelling, "Kill the Commie bastards." He was treated at Beekman-Downtown Hospital with his right eye completely closed, a large welt on his head and five bootmarks on his back.

Mr. Berknap said the police had stood by and made no attempt to stop the assault.

"These people are rampaging and the police are not arresting them," he complained.

Among the student demonstrators taken to Trinity Church for first aid was Drew Lynch, a teacher in the Human Resources Administration's Brooklyn street program.

Mr. Lynch had both eyes blackened and was bleeding from the mouth. He said "at least four" workers had pummeled him to the street, then kicked him.

"A policeman finally grabbed me by the collar, dragged me away, and said: 'Get out of here,' " Mr. Lynch said.

The workers led a mob to City Hall, where an unidentified mailman went to the roof and raised the flag that Mayor Lindsay had ordered lowered to half staff for the slain students. The crowd cheered wildly.

But moments later an aide to Mayor Lindsay, Sid Davidoff, stalked out on the roof and lowered the flag again.

The mob reacted in fury. Workers vaulted the police barricades, surged across the tops of parked cars and past half a dozen mounted policemen. Fists flailing, they stormed through the policemen guarding the barred front doors.

Uncertain whether they could contain the mob, the police asked city officials to raise the flag. Deputy Mayor Richard R. Aurelio, in charge during the absence of Mayor Lindsay, who was at Gracie Mansion, ordered the flag back to full staff.

Two plainclothes policemen, Pat Mascia and Bob Rudion, and the City Hall custodian, John Zissel, walked out on the roof and struggled with the flapping lanyard.

As the flag went up, the workers began singing "The Star-Spangled Banner." A construction worker yelled to the police: "Get your helmets off."

Grinning sheepishly, about seven of 15 police who were on City Hall steps removed their helmets.

Meanwhile, a group of workers had charged Pace College, across the street from City Hall Park, angered by a peace banner hanging from the roof. Some of them gained the roof of the modernistic four-story building, seized the banner and brought it down to the street, where it was burned. Others smashed windows in the lobby of the college and beat some students.

The scuffle over the flag at City Hall was accompanied by chants of "Lindsay's a Red."

"Stop being juvenile," a Lindsay aide, Donald Evans, admonished a construction worker.

"What do you mean, being juvenile?" he replied, punching Mr. Evans on the chin.

Suggested Reading

Depression and New Deal

Two books by Irving Bernstein offer a panoramic and absorbing account of workers and their unions during the depression years: *The Lean Years: A History of the American Worker, 1919–1933,* Part II (Boston, Houghton Mifflin, 1960), and *Turbulent Years: A History of the American Worker, 1933–1941* (Boston, Houghton Mifflin, 1969), both also in paperback. Walter Galenson, *The CIO Challenge to the AFL: A History of the American Labor Movement, 1935–1941* (Cambridge, Mass., Harvard University Press, 1960), and James O. Morris, *Conflict Within the AFL: A Study of Craft versus Industrial Unionism, 1901–1938* (Ithaca, Cornell University Press, 1958), are the best studies of the split in the AFL and the emergence of the industrial-union movement associated with the CIO. For a somewhat different version of labor's civil war, see David Brody, "The Emergence of Mass-Production Unionism," in John Braeman, *et al.,* eds., *Change and Continuity in Twentieth-Century America* (Columbus, Ohio State University Press, 1964), also in paperback. The fullest history of the AFL since 1933 is Philip Taft's scholarly *The A. F. of L. from the Death of Gompers to the Merger* (New York, Harper, 1959). Unlikely to be surpassed as an account of the Flint strike is Sidney Fine, *Sit-Down: The General Motors Strike of 1936–1937* (Ann Arbor, University of Michigan Press, 1969). Still worth consulting is the lively journalistic narrative of the rise of the CIO by Edward Levinson, *Labor on the March* (New York, Harper, 1938). For the lives and careers of the decade's outstanding labor leaders, one should read Saul Alinsky, *John L. Lewis* (New York, Putnam, 1949), and Matthew Josephson, *Sidney Hillman: Statesman of Labor* (New York, Doubleday, 1952). Donald G. Sofchalk, "The Chicago Memorial Day Incident: An Episode in Mass Action," *Labor History,* VI (Winter 1965), 3–43, is the best analysis of that violent event. For a collection of sober but informative essays which discuss the relationship between the New Deal and the labor movement, consult Milton Derber and Edwin Young, eds., *Labor and the New Deal* (Madison, University of Wisconsin Press, 1957). The most revealing studies of working-class life during the depression are Robert and Helen Lynd, *Middletown in Transition* (New York, Harcourt Brace, 1937), and E. Wight Bakke, *Citizens Without Work* (New Haven, Yale University Press, 1940).

Labor Since 1940

Still the basic study of trade-union history during World War II is Joel Seidman, *American Labor from Defense to Reconversion* (Chicago, University of Chicago Press, 1953). A much-flawed but informative study of postwar labor policy is Arthur F. McClure, *The Truman Administration and the Problems of Postwar Labor* (Rutherford, N.J., Fairleigh Dickinson University Press, 1969). The Cold War in the unions is treated from an anti-communist perspective in Max M. Kampelman, *The Communist Party versus the C.I.O.* (New York, Praeger, 1957), and in David J. Saposs, *Communism in American Unions* (New York, McGraw-Hill, 1959). Somewhat different versions of the struggle against the left-wing unions are offered by F. S. O'Brien, "The Communist-Dominated Unions in the United States since 1950," *Labor History,* IX (Spring 1968), 184–209, and by James R. Prickett, "Some Aspects of the Communist Controversy in the C.I.O.," *Science and Society,* XXXII (1969), 299–321. Ronald Radosh, *American Labor and United States Foreign Policy* (New York, Random House, 1970), also in paperback, discusses the foreign-policy role of trade-union leaders. On corruption and crime in the labor movement, Robert Kennedy, *The Enemy Within* (New York, Harper, 1960), also in paperback, is a journalistic discussion by the former chief counsel of the McClellan Committee; John Hutchinson, *The Imperfect Union* (New York, Dutton, 1970), is more scholarly and complete. Ralph and Estelle James, *Hoffa and the Teamsters: A Study in Union Power* (Princeton, Van Nostrand, 1965), is a revealing portrait of the now-jailed Teamsters' leader. A more complete analysis of America's postwar labor leaders is available in C. Wright Mills, *New Men of Power: America's Labor Leaders* (New York, Harcourt Brace, 1948).

The two best brief yet full histories of contemporary American labor are William H. Miernyk, *Trade Unions in an Age of Affluence* (New York, Random House, 1962), also in paperback, and Frank C. Pierson, *Unions in Postwar America: An Economic Assessment* (New York, Random House, 1967), also in paperback. Critical evaluations are presented by Paul Jacobs, *The State of the Unions* (New York, Atheneum, 1966); Solomon Barkin, *The Decline of the Labor Movement and What Can Be Done About It* (Santa Barbara, Calif., Center for the Study of Democratic Institutions, 1961), also in paperback; and Ronald Radosh and Philip S. Foner, "The Corporate Ideology of American Labor," *Studies on the Left,* VI (November–December 1966), 66–96. More sanguine views of the labor movement are taken by Gus Tyler, *The Labor Revolution: Trade Unions in a New America* (New York, Viking, 1967), and Irving Bernstein, "The Growth of American Unions, 1945–1960," *Labor History,* II (Spring 1961), 131–157, 361–380. Frank Cormier and William J. Eaton, *Reuther* (Englewood Cliffs, N.J., Prentice-Hall, 1970), is a complete biography. The black worker's relation to the trade unions is amply covered by F. Ray Marshall, *The Negro and Organized Labor* (New York, Wiley, 1965), as well as by the relevant essays in Julius Jacobson, ed., *The Negro and the American Labor Movement* (New York, Doubleday, 1968), also in paperback. John Gregory Dunne, *Delano* (New York, Farrar, Straus, 1967), is a sympathetic treatment of César Chavez and the grape pickers' strike in California. A perceptive study of automation's impact on American society is Ben B. Seligman, *Most Notorious Victory: Man in an Age of Automation* (New York, Free Press, 1966). For some of the problems and attitudes of the rank-and-file worker in contemporary America, see Paul Sultan, *The Disenchanted Unionist* (New York, Harper, 1963); Bennett Berger, *Working-Class Suburb: A Study of Auto Workers in Suburbia* (Berkeley, University of California Press, 1960), and Ely Chinoy, *Automobile Workers and the American Dream* (New York, Random House, 1955), also in paperback.

Index

A Note on the Editor

Melvyn Dubofsky was born and grew up in Brooklyn, New York, and studied at Brooklyn College and the University of Rochester, where he received a Ph.D. The author of *We Shall Be All,* a highly praised, definitive history of the IWW, and of *When Workers Organize: New York City in the Progressive Era,* Mr. Dubofsky is now Professor of History at the State University of New York at Binghamton.

NEW YORK TIMES BOOKS published by QUADRANGLE BOOKS

AMERICAN FISCAL AND MONETARY POLICY
edited with an Introduction by Harold Wolozin
AMERICAN FOREIGN POLICY SINCE 1945
edited with an Introduction by Robert A. Divine
AMERICAN LABOR SINCE THE NEW DEAL
edited with an Introduction by Melvyn Dubofsky
AMERICAN POLITICS SINCE 1945
edited with an Introduction by Richard M. Dalfiume
AMERICAN SOCIETY SINCE 1945
edited with an Introduction by William L. O'Neill
BLACK PROTEST IN THE SIXTIES
edited with an Introduction by August Meier and Elliott Rudwick
BRITAIN, 1919—1970
edited with an Introduction by John F. Naylor
CITIES IN TROUBLE
edited with an Introducton by Nathan Glazer
THE CONTEMPORARY AMERICAN FAMILY
edited with an Introduction by William J. Goode
THE CORPORATION IN THE AMERICAN ECONOMY
edited with an Introduction by Harry M. Trebing
CRIME AND CRIMINAL JUSTICE
edited with an Introduction by Donald R. Cressey
EUROPEAN SOCIALISM SINCE WORLD WAR I
edited with an Introduction by Nathanael Greene
THE MEANING OF THE AMERICAN REVOLUTION
edited with an Introduction by Lawrence H. Leder
MODERN AMERICAN CITIES
edited with an Introduction by Ray Ginger
MOLDERS OF MODERN THOUGHT
edited with an Introduction by Ben B. Seligman
NAZIS AND FASCISTS IN EUROPE, 1918—1945
edited with an Introduction by John Weiss
THE NEW DEAL
edited with an Introduction by Carl N. Degler
POP CULTURE IN AMERICA
edited with an Introduction by David Manning White
POVERTY AND WEALTH IN AMERICA
edited with an Introduction by Harold L. Sheppard
PREJUDICE AND RACE RELATIONS
edited with an Introduction by Raymond W. Mack